ISSN 2186-6991

# Kindai Management Review

**Vol.6** April 2018

The Institute for Creative Management and Innovation, Kindai University

ICMI

Publisher: **MARUZEN PLANET CO.,LTD.**
Distributor: **MARUZEN PUBLISHING CO.,LTD.**

Kindai Management Review Vol. 6 2018

©2018  Kindai University

All rights reserved. This journal may not be translated or copied in whole or in part without the written permission except for brief excerpts in connection with reviews or scholarly analysis. Use in connection with any form of information storage and retrieval, electronic adaptation, computer software, or by similar or dissimilar methodology new known or hereafter developed is forbidden.

The original English language edition published by Maruzen Planet Co., Ltd.

PRINTED IN JAPAN

# Contents

*Editorial Board of Kindai Management Review*   Inside front cover
*Preface*   4
*Call for Papers*   7

Is American Capitalism Still Working for Us?   9
Philip Kotler, Kellogg School of Management, Northwestern University, USA

Managing–According to Williamson, or to Coase?   13
J.-C. Spender, Kozminski University, Poland

Japan's Incentive System in Medical Care: Preliminary Research on Psychiatric and General Hospitals   35
Masahiko Takaya, Faculty of Medicine, Kindai University, Japan

Creativity, Innovation and Organizational Performance: Does HRM Bind Them Together?   46
Joseph Heller, Bar-Ilan University, Israel
Jacob Weisberg, Bar-Ilan University, Israel

Creative Industries: Managers' Perceived Creativity and Innovation Practices   64
Fernando Cardoso de Sousa, University of the Algarve, Campus de Gambelas, Portugal
Florbela Nunes, University of Evora, Colégio do Espírito Santo, Portugal
Ileana Pardal Monteiro, University of the Algarve, Campus de Gambelas, Portugal

The Early Investment Ecosystem for Startups in Canada, a Preliminary Study   76
Kenneth A. Grant, Ted Rogers School of Management, Ryerson University, Canada
Divya Padmanaban, National Angel Capital Organisation, Canada
Amr El-Kebbi, Ted Rogers School of Management, Ryerson University, Canada

Inter-linkages between Educational Institutions and White Collar Labor Mobility:
A Comparative Study in Japan, Germany, and the U.S.A.   100
Patricia (Tish) Robinson, Hitotsubashi University, Graduate School of International Corporate Strategy, Japan
Kiyohiko Ito, Shidler College of Business, the University of Hawai'i at Manoa, USA

Growth Aspirations and Financing Choices of Immigrant-Owned New Ventures in Canada   116
Miwako Nitani, Telfer School of Management, University of Ottawa, Canada
François Neville, DeGroote School of Business, McMaster University, Canada

BOOK REVIEW
*My Adventures in Marketing: The Autobiography of Philip Kotler*
By Philip Kotler   132
Fangqi Xu, The Faculty of Business Administration, Kindai University, Japan

*Wise Family Business: Family Identity Steering Brand Success*
By Joachim Schwass and Anne-Catrin Glemser   133
Joachim Schwass, Professor emeritus of Family Business, IMD

# *Preface*

Four years ago the Institute for Creative Management and Innovation launched "*Kindai Management Review*" as the research bulletin. Aimed at becoming a representative academic journal of management in English published in Japan its appearance from Maruzen has been widely and immediately acclaimed by the academics both inside and outside Japan. We have received a huge number of congratulatory messages, words of encouragement, and valuable comments from readers. Unable to publish all such messages due to the constraint in the space I would like to cite some of them.

"I would congratulate the first issue of *Kindai Management Review*. As you know, only a very limited number of the publications by Japanese scholars have been known outside Japan and this trend does not seem to improve, wherefore, the Institute for Creative Management and Innovation at Kindai University has focused from its very inception its effort on the strengthening of the diffusion of new management thinking originated in Japan. I am convinced that the journal is a commendable and valuable effort to serve such a challenging attempt."

**Ikujiro Nonaka**, Professor Emeritus, Hitotsubashi University

"I am pleased to be part of the inaugural issue of the *Kindai Management Review*. This new publication is a rare breed—a management journal that can attract international scholars and also spread new management thinking from Japan to the rest of the world. I will follow its development with great interest."

**David J. Teece**, Professor, University of California, Berkeley

"The publication of English-language peer-reviewed academic journal is a remarkable endeavor, quite rare among Japanese universities. I trust that this journal will become a gateway to success for young scholars. In our generation, Dr. Nonaka's international activities outstands. I hope that this journal fosters the coming on stage of world-class scholars capable of emulating Professor Nonaka."

**Tadao Kagono**, Invited Professor of Konan University

"There are many outstanding technologies and wonderful businesses in Japan. Yet far too little of the management processes and thinking that create these achievements is accessible in English. The Kindai Management Review thus fills a critical gap in our knowledge of creativity and innovation in Japanese industry. There are lessons for businesses in all countries, based on this knowledge."

**Henry Chesbrough**, Professor, UC Berkeley Haas School of Business

"Innovation management is a discipline in constant flux. It requires that researchers and leaders alike stay in front of the dynamic and fast changing developments in the field. *Kindai Management Review* is one of the best journals for keeping pace with the newest research and methods for leading organizational innovation."

**Jeff DeGraff**, Clinical Professor, Ross School of Business, University of Michigan

"I congratulate heartily the publishing of the *Kindai Management Review* as the bulletin of ICMI. Many leading scholars on management in the world submitted their newest papers. It means KRM is highly recognized as the socially and academically valuable publication."

**Mieko Watanabe**, Professor Emeritus, University of Tsukuba

"I was delighted and impressed by the contents and design appearance of *Kindai Management Review* which I received recently. It is clear that your journal will become a great success internationally for the quality of materials. Congratulations!"

**Tudor Rickards**, Professor, Manchester Business School

"It was beautifully composed and very interesting content."

**Roderick M. Kramer**, Professor, Stanford Graduate School of Busines

"*Kindai Management Review* has joined the important group of publications aimed at informing managers, leaders, and researchers about critical issues and trends facing organizations. Being based in Asia, yet including global thought leadership on topics such as managing innovation and creativity, KMR provides an excellent and continuing resource to the management field."

**Scott G. Isaksen**, Professor, Norwegian Business School

"The content looks great and the design and production are elegant. Congratulations!"

**Vijay Sathe**, Professor, Claremont Graduate University

"It is very impressive, both in terms of its look and in regard to content."

**Gerard J. Puccio**, Chair and Professor, International Center for Studies in Creativity,
Buffalo State College

"It is not an easy feat to launch and maintain a leading academic journal especially in Japan where the research projects are abundant but not many researchers are publishing in top journals outside Japan. The very existence of Kindai Management Review is a strong stimulus for the researchers in the world but especially so for those in Japan and Asia."

**Kimio Kase**, Professor, International University of Japan

"After reading carefully the Kindai Management Review I would like to commend you and your team for setting up such a quality publication. I strongly believe that the journal will soon get its place in academia thus it will be appreciated by academics and practitioners in the field on Innovation and Management."

**Dimitrios V. Nikolaidis**, Head, Business Administration & Economics Department,
The University of Sheffield

"My comment is WOW! I have shared it around here and others have said the same. Your big challenge now is delivering on the high expectations that come from the first volume—but I think that's a good challenge."

**Stuart Read**, Professor, IMD

"I find it very interesting and informative. I will circulate your request for papers for the journal to the staff in the Business School."

**George Benwell**, Dean and Pro-Vice-Chancellor, Otago Business School

On behalf of the editorial board, I should express our gratitude to all the readers who sent in their comment to us. Please kindly continue to support us.

Fangqi Xu
Director of the Institute for Creative Management and Innovation,
Kindai University
Editor-in-Chief of *Kindai Management Review*

# *Call for Papers*

*Kindai Management Review* is the bulletin of the Institute for Creative Management and Innovation (ICMI) at Kindai University in Japan. The first volume (only inaugural issue) was published by Maruzen Planet in February 2013. We are now calling for submissions to be reviewed for possible inclusion in Volume 7. Everybody who is a research, practitioner or Ph.D. candidate in management is welcome to submit a paper. However, it is limited in an unpublished paper. And the copyright of papers published in the journal belong to Kindai University..

*Kindai Management Review* plays two roles. One is to promote the results of research on management in Japan to the world. The other is to receive new theories and methods of management that were developed elsewhere in the world and introduce them into Japan.

*Kindai Management Review* is a refereed journal. We welcome original papers that have not been published elsewhere that are related to the following topics.

- Creative management and open innovation
- Knowledge creation theory (Nonaka Theory) and knowledge management
- Enterprise's sustainable growth and new business model
- Venture business and entrepreneurship education
- Research on people (management scholar or practitioner, for example, Peter Drucker or Steve Jobs) and management history
- Global management and competitive strategy
- Marketing and customer
- Human resource management and creativity development
- Learning organization and organizational behavior
- Intellectual asset and accounting innovation
- Corporate culture and management philosophy
- Corporate governance and corporate social responsibility
- Other research about new theory or method on management

Manuscripts should be 10-15 pages (A4 size) and the maximum is 20 pages including tables and figures. Please refer to the sample paper for details. The sample paper is available from the following web site. http://www.kindai.ac.jp/sangaku/kenkyu/icmi/

Manuscripts should be submitted by email. We will contact the author when we have received the manuscript. The deadline of the Call for Papers for Volume 7 is October 31, 2018.

Contact us:   The Institute for Creative Management and Innovation
3 – 4 – 1, Kowakae, Higashi-Osaka, Japan 577-8502
Email: journalofkmr@bus.kindai.ac.jp

Editorial Committee of *Kindai Management Review*

*Kindai Management Review* Vol. 6, 2018 (ISSN: 2186-6961)

# Is American Capitalism Still Working for Us?

## Philip Kotler

*Kellogg School of Management, Northwestern University, USA*

---

***Editor's Note:*** We are extremely delighted to publish this article, contributed by Professor Philip Kotler, who, needless to say, is the "father of modern marketing." We are to stress that this is an unpublished article specifically written by Professor Kotler for Kindai Management Review. It is a great honor not only for KMR, but also for our readers. We thank Professor Kotler for his support. It includes much insights, suggestions and ideas on politics, economics and management of the United States. We are convinced that our readers will benefit a great deal from the article.

---

I want to discuss our changing ideas about our two fundamental systems, Capitalism and Democracy. Each system delivers many great benefits. But each system is also creaking now and displaying some serious weaknesses.

In 2016, I published *Confronting Capitalism* that examined 14 thorny problems of American Capitalism. In 2017, I published *Democracy in Decline*, examining 14 problems in American Democracy. For each problem, I examined and compared the major proposed solutions.

I am going to comment on a few problems and then propose a third course of action. Let's start with the insights of a very wise man, Winston Churchill. He offered the following comparison between Capitalism and Socialism:

- "The inherent vice of Capitalism is the unequal sharing of blessings." "The inherent virtue of Socialism is the equal sharing of miseries."

Is this our real Hobson's choice? Must we choose between Capitalism and Socialism? Does Socialism or Social Democracy only produce an equality of misery? Is there a Middle Way? Can we call it Social Capitalism or Social Democracy? What would it be like? What would be the gains? What would be the risks and losses?

Churchill then offered another insight, this one about Democracy.

- "Democracy is the worst form of government, except for all the other forms that have been tried from time to time."

Churchill went on to claim the superiority of Democracy on two counts. The first: "It is the only political system with *moral legitimacy*." He says that Democracy is a better system because it puts a country's future in the hands of its people, not its rulers.

Churchill made a second point about Democracy: "Its major virtue is that it has the capacity to be 'self-correcting.' Inept leaders and policies can be replaced."

We can make the same claim about Capitalism. We can say: "Capitalism is the worst form of economy, except for all the other forms." But we have to address the same two questions that he addressed about Democracy. Does Capitalism have 'moral legitimacy?' Does our capitalism make everyone better off? And does our Capitalism have "the capacity to be self-correcting?" Can it stop making the rich richer and start showering a better life on most Americans? These are legitimate and disturbing questions about our current Capitalism.

Most of us can list the good things about Capitalism.

- Capitalism allows persons with means to start a business or to raise money from others to start a business.
- Capitalism has produced impressive economic growth in the past. It has been able to supply a growing number of jobs to a growing population.
- Capitalism has helped foster much innovation that has made our lives better.
- Capitalism has enabled business people to choose where they want to invest and enabled buyers to choose what they want to buy.

What are the current "bads" of Capitalism?

- Capitalism has been marked by a growing concentration of income and wealth in the hands of a small number of people who have extra influence on our politics and economy. Capitalism produces a few winners and many losers. We live in "a winner-take-all" economic system. We must acknowledge the great cost in human misery and everyday hardship for millions of people just struggling to survive. Where is the moral legitimacy?
- Capitalism has not succeeded to eliminate poverty. Our poverty rate remains at 15%. Over 40 percent of our working class are in deep depth because they don't earn a living wage. Many of our vital safety nets are frayed and fraying.
- Capitalism is moving into a stage where more jobs will be done by machines. We probably will need a system of either Earned Income Tax Credits, or a system of Universal Basic Income, to support persons unable to find a job requiring human labor.
- Capitalism encourages a high level of individualism and neglects building community and cooperation for the Common Good. Capitalists want to keep government small

and this results in neglecting our infrastructure, public goods, and the environment.

- Capitalism is subject to regular cycles of recession. We have had a recession every five to 10 years. Many times, our economic growth is riding on a bubble.
- Capitalism favors short term investment and payout rather than long term investment and innovation.
- Capitalism measures the value of the goods produced but does not measure whether human well-being and happiness are advancing.
- Capitalism is "eating" our democracy. Capitalism can lead to the decline of democracy. Political candidates are "bought" and work more for their donors, secondarily for the lobbyists, third for their party, and last for their citizens. Citizens are not running the country. It is not "one citizen, one vote." And Congress is not really running the country. The country is run by two overlapping groups, the major corporations and the super-wealthy. The policies are largely determined by what lies in the interests of major corporations and the super-wealthy.

Peter Georgescu, who wrote Capitalists Arise!, and who ran the great Advertising Agency, Y&R, has been going around the country telling business people that they need to recognize that Capitalism is in trouble and the pitchforks might attack the Capitalists if they don't make our American economic system work better for more people.

Here are some of the problems:

- Too much business decision making is short term and myopic. The mantra is "Grow profits every year for the shareholders." The company focuses on enriching the shareholders on the grounds that they own the company. They own shares but not the company. (The company owns itself).
- The company professes that the major route to serving the shareholders is to serve the customers. But the other stakeholders – employees, distributors and suppliers - are treated as a cost to be minimized.

- When productivity rises, profits rise and end up as higher capital gains and dividends going to the shareholders, bonuses to management, rebuying corporate stock, but little in the way of rising wages. Management does not use the higher productivity to reward their workers. The earnings of the working class have been flat for 37 years.
- The working class survives only by borrowing money. Many working Americans on payday have to pay off their loan or borrow more money. Getting out of this debt is nearly impossible. So the dream of opportunity and upward mobility has disappeared.
- The dire result is that the American working class does not have enough earnings to buy what they need. This means companies can't grow larger and employ more workers.
- Businesses have been blind to this problem. American Capitalism, which is largely financial capitalism, benefits the few, not the many. The rich get richer and most Americans can barely make ends meet.
- Many business leaders agree that 1. there is a problem and 2. they need to act. But no leader really feels he or she can do much. It is risky not to make good profits in the short run. If the CEO fails, activist shareholders will call for the Board to fire the CEO.
- Fortunately there are some enlightened business leaders. They do long run planning to achieve certain large goals, even if they have to absorb extra costs in the short run. These leaders treat their employees and other stakeholders well and achieve greater profit in the long run. Unilever, Starbucks, Home Depot, Google, Publix, Wegman, Costco, and Johnson & Johnson.
- Johnson & Johnson pursues the right values. They think of the customer first. Second, they serve the employees well. Third, they serve the communities well. Fourth, they serve the shareholders well, in that order.
- We need to restate capitalism's job to be optimizing benefits for all the stakeholders, not only the shareholders.
- We need corporate boards, financial institutions, and pension groups, to celebrate companies that act in the long run. We need to honor and buy from companies that pursue the 4Ps: people, the planet, progress and profits. We need companies that invest in people, care about the planet, and invest in creativity and innovation.
- Company boards need to make management accountable for the long run. We prefer companies in which we can invest and stop watching them from day to day. These companies are committed to long-term growth. That is Warren Buffet's view.
- We need public/private partnerships in our cities to build infrastructure, encourage job creation and improve our education and health.
- I have a cynical concern that many business leaders recognize that our Capitalism is failing and simply want to get the most before the system falls apart. They put their money overseas, move their company to another country (inversion), and fight for still lower taxes on the rich. Anthony Scaramucci warned at a recent SALT Conference: "The rich people in this room, the wealthy people, you don't want to live in a barbed-wire-encased security perimeter in your McMansion like they do in Latin America. So we have to fix this problem."
- Too many businesses rage against tax increases that support entitlements, unwilling to recognize that the rich have entitlements: capital gains, carried interest, mortgage deductions, and tax loopholes. The government continues to subsidize agricultural giants, pharmaceutical companies, oil companies, sugar companies.
- The wealthy are gaining more wealth without risk or effort by becoming rentiers.
- If business refuses to reform, then government will step in, and we will end up with the European model.
- Our taxes are low by international standards and our social welfare programs are less than those in Europe. Just consider European vacations.
- We think that we have economic growth but most of the time we are riding bubbles.

- My Conclusion: Free market capitalism has been hijacked to serve a smaller and smaller population. Inequality is a cancer. Plutocracy must end. We need to produce wealth for the many, not the few. We need to commit to steady economic growth for those at the bottom of the pyramid.

May I be so bold as to propose a Manifesto where I hammer 3 points on the wall:

1. The current systems of Capitalism and Democracy might be sowing the seeds of their own destruction.

- People will get poorer and they will feel more oppressed. They will turn to elect leaders who will try to preserve the privileges of the wealthy while promising, but not delivering, better conditions to the working class. Fascism or Communism might be inevitable.

2. Capitalism needs to enact a number of palliative measures that will favor the working poor and the middle class. Many good measures have been proposed by Senators Bernie Sanders and Elizabeth Warren.

- A single payer health care system
- A higher minimum wage
- A lowering of the cost of college
- Controlling climate by passing a tax on carbon
- Enacting major criminal justice reforms
- Enacting immigration reform
- Breaking up too-big-to-fail banks

- Closing tax loopholes

3. Capitalism's reform will require a tax system that will restrain and redistribute wealth. Find a way to convince the wealthy to do more public good with their wealth as in the Giving Pledge. Raise taxes on high income and wealth.

We have to make a choice between Free Market Capitalism (Financial Capitalism) and Social Capitalism, the form of Capitalism found in Europe. Europe does not have high growth but it has less homelessness and fewer people going hungry. And vacations are longer.

I believe that Free Market Capitalism has lost its "moral legitimacy." It is a Capitalism run by the 1% and the Koch brothers. It is a Capitalism that would cut down the health of its people in order to cut taxes on the wealthy. I believe that Free Market Capitalism lacks the capacity for "self-correction." I think that the system will continue to make more people poorer. I know the choice between Free Market Capitalism and Social Capitalism is hard to make. Which economic system would give you more confidence in our future? One economic system is run with cooperation, compassion and co-sharing the benefits. The other economic system is run with individual economic gain being the measure. Which economic system is better for the people?

Our philosophers are of no help. When Woody Allen was asked, he answered with prophetic wisdom: "More than any time in history mankind faces a crossroads. One path leads to despair and utter hopelessness, the other to total extinction. Let us pray that we have the wisdom to choose correctly."

---

Dr. Philip Kotler is Professor of marketing at the Kellogg School of Management, Northwestern University, Evanston, Illinois, USA. Email:phil@philkotler.com

*Kindai Management Review* Vol. 6, 2018 (ISSN: 2186-6961)

# Managing–According to Williamson, or to Coase?

## J.-C. Spender

*Kozminski University, Poland*

### Abstract

In 1937 Ronald H. Coase famously suggested micro economists did not understand the 'nature of the firm' and could not answer his 'killer questions': Why firms existed? Why their boundaries and internal arrangements were as they were? Why their performance was so varied? Given private firms are the 'engines' of our capitalist system Coase's charge was piercing. What could management schools teach without a clear notion of the entity/phenomena being managed? Faced with the same questions, management theorists adopted two 'Mother-metaphors'; the firm as (1) a rationally designed and administered 'machine' or (2) an integrated community. The first presumed good management led to more efficient resource-use; the second to employees' greater commitment to the firm's goals. Strategy theorists adopted a third metaphor, (3) the firm as an actor pursuing profit in imperfect lumpy markets. Yet few management theorists conceded Coase's critique also applied to these metaphors. The reason is 'economic entropy'; all transactions incur 'positive transaction costs'—frictions—so firms must create fresh economic value to overcome these. None of the metaphors explained this. Nor could the questions be answered by theories of leadership or entrepreneurship based on the same metaphors. A fourth 'positive transaction economics' metaphor was needed to help economists and management theorists deal with real-world managing, leadership, and entrepreneurship. Crucially, Coase suggested it would hinge on the Knightian uncertainties that made the neoclassical assumptions of perfect markets and zero-cost transacting irrelevant. In the 1970s micro economists took up Coase's ideas and created New Institutional Economics (NIE). The paper explores NIE's genesis, viability, and managerial implications. Among our conclusions; Williamson's theories are limited and Coase's subtler intuitions have yet to be fleshed out.

**Keywords:** *Transaction Cost, Coase, Williamson, entrepreneurship, theory of the firm*

### BACKGROUND

The popular story is that in the 1950s, after many decades of being 'much cited but little used', Coase's 1937 paper was rediscovered as a less mathematical and more realistic way of looking at firms; its key novelty being 'transaction cost' (TC) the unavoidable costs of doing business in our real and uncertain world. In the 1970s micro economists used TCs to construct a new analysis—New Institutional Economics (NIE). Several NIE authors have since won the Swedish Riksbank Prize (the 'Economic Nobel'); including Coase in 1991 and Oliver E. Williamson in 2009. Management theorists could then add NIE metaphors to their current inventory of ideas about firms. But they were slow to appreciate that Coase's intuitions threatened their preceding metaphors; the firm as a machine, or as a community, or as a profit-seeking entity in imperfect markets. Positive transaction costs show managing could not be abstracted from the real world, a 'state of nature' that must be explored empirically. In which case, rational decision-making alone was no longer sufficient to theorizing managing, whether that be designing, motivating, or strategizing. Managers had to deal with their firm's situation and its specific facts. No general model would suffice. For example, marriage may seem a general concept, but is specific, even unique, for the parties concerned. Coase implied the essence of managing was not adjusting a universal model to a unique situation. Rather the other way around. Actors are engaged with details; generalizations might inform their situation, but could never dictate their actions. Notwithstanding this, most of us continue take rational models of firms 'for granted', vainly searching for their general characteristics. Coase showed this project was no longer viable—triggered by the option to work 'across markets' —to 'buy' instead of 'make'. Post NIE, many management theorists find comfort in viewing firms as loci of 'less loss', that managing's basic logic is loss-reduction—in Williamson's language, 'economizing' TCs.

This overlooks the corollary. TCs threaten the entire economic analysis unless there are complementary mechanisms to create new economic value—at least sufficient to cover the losses remaining after managers have reduced them as far as they are able. This paper treats 'the firm' as a locus of value-creation by contrasting Coase's and Williamson's treatments of TCs. Its initial sections explore how the new economic metaphor emerged from denying perfect markets and naïve rationality. But the implications remain muddy. One conclusion is that TCs are the costs of dealing with Knightian uncertainty; they are not factor costs. No uncertainty, no TCs, and no firm. A second is that Williamson's views, now mainstream, overlook the value-creation necessary to the 'positive-TC' approach Coase called for in his Nobel speech. At the same time, Coase's intuitions were promising but not explicated. Note, though, that he used 'entrepreneur' 24 times in his 1937 paper; 'transaction cost' not once.

Making sense of Coase is a cottage industry, given his idiosyncrasy, sharpness, and the stories he told about himself (Coase, 1991a, 1991b, 1991c, 1991d, 1991e). Yet his intuitions about how economic activity might lead to new economic value were based on personal experience of business and business people. While profound they were never well-articulated—so we risk crediting him with responding to influences he eschewed and ideas he would have rejected. But some things are clear. While often considered similar, Williamson's TC analysis differed substantially from Coase's. Given the considerable impact of NIE on the management literature (e.g. Foss, Foss, & Klein, 2017; Furubotn, 2001; Hodgson, 1998; Hovenkamp, 1990; Khalil, 1995; Macher & Richman, 2008; Madhok, 1996; Masten, 1993; Vanberg, 1989) there is less critique than seems due (Ankarloo & Palermo, 2004; Ghoshal, 2005; Ghoshal, Bartlett, & Moran, 1999; Hodgson, 2010; Kay, 2015).

Coase and Williamson differed on 'transaction', 'transaction cost' and, most fundamentally, on 'uncertainty'—and thus on 'the firm'. One key to this intellectual archeology is Frank Knight's *The Economic Organization*, sometimes considered the most influential economic text of the modern era (Knight, 2013:vii). The paper turns on our protagonists' different appreciations of Knightian uncertainty (KU) and its impact on the economic activity (Knight 1921; Knight, 2013). A second key is Wesley Hohfeld's work, influential in the US from the 1920s onwards, especially in 1948 when Coase spent 9 months in the US researching broadcasting regulation (Wang, 2014). Hohfeld is little cited today and no mention of his work can be found in Coase's *oeuvre*. But Hohfeld was pivotal for John R. Commons, generally credited with introducing the term 'transaction' into economics as well as to shaping the 'old' institutional economics (Hodgson, 2003; Langlois, 1989, 2017; Schweikhardt, 1988). Coase's immersion in US 'legal realist' or 'functionalist' thinking while researching broadcasting regulation (Calabresi, 2003; Kalman, 1986; Williamson, 1996b) informed his BBC book (Coase, 1950).

Coase's paper on the Federal Communications Commission (FCC) raised the possibility of auctioning broadcasting spectrum (Coase, 1959:15), citing Herzel (Herzel, 1952). Herzel's suggestion reflected Hohfeld's views on 'rights, duties, and obligations'. Earlier property law was dubbed 'sovereign'. Property rights were absolute; an owner was free to do whatever s/he willed with the property 'owned'. Against this doctrine Hohfeld pointed out property rights were always problematic in a political economy based on laws; for property-rights were never absolute. Rather than being sovereign, they were better specified as their 'owners' rights to use, dispose, and exclude', complementing the owners' 'obligations and duties'. Owners were neither sovereigns nor States but always citizen-subjects whose rights were defined and bounded by the superior authority's laws. Wireless spectrum property rights were especially problematic given there was nothing tangible about them.

This paper suggests Coase was significantly influenced by Hohfeldian thinking and thereby carried over aspects of the 'old institutionalist' program—in spite of his famous dismissal of it as 'piles of data waiting for a theory or a fire' (Coase, 1984; Schweikhardt, Scorsone, & Doidge, 2015). He welcomed institutional attempts to bring aspects of social analysis into economics (Calabresi, 2003:2119; Madhok, 1996; Merrill & Smith, 2001; Vanberg, 1989; Williamson, 1996a, 1996c). Though not a legal scholar, he focused on the impact of the law—building up the *Journal of Law and Economics* to push this line of thought. He felt that any economics detached from law, surely a crucial feature of the real world, was irrelevant 'blackboard mathematics'. Throughout his long life he pilloried his colleagues' labors on the irrelevant, insisting they attend to the specifics of the situation, as in the 'case studies' he favored over mathematical models. But where did Coase look for realism and relevance? Philosophers know realism is a tricky notion. One discussion is around the realism of an analysts' assumptions. Much influenced by Karl Popper, Milton Friedman argued prediction was the true test of theory, that the realism of the theory's assumptions was irrelevant (Friedman, 1953; Williamson, 2008). Herbert Simon countered that the purpose of theory was explanation, that assumptions connected theorizing to the world we experience (Simon, 1963).

Coase aligned with Simon, believing 'the specifics' were where realism and relevance—and

profit—were to be found. This had profound methodological implications. The Aristotelian distinction between the general and particular runs throughout this paper (Devereux, 1986). As William Blake wrote in the margins to his Reynolds' *Discourses*, ca. 1808: "To generalize is to be an idiot. To particularize is the alone distinction of merit. General knowledges are those knowledges that idiots possess". The positivist assumption is that theory, being general, even universal, thereby captures what is objective and real, independent of what we think. It may be that an economy is an objective reality, independent of those involved, whose iron laws can be discovered and presented as determining or limiting our practice. But a more relevant epistemology starts out by focusing on our experiences, always particular, specific, and situated. We live one moment at a time and in only one time and place, never in 'the general'.

Neoclassical economists adopt 'rational man' (homogeneous and universal) specifically to escape the heterogeneity, uniqueness, and idiosyncrasies of experience. Though some psychologists seek general rules of perception, bias, behavior, etc., others explore the nature and drivers of the individuality we experience. Allport distinguished between (a) human personality (a universal construct) and (b) Bill's personality (something specific and experienced), and adopted Windelband's terms 'nomothetic' and 'idiographic'(Allport, 1962:405). Prediction is nomothetic, the aim of scientific theorizing about what we presume real; explanation is idiographic, paying attention to the specifics, experience, observation, uniqueness, initial conditions, etc. (Tsoukas, 1989). Note history's stories are idiographic, though expressed in language with a degree of generality—unavoidable, for that is how language communicates, never able to capture experience fully.

The new economic metaphor for managing must bring nomothetic and idiographic together. The deepest differences between Coase and Williamson were that Coase was inclined to the idiographic, methodologically prioritizing attention to the particulars. This could illuminate the actor's options and help them deal with the challenges of inhabiting a real socio-economy. Williamson, in contrast, engaged the neoclassical nomothetic project, today's mainstream, searching for theory that would dictate optimal choosing. They also differed crucially on Knightian uncertainty (KU). While Williamson wrote of 'uncertainty', his understanding differed greatly from Knight's (Boudreaux & Holcombe, 1989; Hodgson, 2011; Nash, 2006). KU was also key to Coase's thinking; it is what inhibited nomothetic theory's relevance to the 'real world'. Knight's intuition was that absent KU there would be no firms. Coase's intuition was similar, that absent positive TCs there would be no firms. It followed that in the context of managing under KU or positive TCs, when firms might exist, there could be no purely nomothetic theory of the firm. The deeper conclusion was that 'the firm' is a profoundly idiographic concept, just as is the human individual. We understand ourselves ideographically, through our differences, not as instances of some nomothetic model. This has many ramifications, especially for those interested in managing in the real world, in creating new economic value rather than playing optimization games.

There are many puzzles about Coase's work, especially its greater impact on legal scholars than on economists. While it has prompted a new generation of scholarship and taken us well beyond the 'firms exist when make is cheaper than buy', Coasian ideas have yet to impact management theorizing thoroughly. The history is that, especially after the 1959 *Foundation Reports* (R. Gordon & Howell, 1959; Pierson & Others, 1959), the management discipline prioritized 'rigorous' nomothetic analysis, pushing aside 'softer', idiographic and historical methods of 'general management'—thus moving away from Coase's program and closer to Williamson's. But management theorists have more pressing reasons than have micro economists to puzzle about profit and the private firm as the politically legitimated apparatus to generate it. A new generation of writers is focusing on entrepreneurship, leadership, innovation, and the dynamics essential to a practical understanding of firms, despite having no tenable theory of the firm. Likewise, few see the firm as the politically situated instrument Coase knew it to be. There is urgency here, for many developed economies are implementing neoliberal policies that 'privatize' and so deliver public sector

agencies into the hands of private firms, even as we know little about how they work (Veldman, 2013). The discussions about globalization, the Precariat, and inequity, such as Piketty's or the protests about 'maximizing shareholder value' (MSV), imply the 'footloose private firm' cannot avoid generating both profit and inequity and is therefore—as Buffett described derivatives in 2002—a 'financial weapon of mass destruction'. Coase's theorizing implied a necessary link between profit and inequity.

Neoclassical economics' focus is on individuals' perfect rationality and maximizing exchange; it is 'hard'. NIE is 'softer', embracing power, culture, and history along with 'imperfect' people. But the resulting inter-penetration of categories leads to confusion and mainstream theorists' displeasure. Coase's insight was to presume the different modes of organization are economic choices—so leading to different costs—and towards an economic explanation of why managers might favor one mode of organization rather than another. The choice would not be based on OB/OT notions of power or personal flourishing. Coase's 1937 paper linked 'organization' and 'cost', but offered no clear 'theory of the firm'. Rather he set out a program for researching the plurality of influences over a specific real-world firm's formation, operation, and survival (Coase, 1988a). He considered his principal achievement was to suggest why firms existed and so set out a research program into how firms divided up the functions they performed for the economy, illuminating the boundary between its private and public sectors (Coase, 1972). Towards the end of his life he saw rejecting neoclassical economics' zero-TC assumption led not only towards understanding 'the firm', a previously unexplained phenomenon of democratic capitalism, but also towards a radically new kind of 'positive TC' economics. This has yet to be articulated.

Williamson was among those leading the effort to flesh out NIE. He saw Coase's insights as 'fundamental' but that his analysis was "not operationalized in a fashion that permits one to assess the efficacy of completing transactions between firms and markets in a systematic way" (Williamson, 1975:3). This critique was extended later (Williamson, 1981:1546; 1985:78n7). At least in principle, OT and OB already offered alternative modes of organizing that could be costed comparatively, so leading to a rigorous theory of managing as 'economizing'. Much current OB and OT research is in this direction. Chandler made suggestions about the efficiency of alternative 'structures' (Chandler, 1962). Williamson showed how OT and OB ideas could reshape the economic analysis of managers' choices. He argued for four levels of analysis; (1) sociological, about society at large, (2) society's existing institutions including firms, laws, and norms, (3) firm-level governance or managerial control, and (4) a rigorous post-NIE economics. He claimed NIE dealt with levels 2 and 3. His 'transaction cost economics' (TCE)—the most recognizable part of NIE—brought 'governance' into micro economic analysis. Specifically, managers had to deal with the costs arising from 'bounded rationality, opportunism, uncertainty, small numbers phenomena, and information impactedness' (Williamson, 1975:257). Williamson argued TCE was an 'empirical success story' because research supported his hypothesis that managers reduced these costs by bringing OT and OB principles into their organizing (Williamson, 1999). Given such support, he anticipated TCE developing into a rigorous nomothetic theory (Williamson, 2016).

Coase accepted the NIE label but that did not stop him berating his colleagues for their failure to develop relevant theory (Coase, 1982, 1984, 2002; Coase & Wang, 2012; Hsiung, 2004). His 1937 paper hoped for an 'exact' analysis that would save Marshallian 'substitution at the margin' as the foundation of the new economics. His letters to his friend Fowler around the time revealed their concern with firm boundaries and size (Coase, 1991d) and, following Knight, they wondered why, if managers were indeed able to reduce costs and so explain a firm's existence, it would not then expand into a monopoly (Knight 1921:xxi). At the same time Coase noted the categories 'firm' and 'market' were muddy. Markets are moving patterns of individual economic events, they do not 'exist' as identifiable entities. Sometimes there are markets within firms.

Legal matters are central to the Coasian discourse; firms hold their assets together using the limited inventory of contract methods available. In his 1937 paper, Coase stressed the 'employment

contract'. He later regretted this, calling it one of the paper's 'main weaknesses' for it led him to ignore the many other types of contract for acquiring and deploying the firm's capital (Coase, 1991b:65). Mangers had to deal with multiple contracts whose character varied even as all were subordinate to the entrepreneur's vision and the relevant social norms and corporate law, again varied. They had to estimate pricing practices, contractual arrangements, and organizational forms (Coase, 1991b:73). Given the uncertainties and complexities, their choices are not likely to be rigorous.

## WILLIAMSON

Coase was Williamson's elder by 22 years, nonetheless it helps to unpack Williamson's work before delving into Coase's subtler story. Williamson has written at length about his sources (Dahlstrom & Nygaard, 2010; Williamson, 1986, 1990a, 1996c, 2005, 2010a, 2010b, 2010c, 2014, 2016, 1990b). He is a product of the Graduate School of Industrial Administration (GSIA) at Carnegie Mellon; Simon was one of its founders (Khurana & Spender 2012). In 1960, on Charles Bonini's advice and with the GSIA Dean's encouragement, Williamson transferred from Stanford's doctoral program to GSIA's (Williamson, 1986:xiii). There, Richard Cyert, James March, and Allen Meltzer became influential. Williamson began work on 'managerial discretion', the managers' freedom to pursue goals other than profit-maximizing. Some of these might be 'personal', precipitating principal-agent issues. Williamson reported Simon's influence was 'massive'. Soon a paper he wrote for Simon's course on mathematical social science appeared in *Quarterly Journal of Economics* (Williamson, 1963)—before he was awarded his PhD in May 1963. He also had a chapter in Cyert & March's *Behavioral Theory of the Firm*, formalizing a managerial discretion model (Cyert & March, 1963:237-252).

Williamson's dissertation won a Ford Foundation Prize, though not everyone understood why (Ankarloo & Palermo, 2004; Kay, 2015; Zannetos, 1965). It was largely mathematical and quickly published by Prentice-Hall as *The Economics of Discretionary Behavior: Managerial Objectives in a Theory of the Firm* (Williamson, 1964). Williamson went on to UC Berkeley, spent the summer of 1964 at RAND, where he met Kenneth Arrow and other leading economists, spent the summer of 1965 at UCLA, and settled at U Penn's Economics Department for almost 20 years before moving back to Berkeley. But in Spring 1966, now an up-and-coming player in the US economics community, he was invited to the US Department of Justice's Antitrust division for a year and worked on several cases: Schwinn, the Ford-Autolite merger, the P&G-Clorox merger, and the Utah Pie case. Returning to Penn, he was asked to teach a course on 'theories of institutions' which introduced him to institutional theorizing.

The DOJ and Penn experiences shifted Williamson from formal modeling towards 'institutional comparison' and a softer TC approach. He published on theorizing the firm's size (Williamson, 1967) but more importantly, on 'economizing' as a defense against charges of monopolization (Klein, Crawford, & Alchian, 1978; Williamson, 1968). His first piece on TCs was 'Vertical Integration of Production: Market Failure Considerations' which appeared in the *American Economic Review* (Williamson, 1971). It was much influenced by Arrow. Williamson cited Coase (1937) but offered no analysis. He also cited Malmgren's much overlooked paper, again without comment (Malmgren, 1961). The importance of Williamson's 1968 and 1971 papers lay in their support for Arrow's 1969 observations on monopolies. At the time monopolies were presumed to be anti-social exercises of capitalist power and so attracted antitrust legislation. Williamson showed there might be circumstances in which monopoly was a socially efficient way of organizing, a conclusion with significant political implications that eventually supported neoliberal policies and Reagan-era 'deregulation'. In these early papers Williamson noted Coase but again only in passing (Kay, 2015). Sensing his TC analysis could be extended from 'vertical integration' to management more generally, *Markets and Hierarchies* (*M&H*) began to take shape (Williamson, 1975). Providentially a graduate student working with Williamson (and the student's lawyer wife) introduced him to labor law. *M&H* was rejected by Brookings but eventually published by Free Press in 1975. It was quickly recognized as a major contribution to the political debate and to micro economics. Williamson was awarded a Nobel in 2009.

Williamson summarized his view of TCE many times. In *M&H* it was a novel analysis to be set against 'received micro theory, the structure-conduct-performance paradigm, the property rights tradition' (Williamson, 1975:250). Its distinctive features were: a 'value-free' focus on transactions, comparative institutional analysis, explicit provision for 'bounded rationality, opportunism, complexity/uncertainty, small numbers bargaining, organizational forms, and atmosphere', and a denial of the fiction of 'frictionless' transacting. (Asset specificity came later.) A few pages on the 'organizational failures' framework was summarized as: bounded rationality, opportunism, uncertainty, small numbers, information impactedness, and atmosphere (Williamson, 1975:257).

In later discussion Williamson cited James M. Buchanan's shift from an 'economics of choice' to an 'economics of contract', pitting the new economics against Lionel Robbins's definition. TCE focused on the costs, merits, and weaknesses of making and enforcing contracts between parties engaged in economic activities. Given real-world contracts were invariably 'incomplete', contracted parties were in a state of 'bilateral dependency'. Efficiencies could arise as the parties 'adapted' their values and intentions, a dynamic and 'inter-temporal' process. Time was drawn into the analysis. Williamson argued that trying to design 'perfect' arrangements was a 'truncated way to study organizations'. The focus should be on contracting with employees, with other firms, and with other agents in markets. This involved 'haggling' and legal process, so was often costly. However, contracts within firms could be treated with 'forbearance', settling things by management 'fiat', so reducing costs. Williamson's Nobel citation noted he had shown how "to regard markets, firms, associations, agencies, and even households from the perspective of their contribution to the resolution of conflict", thereby introducing 'governance' into neoclassical economics. His goal was to develop a 'predictive theory of economic organization' (Williamson, 2010b:215).

## COASE

Some aspects of Coase's story are well known (Coase, 1988b), how he was thought a semi-invalid, attended grammar school (an artifact of the British class system), enrolled in a University of London chemistry degree, discovered a life-long distaste of mathematics, and being debarred from studying history, switched to a Bachelor of Commerce. This included a correspondence course in accounting. It all helped him enroll at LSE. He chose 'industry' for its Part 2, given the strong UK tradition of studying the nature and history of the commercial concerns on which the Empire stood (Pollard, 1968). Ironically, by the time Coase completed his BComm he had taken no economics courses. He felt attracted to Industrial Law. But he had also taken courses with Arnold Plant, LSE's new Professor of Commerce 'with special reference to business administration'. Plant befriended Coase and his support and mentoring was crucial to Coase's career. In Plant's seminar Coase stumbled into the question that defined his life's work; when to organize economic relations within a firm, when in a market. The rest, it seemed, was history.

But it was not so simple. Coase's question presumed some fundamental, unspecified, distinction between firms and markets; but how did they differ? Coase queried the taken-for-granted. Even in his 1937 paper, there was an echo of 'why markets?' But how could his thinking develop unsupported by the concepts of firms and markets that most adopt uncritically? Coase conceded he was not an outstanding student but nonetheless, with Plant's support, was awarded a traveling scholarship to spend the academic year 1931-1932 in the US. Before the trip, Coase attended Hayek's lectures and learned about the political impact of limited knowledge and information and how it was central to any economics that dismissed perfect knowledge as irrelevant—to whit, an economics of the real world. Hayek was using Knight's *Risk, Uncertainty, and Profit* as a text (Knight 1921). Likewise Knight's *The Economic Organization* was circulating in mimeograph (Knight, 2013:x). Knight defined economics as the study of alternative modes of socio-economic organization; caste, authority, democracy, exchange (Knight, 2013:20). He also discussed the firm's boundaries and 'substitution at the margin'.

Feeling ill-equipped to talk with US economists, Coase spent most of his time with businessmen—to whom he had good access with letters of commendation from UK government and trades union officials (a benefit of the UK class system available to him as an LSE student). He also devised clever methods of gaining access. He reported talking with a Union Carbide purchasing manager in Chicago and getting a 'lively sense of the possibilities of substitution'(Coase, 1991d:39). He also attended some of Knight's lectures, but seemed not to make much of them (Coase, 1937, 1991d). In contrast, Coase's accounting courses covered both financial and managerial accounting; the latter then called 'cost and works accounting'. It dealt with estimating manufacturing costs. You qualified as an 'estimator'. It was forward-looking, anticipating costs, not backwards-looking ledger-keeping. It helped Coase appreciate that firms comprised many varied parts with dynamic inter-relations, in contrast to the financial accountants' work to condense everything into a single P&L figure. Today's accounting students learn little about what goes on within firms, or how to cost it (Johnson & Kaplan, 1987). These courses gave Coase a novel way to address Knight's questions about firms' organization and boundaries.

Returning from the US, Coase taught at Dundee, then Liverpool. His heavy teaching load delayed the paper, eventually published in 1937 with many comments on Knight's thinking—not all favorable. To his surprise—and disappointment—the paper dropped into oblivion immediately. But by then he had joined LSE's teaching staff and married Marian Hartung, the life-long partner he met at Northwestern U during his US trip. He was asked to teach a course on the economics of the public sector, something else he knew little about. With Plant's help he discovered others knew as little, beyond the suspicion that regulation's impact was often contrary to the public interest. Which helped move Coase towards more libertarian views. In 1938 he wrote a series of articles for *The Accountant* that laid out what was later dubbed the 'London Tradition on Opportunity Costs' (Coase, 1981a). That these were 'forward looking' was crucial to his later work.

A chance LSE assignment led Coase to study the

regulation of broadcasting. This turned into a life-long project with huge impact on his thinking. Throughout WW2 Coase worked for Churchill's Cabinet operations as a statistician. In 1946 he was at the UK government's office in Washington DC. There, noting military and industrial planning's ineffectiveness, he moved closer to Hayekian libertarian ideas. He also was deeply immersed in the UK government's contracts with US suppliers and discovered most were vague and 'incomplete', only functioning through the parties' 'trust'. But intra-firm politics often severely impacted their implementation. A 1948 Rockefeller grant enabled a further 9-month visit to study US broadcasting regulation, which was complicated in the intensely competitive US market, in sharp contrast with the BBC's Crown monopoly. Coase completed his BBC report in 1950 (Coase, 1950). Invited to attend hearings, he told the panel about the US idea of auctioning broadcast spectrum. Astounded, they presumed he was making a tasteless joke. Coase saw it as a comparative institutional arrangement, that a government might either assign spectrum or make a market to trade rights to use and exclude other broadcasters.

In 1950, unhappy about the UK political situation, Coase accepted the University of Buffalo chair vacated by Fritz Machlup, leaving there to join Buchanan, another of Frank Knight's students, at the University of Virginia. In 1958-1959 Coase spent a year at Stanford as a Fellow, finding Thomas Kuhn's work formative. He worked up a paper about the comparative institutional arrangements in broadcasting and submitted it to the new *Journal of Law and Economics* at the Chicago Law School. He was invited to Chicago to present it. He famously overcame objections to his anti-Pigovian treatment of 'social costs' from Milton Friedman, George Stigler, and others from the Chicago School of Economics (Klink, 1994; Simpson, 1996). Coase pondered why they had difficulty, concluding it was because they misunderstood 'opportunity costs'. He later discussed this with fellow LSE student Abba Lerner who shared the London Tradition. Lerner understood it 'in a minute'. The *JL&E* editor advised Coase to cut the offending parts of the 1959 paper but he declined. But he was more successfully persuaded to re-write the paper completely (Coase,

1960:n1), which was published in 1960 as "The Problem of Social Cost". Coase's Nobel citation stands on his 1937 and 1960 papers. He was invited to a joint appointment at the Chicago Law and Business Schools where he remained until his death in 2013.

Coase's 1959 and 1960 papers were very different. In 1959 Pigou was touched on; in 1960 demolished. In 1959 there was less economics, more law, an extensive discussion of the evolution of US broadcasting regulation. Coase noted the suggestion for using the price mechanism (auctioning) had come from Herzel, a Chicago Law student (Coase, 1959:14; Herzel, 1952, 1998). Coase later asked Herzel where he got the idea and was told it came from Lerner's lectures and book (Lerner, 1944). The 1951 *Chicago Law Review* 'Comment' that precipitated Herzel's suggestion showed the scholars involved were familiar with Coase's BBC work (Chicago Law Review, 1951:810n54) and with Lerner's 1944 *Economics of Control* (Chicago Law Review, 1951:810n53). They were also familiar with Knight's *Economic Organization*. Coase's 1950 BBC monograph did not include Herzel's suggestion; which he must have read in 1952—but before the BBC hearings.

## COMMONS & HOHFELD

A happy aspect of Coase's and Williamson's work is that interviews with both are available on You-Tube[1]. They add a personal dimension to their writings. Coase had a sharp sense of humor. He was committed to managers and their practices, reiterating the importance of looking at their situation's specifics, especially its legalities. He endorsed case studies and working inductively towards the general. In contrast, Williamson saw himself in the nomothetic tradition, searching for better models. He anticipated developing TCE into rigorous theory by 'uncovering and explicating the micro-analytic features' of organizational governance (Williamson, 2000:596). He proceeded from TCE's axioms: bounded rationality, opportunism, uncertainty, small numbers, asset specificity, etc. In *M&H* he set off by noting Coase (1937) and Commons (1934) and presumed managers could mitigate the TCs arising from employees' imperfection. His 'model of man'— 'imperfect' or 'opportunistic', to be monitored and managed—has been widely attacked (Ghoshal, 2005).

Williamson told readers he was picking up the Coasian program. But was he? (Kay, 2015) He also claimed Commons as a major influence, but there is a curious lacuna; he cited only Commons's 1934 book. Only later did he cite, perhaps for the first time, Commons' more influential 1924 book (Williamson, 1993). In this book Commons went to great length to define 'transaction' (Commons, 1924:68). Many of those writing about TCs seem unaware of this definition. There was no evidence of Commons' thinking in Williamson's writings. Even today there is considerable disagreement about the nature of a 'transaction' (e.g. Allen, 1991; Barzel, 1985) and about how much TCE has achieved, indeed whether it can be tested at all (Crook, Combs, Ketchen Jr, & Aguinis, 2013; Geyskens, Steenkamp, & Kumar, 2006; Hodgson, 2010). Williamson showed little doubt and defined transactions, both external and internal to the firm, as 'exchanges' (Williamson, 1975:124).

Rather than presuming 'in the beginning there were markets' (Williamson, 1975:20), Coase presumed individuals with a 'propensity to truck, barter, and exchange'. The problem is to know what to consider. Institutional theorists divide on whether they focus on the details of the institutional environment, in the Douglass North tradition, or on the interpersonal relations and governance processes within institutions (Williamson, 1993:457). Coase was in the second camp and began his 1960 paper by claiming economic relations are 'reciprocal', between independent parties who have incommensurate ideas and interests, but whose negotiations are constrained by relevant law (Coase, 1960). Following Plant's suspicion that laws and regulations were often 'inefficient', Coase pilloried legislators who could not or did not pay attention to the economic consequences of their legalizing.

Coase's axiomatizing 'reciprocity' (Coase, 1960:2) suggested common ground with Commons—again not cited in Coase's *oeuvre*. Commons' 1924 analytic scheme emerged from a lengthy analysis of two Hohfeld papers (Commons, 1924:65-142; Hohfeld, 1913, 1917). These had huge impact on US corporate law, yet were likewise not

**Figure 1: Parties to every transaction
(Commons 1924:68)**

cited by Coase. Hohfeld's work was extremely difficult (Andrews, 1983; Corbin, 1919; Pagano & Vatiero, 2014; Radin, 1938; Schlag, 2015; Singer, 1982; Vatiero, 2010). A 1996 Williamson paper cited Hohfeld but without comment (Williamson, 1996b:390). Borrowing greatly from Hohfeld, Commons argued every real transaction was (a) reciprocal, and (b) took place between at least five notional parties whose rights, obligations, and duties varied (Figure 1). The deal was always between A and B, buyer and seller, but also with A' and B', 'opportunity' buyers and sellers who would have 'done the deal' had A and B not closed it (Commons, 1924:68). Finally, there was C, the instrument of the legal power standing over the negotiation, setting its rules and boundaries, limiting the uncertainties engaged.

The deeper point was that the economists' notion of 'the market', the locus of a mathematically analyzable 'perfect' deal between powerless actors, was displaced by an alternative idiographic metaphor of a real negotiation process between parties in a real society. Hohfeld pushed back against nomothetic market-based views, presuming each deal unique. The resulting analysis was idiographic and 'time-bound' rather than nomothetic and 'time-less'. As business people say, "timing is everything".

Williamson put epistemological and methodological distance between himself and Coase as he drew on the nomothetic OT and OB he learned at GSIA. Ultimately Williamson presumed 'the firm' already existed, essentially bureaucratic, so dodging Coase's first 'killer question'. Williamson then focused on the way 'bounded rationality' and so on would impede the firm's otherwise costless operation. He saw TCs as a 'loss of grace' story. TCE would collate every discoverable way in which people fail to live up to 'rational man'. But was Coase headed in a better direction? The charge the 'old institutionalists'—such as Ely, Veblen, Mitchell, and Commons—'had no theory' hides the more precise charge—they had no nomothetic theory. This, we know, is the issue that leads many to complain about economics' irrelevance despite its vast research funding, teaching, and many Nobel Prizes. As Queen Elizabeth II famously asked 'why didn't anybody notice the 2008 collapse coming?' (Power, 2012). The old institutionalists were closer to the English tradition of Alfred Marshall and John Maynard Keynes; spelt out for a generation in John Neville Keynes's *Scope and Method of Political Economy* (Keynes, 1904). This was written at Marshall's request by John Maynard's father to head off an academic catastrophe in England like the *Methodenstreit* that ultimately wiped out the German economics tradition, opening the way for the Anglo-American disciplinary dominance that lives on today, both in the literature and the Nobel count.

Keynes *Pére* argued 'useful economics' stood on three pillars (a) rigorous economic science, (b) political theory, and (c) artful execution (skilled practice). While many saw, and still see, economics as 'science', remote from life's exigencies, Keynes (and Marshall) saw it differently, as an effort to inform those inhabiting our capitalist society about the way in which its economics works—thereby to inform, not determine, their practice. In today's terms, help them act mindfully. Ironically *Scope & Method* became the 'straw man' in Friedman's famous essay "The Methodology of Positive Economics" (Friedman, 1953). Helped along by Stigler, Friedman dismissed (b) and (c), valuing theory on its ability to predict. Knight emphasized the art (Knight, 1923; 2013:8). The discussion was muddied by Coase pointing out that if transactions were costless the initial assignment of the parties' legal rights would not affect the deal they ultimately negotiated. In Stigler's hands this became the 'Coase Theorem' or 'So-Called Coase Theorem', rejected by Coase himself (e.g. Allen, 2015; Coase, 1981b; D. A. Farber, 1997; Medema & Zerbe Jr, 1999; Schlag, 2013). Coase abhorred the 'blackboard' wherein

law was immaterial to the economics. Although an often a gifted writer, he chose a maladroit way to persuade his readers to focus on positive TCs, that the law's allocation of property rights was always material, and that economists could not ignore it.

The switch from nomothetic to idiographic analysis opens the analysis to much methodological criticism—some evident in the long running debates about the 'case method'. As Coase grew older and his fame increased, eventually sealed by his Nobel and the success of *JL&E*, he grew less patient with those hewing to the nomothetic path. How, he wondered, could they find professional satisfaction theorizing a world that could not exist, in reasoning that had no impact on the urgent economic issues facing the living? At the same time the implications of his own 1937 and 1960 papers were not much clarified. Neither was the contrast between his methods and those of the mainstream. Yet to the end of his life, following Knight's direction, Coase found the energy to shake his fist at his colleagues for what he felt was their moral failure to help those living in the real socio-economy (Coase, 2003; Coase & Wang, 2012).

## UNCERTAINTY & VALUE CREATION

Knight's thinking shapes today's discussions about a useful and thus inherently moral and political economics—and thus about business ethics, corporate social responsibility, and much else. His influence over the Chicago school and thereby the entire field of economics was massive (Emmett, 2009; Knight, 2013; Mirowski & Nik-Khah, 2017; Overtveldt, 2007; Van Horn, Mirowski, & Stapleford, 2011). Much turns on 'taking KU seriously' (Bewley, 1998; Hoogduin, 1987; Hoogduin & Snippe, 1987; Korsgaard, Berglund, Thrane, & Blenker, 2016). Despite Coase's doubts about Knight's work in his 1937 paper, he sensed KU as key to the 'realism' he advocated throughout his life. No KU, no firms, no exchange, no economics. Knowledge, it turns out, is our imaginative response to KU, not the result of a privileged 'scientific' communication with reality. No KU, no knowledge, and even Hayek got lost here (Hayek, 1945). Ironically, no KU, no realism; if nothing is uncertain there is no contrast between the real and the not-real. Williamson and others dodged KU, preferring the 'blackboard' world of 'certainty presumed'. Williamson thought uncertainty a source of imperfection and inefficiency in this certainty, curiously citing his teacher, Herbert Simon, while missing the essence of Simon's thinking (Spender, 2013a). Note that Simon attended Knight's department as an undergraduate and surely read Knight's discussion on man's bounded rationality (BR) (Knight, 2013:15). BR is not incomplete understanding of what is known or even knowable. Rather it paints the human condition as both (a) conscious, and (b) conscious of never knowing reality, of not standing at the Archimedean Fulcrum.

Despite KU implying 'knowledge-absence', there are ways to frame it as the locus of economic value creation. The focus switches from pursuing 'perfectible knowledge', especially about markets and human weakness, and onto our creative responses as we collide with the 'knowledge absences' that impede our progress towards our chosen goals. Coase (1960) sketched an analysis of how micro-institutional inter-personal acts of imagining, negotiating, and deal-making enabled heterogeneous parties (real actors rather than 'rational men' who see the world similarly) to create mutuality, common ground, and collaborative practice—and thereby new economic value. His 1960 paper showed how legislators often failed to 'design' optimal solutions and how, left to negotiate their own interests, the parties engaged might 'micro-institutionalize' a new 'win-win'. This micro-institutionalization provides the core to a Coasian metaphor of the firm. It is what entrepreneurs and leaders strive to make happen. It is absent from nomothetic theorizing, precisely because KU is ignored or dismissed.

Clarifying this requires some groundwork on 'transaction' and 'uncertainty'. First, as noted earlier, 'transaction' may mean 'exchange' or it may mean 'contract'. It is economical to treat it as both, mutually defining. In a Von Neumann machine computation flip-flops between two states: instruction and execution. A firm is a species of computer with (a) a knowledge-identity—perhaps labeled the entrepreneurial idea, business model, or strategy—and (b) a physical or ontological identity, assets (perhaps VRIN) and a production function, the font of

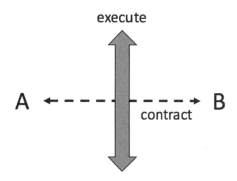

**Figure 2: Bi-Modal Contract/Execute Process**

entropy and, sometimes, economic value (Kraaijenbrink, Spender, & Groen, 2010). Profits arise from practice, not ideas, as the bi-modal firm 'flip-flops' between contracting and executing, direction and action, strategizing and implementing (see Figure 2). The states cannot be separated definitively without the razor of certainty; in KU circumstances, they are inherently dynamic, intertwined and mutually defining.

Writers such as Klapp and Pitelis & Teece explored dynamic models of the firm by contrasting their different states of being (Klapp, 1975; Pitelis & Teece, 2010). Nonaka & Takeuchi's SECI analysis is the most pertinent model as 'knowledge' cycles from the development lab, where practice leads to knowledge creation, which is then transformed into economic value as senior management allocate resources (Nonaka & Takeuchi, 1995; Spender, 2013b). To those in the neoclassical tradition this is utter nonsense; no testable theory or predictions emerge (Cohen, 1935). But, countering this, rigorous economics appears incapable of explaining value-creation—or addressing Coase's questions. Rigorous choice does not create economic value. It explores correlations not causes. The methodological choice is brutal; no KU, no space for entrepreneurial judgment and imagination, so no firms and no value creation. How then to engage or 'theorize' KU with informative results?

The types of KU actors face can be parsed into (1) ignorance, (2) indeterminacy, (3) incommensurability, and (4) irrelevance (Spender, 1989:45). First, we may be **'ignorant'** of what is knowable. As Hayek and others insisted (Knight, 2013:73), the price system helps actors deal with ignorance of the information they need to make rational decisions. They can turn to 'the market' for the relevant facts, taken as 'objective'. Admitting that no mind can grasp them all does not diminish the facts' relevance. The actor/market relationship is nomothetic so long as no actor's choices affect the market. Goal pursuit can be analyzed without reference to other actors.

But, second, competition implies a completely different knowledge-universe, one of actors, not markets, in which the actors' relationships are reciprocal, idiographic, rather than between the actor and Mother Nature. Ignorance of 'objective facts' is not the issue. Under KU individuals are heterogeneous, they differ in interest and capability. The relevant knowledge is idiographic or 'subjective'. The socio-economy is in motion as the actors push to better themselves. There is no equilibrium, no single coherent body of 'true' knowledge. There is never-ending '**indeterminacy**' between the actors and their knowledge. This is the core axiom of game-theory (Shubik, 1954). Instead of uncertainty being at a general level, between a stylized (scientist) actor and a higher truth—such as the market—there is a relationship between BR individuals. Indeterminacy will not yield to the scientific method for it only becomes ignorance under conditions of certainty. Third, from Adam's fall and the Book of Job onwards to Simon, we know the human condition is of BR. Plus we know many things but always in limited ways and 'differently' since everything we take as knowledge stands on specific assumptions (axioms) that can never be fully justified. As Descartes or Popper reminded us, no axioms are universal, no knowledge is irrefutable. We experience our knowledge as bounded, fragmented into '**incommensurate**' chunks Kuhn called paradigms.

Fourth, as Wittgenstein argued, knowledge claims must be expressed in language. So long as we define 'tacit knowledge' as that which is un-codified, we cannot speak it to others. There is no 'truth criterion' for tacit knowledge (Polanyi, 1962). Knowledge is public shareable language. There is no knowledge outside language, no private language. Mathematics is a powerful 'formal' language but not the only one we use. It cannot capture our uncertainties or responses—or the Coasian firm.

Our formal languages are complemented by the un-formal 'natural' languages we use to negotiate living. Their open-ness helps us capture, somewhat, the emotions and anxieties we experience as we inhabit uncertain circumstances. In real-world KU circumstances, what we treat as 'objective facts' cannot be separated from the feelings and judgments we label religious, political, aesthetic, moral, social, cultural, and so on. Ultimately the institutional approach stands on taking our chosen natural languages seriously, trying to capture the specifics of our experience (Crémer, 1990; Crémer, Garicano, & Prat, 2007). Neoclassical approaches disregard them, presuming objective facts, perhaps falsifiable, putting distance between our analysis and our experiences. The blooming, buzzing confusion of realism is abandoned in favor of formalization—so risking our chosen language's **irrelevance**.

With these four stylizations of KU—ignorance, indeterminacy, incommensurability, and irrelevance—we can turn to the analysis of how we respond to KU imaginatively—as practice, as opposed to analytically. We respond differently depending how we categorize the uncertainty confronted. We enact different practices. Ignorance is addressed by 'researching' where we presume answers findable, sometimes formalized into using the 'scientific method'. Fetishizing science implies everything worth knowing can be obtained with such methods. But we also experience the other types of KU, when 'researching the market' is not an effective strategy. Again, uncertainties are aspects of us and how we know (both nomothetically and ideographically) not aspects (essences) of the things known. Managers must deal with indeterminacy and incommensurability as well as ignorance. Game theorists show that few indeterminacies can be framed conclusively, so establishing 'a strategy', as they define the term. Most game-like circumstances have no determinable strategy. One response is bargaining, and this requires the parties to adapt as they move towards agreement, overcoming the incommensurabilities of views and objectives. When Coase defined economic relationships as reciprocal he focused on the indeterminacies and incommensurabilities of real-world economic activity, not with the actors' ignorance of market prices or the computational impediments to rigorous choosing.

## THE FIRM

The Hohfeld/Commons notion of transaction is defined by the parties A, B, A', B'—and maybe C too—as independent, incommensurate, and incommensurate, interacting with each other, not optimizing within a coherent market. The interactions 'construct' them as economic actors; their nature is not presumed *ex ante*. The negotiation resolves the parties' uncertainties into multiple contracts—a process of micro-institutionalization that shifts how they are defined as identities and values. Coase followed Knight's dismissal of absolutes; the individuals involved are adaptable, they learn, change, and forget (Knight, 2013:15). Contracts cannot be written in formal language, such as mathematical formulae, only in ways shaped by the natural language of the relevant law, expressing the parties' heterogeneous interests and the uncertainties addressed; more idiographic than nomothetic. No KU, no contracts, just spot exchanges. If there are no divergences between the parties, there is neither need nor possibility of contract. Different kinds of uncertainty are resolved in different ways. Contract deals with inter-party indeterminacies and incommensurabilities, converging on the shared natural language constructed specifically for the situation. The overarching idea is Knightian, that 'the firm' is a socially and legally legitimated apparatus of multiple contracts—written to grasp and resolve some specific uncertainties discovered in the socio-economy, in pursuit of increasing the various parties' differing values. Indeterminacy and incommensurability call forth imaginative practice that shifts collaborating individuals' economic values. Resolving ignorance and irrelevance merely support this as the nub of the human process of value-creation.

Coase's 1960 illustrations were of Hohfeldian 'entrepreneurial acts', the reciprocal creation of economic value by actor A and actor B in a social context that also comprises A', B' and C. The intuition can be generalized into the 'nexus of contracts' model which recognizes that real firms entail more than one contract—and more than one discovered uncertainty (Aoki, Gustafsson, & Williamson, 1990). There can be no less than three, another manifestation of the medieval Rule of Three. The investors' intentions differ from those of employees, suppliers, customers, regulators, the courts, and so on. The 'model of man' invoked was Adam Smith's 'propensity to truck, barter, and exchange'—economically imaginative beings. The neoliberal inclination to see only exchange, presuming all values can be expressed as prices, denies Adam Smith's subtleties. Every exchange presupposes the parties value differently what is being exchanged; indeed, different 'things' are being exchanged. As Vernon Smith showed, the values that matter to the negotiation reflect the individuality and reciprocity of the parties engaged, nothing to do with markets (Smith, 1998). Farber shows the process of bartering not only leads to individuals 're-valuing' the exchange and themselves, the process cascades out into a changed sense of community (L. Farber, 2006).

It is useful to think of 'a firm' as a specific 'opportunity space' realized and occupied by the complex of languages implied by a nexus of contracts negotiated (See Figure 3) (Aoki et al., 1990; Gustafsson, 1990; Spender, 2014a, 2014b). As these connect towards 'closure' the actors' confidence rises to the point they 'plunge in' and act, shifting from thought to action. The parties' various personal aims and uncertainties get traded-off as they move into this collaborative action.

The firm as a negotiated language is an economic metaphor that codifies the parties' agreement. It is relevant when it enables discussion of the breaches and remedies that arise in practice, linking to wider-reaching legal doctrines. Recalling the computer analogy (Fig. 2), the firm is characterized as a dynamic interaction between the parties' constructed languages and the contexts of their practices—interplaying the parties' imaginations and the constraints on their practices. Not all we can imagine and capture in language is actionable—think perpetual motion machines. Unavoidably the language constructed is prey to 'irrelevance', of failing to explain, shape, or anticipate the parties' practice. Arriving at and executing a contract changes how the parties view the values committed. The value changes are personal to the parties, not related to any market. Markets are evidence of individuals' re-valuing in the interests of executing

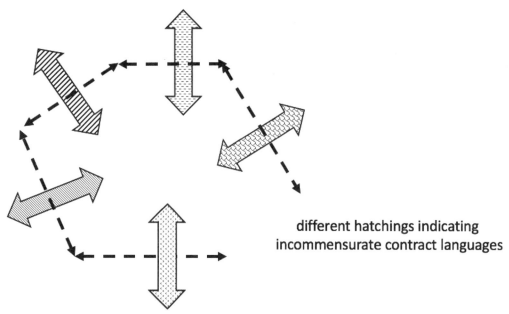

Figure 3: Multiple Contract/Execute Transactions Framing an Opportunity Space

exchanges. Thinking that market values are 'more correct' shifts attention away from the parties and onto economy-wide issues. But the firm is not an economy-wide phenomenon; it proceeds one transaction at a time. In its bi-modal flip-flops, the judgment fueling valuation and negotiation is transformed into the practices that comprise the production function.

Coase assumed actors 'estimated' costs based on information gathered from the parties and the situation, not on 'price taking'. He focused on 'opportunity cost' (Coase, 1981a). Just as his use of 'cost' led to miscommunication with the Chicago economists in 1958, so it has led to confusion about his 1937 paper's message. Most see cost as the price paid to acquire an asset. Instead, Coase focused on the value of the asset already owned and what was to be realized by trading it. His 1960 paper explored arrangements to maximize this, covering the costs of discovery and contracting, informed by the costs of discovering the 'next best' deal. But his TCs are idiographic, situated, nothing to do with the 'price system'. They are bound into the specific situation rather than into markets. They are the 'costs' of overcoming the situation's uncertainties; especially those of identifying the parties A, B, A', B' and C, and of doing a deal. These costs cannot be treated as matters of ignorance, absent price information; they can only be estimated relative to the firm's current operations. As business people say "What does it mean to us?" The London Tradition on opportunity costs separated Coase's analysis from Williamson's. Williamson sought market-based prices for the factors of production, including labor and, most crucially, management. Thus, Coase also suggested a paradox—that TCs were the least avoidable costs but also the least determinable. If determinable why are they not factor costs? (Barzel, 1985). If not determinable how can they be fitted into rigorous theory? Likewise, contracts are invariably incomplete, their consequences under-determined and therefore inherently political (e.g. Calabresi, 1982; Medema, 1996; Merrill & Smith, 2011).

## CONCLUDING COMMENTS

The Coase and Williamson discourses were far apart, immiscible. Williamson's model was essentially static, only analyzable as in equilibrium or headed there. The Coasian model was open-ended and dynamic, inevitably escaping attempts to express it formally because it is built from creative responses to the actors' selected KUs. Entrepreneurship begins by discovering and selecting the specific KUs to be engaged (Alvarez & Barney,

2007). Right now, the TC literature is stuck between one discourse that presumes TCs are both general and determinable, so indistinguishable from factor costs, and another that presumes TCs are particular, un-determinable, and so not theorize-able. What is to be done?

First, to presume 'TCs explain why firms exist' is to fall into a tautological trap of one's own making. Williamson treated TCs firms, and markets axiomatically—firms exist and engage markets, which exist, and incur a special class of costs that can be reduced by managers who are not subject to the same shortcomings as their 'opportunistic' employees. But there is no such 'special class' of determinable costs; nor are real employees predictably opportunistic. Coase's intuitions were less totalizing and more realistic, driven by axiomatizing individuals' heterogeneous propensity to truck, barter, and exchange.

Second, he noted Penrose's intuitions complemented his own (Pitelis & Teece, 2009:8). This helps clarify how, perhaps under the combined influence of Knight, Kuhn, and Hayek, Coase distanced himself from the mainstream that saw values as prices. He moved towards values based on the parties 'personal knowledge'. Penrose 'personalized' the firm—which creates new knowledge and new value from the management team's imaginative interaction (Spender, 1999). The Coasian firm is likewise no more than a 'term of art' that points towards a fuzzily bounded bundle of inter-party contracts of varying incompleteness. The firm as a theorize-able entity dissolves (J. N. Gordon, 1989).

Third, many miss the idiographic aspects of Coase's TCs because they presume, perhaps unwittingly, 'the firm' can be distinguished from such 'costs', that firms exist and have TCs. But Coasian TCs point to the contracting processes that are the firm, that execute its idiographic flip-flop between idea and practice. Firms exist only as contracts made and executed. No contract/execute, no firm. If the resulting TCs are zero, neither positive nor negative, the contracts are revealed as irrelevant to the firm's identity and process; no KUs are engaged, no new value created to be held or distributed (Alchian & Demsetz, 1972). Pursuing nomothetic theory, Williamson viewed TCs determinable, arising from resolvable ignorance, even when discuss-ing principal-agent issues. Coase dealt with indeterminacy and incommensurability. Williamson's managing was economizing, Coase's was strategizing, creatively bundling and administering contracts to net-positive result, not merely economizing.

Fourth, Coase's work was a masked but nonetheless full-throated attack on mainstream 'market-based' analysis. His Nobel Lecture appeal to 'study the world of positive transaction costs' (Coase, 1991e; 1992:717) was a direct slap at Friedman's earlier use of the term 'positive'. Many explain the popularity of Friedman's 1953 *Essay* as defending an eroding mainstream position; there is much politics involved (Backhouse & Fontaine, 2010). But axiomatizing less-than-fully-rational actors brings their politics to the center of the analysis—as well as their psychology (Mirowski & Nik-Khah, 2017). More than behavioral economics results. Economics is revealed as the 'continuation of politics by other means'.

Fifth, Coase implied a theory of entrepreneurship—micro-institutionalization under the entrepreneurial 'gaze'. Positive TCs fragment 'the firm' into multiple incommensurate contracts that the entrepreneur must (a) synthesize into a functionally adequate vision, and (b) execute into somewhat ordered practice. Positive TCs bring the 'theory of the firm' and the 'theory of entrepreneurship' together. Coase's call to 'running the business' implied entrepreneurship was not simple 'price-taking' and rational decision-making, rather the puzzling practice of constructing new knowledge (Pitelis, 2002:34).

Sixth, Coase's method stood against the mainstream economist's, recapturing Keynes's richer pluralist methodology (Keynes, 1904). Williamson's mainstream approach set out from TCE's axioms and sought nomothetic and testable implications. Coase started from idiographic observation and experience and advanced inductively to shareable knowledge.

Seventh, Williamson misread Coase's *mea culpa* on the employment contract (Coase, 1991b:64). Including other contracts did not re-establish the priority of market prices in the analysis. It simply pointed to actors other than employees that entrepreneurs had to draw into the contracting process.

OT folk might call this 'stakeholder theory'. The proposal to identify everyone influenced by a firm's decision, and to take their views into account, is a ludicrous mask of the political reality; the only actors taking part are those with the power to seize a place at the strategizers' table. No-one speaks for the powerless, such as those affected by externalities like pollution and loss of natural resources, especially those unrepresented by other agents, such as those charged to serve the public interest. This points towards a fifth 'killer question' implied in Coase's 1937 paper—"Why would you, a free citizen, contract with this entrepreneur since it means giving up rights and subordinating yourself—'within certain limits'?" Given the rapidly changing nature of work, the gig economy, the erosion of employment benefits, etc. the question is becoming central to any 'useful economics' that claims to illuminate today's society. Finally, eighth, Coasian managers engage KU in the pursuit of new value and profit—a foreword looking entrepreneurial practice on which our democratic capitalism depends (McCloskey, 2010). Williamson's managers are suspicious scrooges, living off past entrepreneurs' imaginations.

Coase gave voice to deep intuitions about private sector firms as practices central to our capitalist democracy, way beyond what can be represented on the economist's blackboard. They can be clarified by comparison with Williamson's more mainstream analysis. The evolution of Coase's political thinking, from naive socialism to committed libertarianism, underscored his attack on Pigou and on mainstream economics' attempt to create an a-political economics. Rather than join Stigler and many recent Riksbank Prize winners, excising the private firms' political and moral implications, Coase aligned with Knight in taking them seriously (Emmett, 2009). Which meant he was pushing against the mainstream's presumption that property-rights were a-political and fully determinable—precisely what Hohfeld denied. Coase's views are increasingly important as 'knowledge' and 'intangible assets' become more central to the private sector firm and its profits.

The deepest puzzle, though, is Coase's personal and intellectual relationship with Knight (Emmett, 2010). Given both men's influence, further research is badly needed if their ideas are to have more impact on the baleful state of management theorizing.

## NOTES

1) https://www.youtube.com/watch?v=fpfi0gsTjrs
https://www.youtube.com/watch?v=04zFygmeCUA&t=59s
https://www.youtube.com/watch?v=u-nu0Q2CQKY
https://www.youtube.com/watch?v=SSYYe-x9r68&t=790s

## REFERENCES

Alchian, Armen A., & Demsetz, Harold. (1972). Production, Information Costs, and Economic Organization. *American Economic Review*, 62(5), 777-795.

Allen, Douglas W. (1991). What Are Transaction Costs? *Research in Law and Economics*, 14, 1-18.

Allen, Douglas W. (2015). The Coase Theorem: Coherent, Logical, and Not Disproved. *Journal of Institutional Economics*, 11(2), 379–390.

Allport, Gordon W. (1962). The General and the Unique in Psychological Science. *Journal of Personality and Social Psychology Bulletin*, 30(3), 405-422.

Alvarez, Sharon A., & Barney, Jay B. (2007). The Entrepreneurial Theory of the Firm. *Journal of Management Studies*, 44(7), 1057-1063. doi:doi:10.1111/j.1467-6486.2007.00721.x

Andrews, Mark. (1983). Hohfeld's Cube. Akron Law Review, 16(3), Article 4.

Ankarloo, Daniel, & Palermo, Giulio. (2004). Anti-Williamson: a Marxian critique of New Institutional Economics. *Cambridge Journal of Economics*, 28, 413–429.

Aoki, Masahiko, Gustafsson, Bo, & Williamson, Oliver E. (Eds.). (1990). *The Firm as a Nexus of Treaties*. Newbury Park CA: Sage.

Backhouse, Roger E., & Fontaine, Philippe (Eds.). (2010). *The History of the Social Sciences since 1945*. Cambridge: Cambridge University Press.

Barzel, Yoram. (1985). Transaction Costs: Are They Just Costs? *Zeitschrift für die gesamte*

*Staatswissenschaft*, Bd. 141(H. 1., 2nd Symposium on The New Institutional Economics (März 1985)), 4-16.

Bewley, Truman F. (1998). Knightian Uncertainty. In Donald Jacobs, Ehud Kalai, & M Kamien (Eds.), *Frontiers of Research in Economic Theory* (pp. 71-81). New York: Cambridge University Press.

Boudreaux, Donald J., & Holcombe, Randall G. (1989). The Coasian and Knightian Theories of the Firm. *Managerial and Decision Economics*, 10(2 (June)), 147-154.

Calabresi, Guido. (1982). The New Economic Analysis of the Law: Scholarship, Sophistry, or Self-Indulgence? *Proceedings of the British Academy*, 85(Maccabaean Lecture in Jurisprudence), 85-108.

Calabresi, Guido. (2003). An Introduction to Legal Thought: Four Approaches to Law and to the Allocation of Body Parts. Faculty Scholarship Series. Paper 2022. doi: http://digitalcommons.law.yale.edu/fss_papers/2022

Chandler, Alfred D. (1962). *Strategy and Structure: Chapters in the History to the American Industrial Enterprise*. Cambridge MA: MIT Press.

Chicago Law Review. (1951). "Public Interest" and the Market in Color Television Regulation. *The University of Chicago Law Review*, 128(4), 802-816. doi:10.2307/1598016

Coase, Ronald H. (1937). The Nature of the Firm. *Economica N.S.*, 4(16), 386-405.

Coase, Ronald H. (1950). *British Broadcasting: A Study in Monopoly*. London: Longmans, Green, and Co.

Coase, Ronald H. (1959). The Federal Communications Commission. *Journal of Law & Economics*, 2(October), 1-40.

Coase, Ronald H. (1960). The Problem of Social Cost. *Journal of Law & Economics*, 3, 1-44.

Coase, Ronald H. (1972). Industrial Organization: A Proposal for Research. In Victor R. Fuchs (Ed.), *Economic Research, Retrospect and Prospect: Policy Issues and Research Opportunities in Industrial Organization* (Vol. 3, pp. 59-73). Cambridge MA: NBER.

Coase, Ronald H. (1981a). Business Organization and the Accountant. In James M. Buchanan & George F. Thirlby (Eds.), *L.S.E. Essays on Cost* (pp. Essay 5). New York: New York University Press.

Coase, Ronald H. (1981b). The Coase Theorem and the Empty Core: *A Comment. Journal of Law & Economics*, 24(1), 183-187.

Coase, Ronald H. (1982). Economics at LSE in the 1930's: A Personal View. *Atlantic Economic Journal*, 10(1), 31-34.

Coase, Ronald H. (1984). New Institutional Economics. *Journal of Institutional and Theoretical Economics*, 140, 229-231.

Coase, Ronald H. (1988a). Industrial Organization: A Proposal for Research. In Ronald H. Coase (Ed.), *The Firm, The Market, and the Law* (pp. 57-74). Chicago IL: University of Chicago Press.

Coase, Ronald H. (1988b). The Nature of the Firm: Origin, Meaning, & Influence. *Journal of Law, Economics & Organization*, 4(1, Spring), 3-47.

Coase, Ronald H. (1991a). The Nature of the Firm (1937). In Oliver E. Williamson & Sidney G. Winter (Eds.), *The Nature of the Firm; Origins, Evolution and Development* (pp. 18-33). New York: Oxford University Press.

Coase, Ronald H. (1991b). The Nature of the Firm: Influence. In Oliver E. Williamson & Sidney G. Winter (Eds.), *The Nature of the Firm: Orgins, Evolution, and Development* (pp. 61-74). New York: Oxford University Press.

Coase, Ronald H. (1991c). The Nature of the Firm: Meaning. In Oliver E. Williamson & Sidney G. Winter (Eds.), *The Nature of the Firm: Origins, Evolution, and Development* (pp. 48-60). New York: Oxford Unversity Press.

Coase, Ronald H. (1991d). The Nature of the Firm: Origin. In Oliver E. Williamson & Sidney G. Winter (Eds.), *The Nature of the Firm: Origins, Evolution, and Development* (pp. 34-47). New York: Oxford University Press.

Coase, Ronald H. (1991e). Speech at the Nobel Banquet. Nobelprize.org.

Coase, Ronald H. (1992). The Institutional Structure of Production. *American Economic Review*, 82(4), 713-719.

Coase, Ronald H. (2002). Why Economics Will Change. *International Society for New Institutional Economics Newsletter*, 4(1, Summer), 1-4.

Coase, Ronald H. (2003). The Present and Future of

Law and Economics [an .mp3 of this lecture.]. In. Chicago IL.

Coase, Ronald H., & Wang, Ning. (2012). Saving Economics from the Economists. *Harvard Business Review*, 90(12), 36-36.

Cohen, Felix S. (1935). Transcendental Nonsense and the Functional Approach. *Columbia Law Review*, 35(6, Jun), 809-849.

Commons, John R. (1924). *The Legal Foundations of Capitalism*. New York: Macmillan.

Corbin, Arthur L. (1919). Legal Analysis and Terminology. *Yale Law Journal*, 29(2, Dec), 163-173.

Crémer, Jacques. (1990). Common Knowledge and the Co-ordination of Economic Activities. In Masahiko Aoki, Bo Gustafsson, & Oliver E. Williamson (Eds.), *The Firm as a Nexus of Treaties* (pp. 53-76). London: Sage Publications.

Crémer, Jacques, Garicano, Luis, & Prat, Andrea. (2007). Language and the Theory of the Firm. *Quarterly Journal of Economics*, 122(1), 373-407.

Crook, T. Russell, Combs, James G., Ketchen Jr, David J., & Aguinis, Herman. (2013). Organizing Around Transaction Costs: What Have We Learned and Where Do We Go From Here? *Academy of Management Perspectives*, 27(1), 63–79. doi:10.5465/amp.2012.0008

Cyert, Richard M., & March, James G. (1963). *A Behavioural Theory of the Firm*. Englewood Cliffs, New Jersey: Prentice-Hall.

Dahlstrom, Robert, & Nygaard, Arne. (2010). Scientific Background: Oliver E. Williamson's Contributions to Transaction Cost Economics. *Journal of Retailing*, 86(3), 211–214.

Devereux, Daniel T. (1986). Particular and Universal in Aristotle's Conception of Practical Knowledge. *Review of Metaphysics*, 39(3, Mar), 483-550.

Emmett, Ross B. (2009). *Frank Knight and the Chicago School of Economics*. London: Routledge.

Emmett, Ross B. (Ed.) (2010). *Elgar Companion to the Chicago School of Economics*. Cheltenham: Edward Elgar.

Farber, Daniel A. (1997). Parody Lost/Pragmatism Regained: The Ironic History of the Coase Theorem. *Virginia Law Review*, 83(2, Mar), 397-428.

Farber, Lianna. (2006). *An Anatomy of Trade in Medieval Writing: Value, Consent, and Community*. Ithaca NY: Cornell University Press.

Foss, Kirsten, Foss, Nicolai J., & Klein, Peter G. (2017). Uncovering the Hidden Transaction Costs of Market Power: A Property Rights Approach to Strategic Positioning. *Managerial and Decision Economics*, early view.

Friedman, Milton. (1953). The Methodology of Positive Economics. In *Essays in Positive Economics* (pp. 3-43). Chicago IL: University of Chicago Press.

Furubotn, Eirik G. (2001). The New Institutional Economics and the Theory of the Firm. *Journal of Economic Behavior & Organization*, 45, 133-153.

Geyskens, Inge, Steenkamp, Jan-Benedict E.M., & Kumar, Dhirendra. (2006). Make, Buy, or Ally: A Transaction cost Theory Meta-Analysis. *Academy of Management Review*, 49(3), 519-543.

Ghoshal, Sumantra. (2005). Bad Management Theories are Destroying Good Management Practices. *Academy of Management Learning & Education*, 4(1), 75-91.

Ghoshal, Sumantra, Bartlett, Christopher A., & Moran, Peter. (1999). *A New Manifesto for Management. Sloan Management Review*, 40(3), 9-20.

Gordon, Jeffrey N. (1989). The Mandatory Structure of Corporate Law. *Columbia Law Review*, 89(No. 7, Contractual Freedom in Corporate Law, Nov.), 1549-1598.

Gordon, Robert, & Howell, John. (1959). *Higher Education for Business*. New York: Columbia University Press.

Gustafsson, Bo. (1990). Foreword. In Masahiko Aoki, Bo Gustafsson, & Oliver E. Williamson (Eds.), *The Firm as a Nexus of Treaties* (pp. vii-x). London: Sage.

Hayek, Friedrich A. (1945). The Use of Knowledge in Society. *American Economic Review*, 35(4), 519-530.

Herzel, Leo. (1952). [Facing Facts about the Broadcast Business]: Rejoinder. *University of Chicago Law Review*, 20(1, Aug), 106-107.

Herzel, Leo. (1998). My 1951 Color Television Article. *Journal of Law & Economics*, 41(S2, Oct), 523-528.

Hodgson, Geoffrey M. (1998). The Approach of Institutional Economics. *Journal of Economic Literature*, 36(1 (March)), 166-192.

Hodgson, Geoffrey M. (2003). John R. Commons and the Foundations of Institutional Economics. *Journal of Economic Issues*, 37(3), 547-576.

Hodgson, Geoffrey M. (2010). Limits of Transaction Cost Analysis. In Peter G. Klein & Michael E. Sykuta (Eds.), *The Elgar Companion to Transaction Cost Economics* (pp. 297-306). Cheltenham: Edward Elgar.

Hodgson, Geoffrey M. (2011). The Eclipse of the Uncertainty Concept in Mainstream Economics. *Journal of Economic Issues*, 45(1), 159-175.

Hohfeld, Wesley Newcomb. (1913). Some Fundamental Legal Conceptions as Applied in Judicial Reasoning. *Yale Law Journal*, 23(1, Nov), 16-59.

Hohfeld, Wesley Newcomb. (1917). Fundamental Legal Conceptions as Applied in Judicial Reasoning. *Yale Law Journal*, 26(8), 710-770.

Hoogduin, Lex H. (1987). On the Difference Between the Keynesian, Knightian and the 'Classical' Analysis of Uncertainty and the Development of a More General Monetary Theory. *De Economist*, 135(1), 52-65.

Hoogduin, Lex H., & Snippe, J. (1987). Uncertainty in/of Macroeconomics: An Essay on Adequate Abstraction. *De Economist*, 135(4, Dec), 429-441.

Hovenkamp, Herbert. (1990). The First Great Law & Economics Movement. *Stanford Law Review*, 42(4), 993-1058.

Hsiung, Bingyuan. (2004). An Interpretation of Ronald Coase's Analytical Approach. *History of Economics Review*, 39(1), 12-32. doi:10.1080/18386318.2004.11682100

Johnson, H. Thomas, & Kaplan, Robert S. (1987). *Relevance Lost: The Rise and Fall of Managerial Accounting*. Boston MA: Harvard Business School Press.

Kalman, Laura. (1986). *Legal Realism at Yale, 1927-1960*. Chapel Hill NC: University of North Carolina Press.

Kay, Neil M. (2015). Coase and the Contribution of 'The Nature of the Firm'. *Managerial and Decision Economics*, 36(1), 44-54.

Keynes, John Neville. (1904). *The Scope and Method of Political Economy* (3rd ed.). London: Macmillan & Co.

Khalil, Elias L. (1995). Institutional Theory of the Firm? Extension and Limitation. *Review of Political Economy*, 7(1), 43-51.

Klapp, Orrin. (1975). Opening and Closing of Systems. *Behavioral Science*, 20(4), 251-257.

Klein, Benjamin K., Crawford, Robert G. , & Alchian, Armen. (1978). Vertical Integration, Appropriable Rents and the Competitive Contracting Process. *Journal of Law and Economics*, 21, 297-326.

Klink, Federico Aguilera. (1994). Pigou and Coase Reconsidered. *Land Economics*, 70(3, Aug), 386-390.

Knight , Frank Hyneman. (1921). Risk, Uncertainty and Profit. New York: Hart, Schaffner & Marx.

Knight, Frank Hyneman. (1923). Business Management: Science or Art? *Journal of Business*, 2(4, March), 5-24.

Knight, Frank Hyneman. (2013). *The Economic Organization* (With a New Introduction by Ross B. Emmett). New Brunswick NJ: Transaction Publishers.

Korsgaard, Steffen, Berglund, Henrik, Thrane, Claus, & Blenker, Per. (2016). A Tale of Two Kirzners: Time, Uncertainty, and the "Nature" of Opportunities. *Entrepreneurship Theory & Practice* (July), 867-889.

Kraaijenbrink, Jeroen, Spender, J.-C., & Groen, Aard. (2010). The Resource-Based View: A Review and Assessment of Its Critiques. *Journal of Management*, 36(1), 349-372.

Langlois, Richard N. (1989). What was Wrong with the Old Institutional Economics (and What is Still Wrong with the New)? *Review of Political Economy*, 1(3), 270.

Langlois, Richard N. (2017). The Institutional Approach to Economic History: Connecting the Two Strands. *Journal of Comparative Economics*, 45(1, Feb), 201-212.

Lerner, Abba. (1944). *The Economics of Control: Principles of Welfare Economics*. New York: Macmillan.

Macher, Jeffrey T., & Richman, Barak D. (2008). Transaction Cost Economics: An Assessment of Empirical Research in the Social Sciences. *Business and Politics*, 10(1), 1–63.

Madhok, Anoop. (1996). The Organization of Economic Activity: Transaction Costs, Firm Capabilities, and the Nature of Governance. *Organization Science*, 7(5), 577-590.

Malmgren, H. B. (1961). Information, Expectations and the Theory of the Firm. *Quarterly Journal of Economics*, 75(3, Aug), 399-421.

Masten, Scott E. (1993). Transaction Costs, Mistakes, and Performance: Assessing the Importance of Governance. *Managerial & Decision Economics*, 14(2), 119-129.

McCloskey, Deirdre N. (2010). *Bourgeois Dignity: Why Economics Can't Explain The Modern World* (Vol. 2 of The Bourgeois Era). Chicago IL: University of Chicago Press.

Medema, Steven G. (1996). Ronald Coase and American Institutionalism. *Research in the History of Economic Thought and Methodology*, 14, 51·92.

Medema, Steven G, & Zerbe Jr, Richard O. (1999). The Coase Theorem. *Encyclopedia of Law and Economics*, 836-892.

Merrill, Thomas W., & Smith, Henry E. (2001). What Happened to Property in Law and Economics? *Yale Law Journal*, 111(2, Nov), 357-398.

Merrill, Thomas W., & Smith, Henry E. (2011). Making Coasean Property More Coasean. *Journal of Law & Economics*, 54(4, Nov, Markets, Firms, and PropertyRights: A Celebration of the Research of Ronald Coase), S77-S104.

Mirowski, Philip, & Nik-Khah, Edward. (2017). *The Knowledge We Have Lost in Information: The History of Information in Modern Economics*. Oxford: Oxford University Press.

Nash, Stephen John. (2006). On the Anticipation of Knightian Uncertainty in Nietzsche's Genealogy of Morals. In Jrgen G. Backhaus & Wolfgang Drechsler (Eds.), *European Heritage in Economics and the Social Sciences* (Vol. 3, Friedrich Nietzsche (1844-1900), pp. 146-171). Secaucus NJ: Springer.

Nonaka, Ikujiro, & Takeuchi, Hirotaka. (1995). *The Knowledge-Creating Company: How Japanese Companies Create the Dynamics of Innovation*. New York: Oxford University Press.

Overtveldt, Johan Van. (2007). *The Chicago School: How the University of Chicago Assembled the Thinkers Who Revolutionized Economics and Business*. Chicago: Agate Publishing.

Pagano, Ugo, & Vatiero, Massimiliano. (2014). Costly Institutions as Substitutes: Novelty and Limits of the Coasian approach. *Journal of Institutional Economics*.

Pierson, Frank Cook, & Others. (1959). *The Education of American Businessmen: A Study of University-College Programs in Business Education*. New York: McGraw-Hill.

Pitelis, Christos N. (Ed.) (2002). *The Growth of the Firm: The Legacy of Edith Penrose*. Oxford: Oxford University Press.

Pitelis, Christos N., & Teece, David J. (2009). The (New) Nature and Essence of the Firm. *European Management Review*, 6, 5-15.

Pitelis, Christos N., & Teece, David J. (2010). Cross-border Market Co-creation, Dynamic Capabilities and the Entrepreneurial Theory of the Multinational Enterprise. MPRAPaper No. 23301.

Polanyi, Michael. (1962). *Personal Knowledge: Towards a Post-Critical Philosophy* (Corrected ed.). Chicago IL: University of Chicago Press.

Pollard, Sidney. (1968). *The Genesis of Modern Management*. Harmondsworth Middx: Penguin Books.

Power, Marilyn. (2012). A History of Heterodox Economics. *On The Horizon*, 20(3), 253 - 259.

Radin, Max. (1938). A Restatement of Hohfeld. *Harvard Law Review*, 51(7), 1141-1164.

Schlag, Pierre. (2013). Coase Minus the Coase Theorem - Some Problems with Chicago Transaction Cost Analysis. *Iowa Law Review*, 99, 175-222.

Schlag, Pierre. (2015). How to Do Things With Hohfeld. *Law and Contemporary Problems*, 78, 185-234.

Schweikhardt, David B. (1988). The Role of Values in Economic Theory and Policy: A Comparison of Frank Knight and John R. Commons. *Journal of Economic Issues*, 22(2, June), 407-416.

Schweikhardt, David B, Scorsone, Eric , & Doidge, Mary. (2015). Commons, Coase, and the Unchanging Nature of the Social Provisioning Process. *Journal of Economic Issues*, 49(2, June), 459-466.

Shubik, Martin. (1954). Information, Risk, Ignorance and Indeterminacy. Quarterly *Journal of Economics*, 68(4), 629-640.

Simon, Herbert A. (1963). Problems of Methodology - Discussion. *American Economic Review*, 53, 229-231.

Simpson, A. W. Brian (1996). "Coase v. Pigou" Reexamined. *Journal of Legal Studies*, 25(1, Jan), 53-97.

Singer, Joseph William. (1982). The Legal Rights Debate in Analytical Jurisprudence from Bentham to Hohfeld. *Wisconsin Law Review*, 975-1059.

Smith, Vernon L. (1998). The Two Faces of Adam Smith. *Southern Economic Journal*, 65(1, July), 1-19.

Spender, J.-C. (1989). *Industry Recipes: The Nature and Sources of Managerial Judgement.* Oxford: Blackwell.

Spender, J.-C. (1999). Organizational Knowledge, Collective Practice and Penrose Rents. In Michael H. Zack (Ed.), *Knowledge and Strategy* (pp. 117-132). Woburn MA: Butterworth-Heinemann.

Spender, J.-C. (2013a). Herbert Alexander Simon: Philosopher of the Organizational Life-World. In Morgen Witzel & Malcolm Warner (Eds.), *Oxford Handbook of Management Thinkers* (pp. 297-357). Oxford: Oxford University Press.

Spender, J.-C. (2013b). Professor Ikujiro Nonaka and KM's Past, Present and Future. In Georg Von Krogh, Hirotaka Takeuchi, Kimio Kase, & César G. Cantón (Eds.), *Towards Organizational Knowledge: The Pioneering Work of Professor Ikujiro Nonaka* (pp. 24-59). London: Palgrave-Macmillan.

Spender, J.-C. (2014a). *Business Strategy: Managing Uncertainty, Opportunity, and Enterprise.* Oxford: Oxford University Press.

Spender, J.-C. (2014b). Management's Role in the Theory of the Managed Firm (TMF). *Kindai Management Review*, 2, 28-45.

Tsoukas, Haridimos. (1989). The Validity of Idiographic Research Explanations. *Academy of Management Review*, 14(4), 551-561.

Van Horn, Robert, Mirowski, Philip, & Stapleford, Thomas A. (Eds.). (2011). *Building Chicago Economics: New Perspectives on the History of America's Most Powerful Economics Program.*

Cambridge: Cambridge University Press.

Vanberg, Viktor. (1989). Carl Menger's evolutionary and John R. Commons' collective action approach to institutions: a comparison. *Review of Political Economy*, 1(3), 334.

Vatiero, Massimiliano. (2010). From W. N. Hohfeld to J. R. Commons, and Beyond? A "Law and Economics" Enquiry on Jurai Relations. *American Journal of Economics and Sociology*, 69(2, April), 840-866.

Veldman, Jeroen. (2013). Politics of the Corporation. *British Journal of Management*, 24(Sept), S18–S30. doi:10.1111/1467-8551.12024

Wang, Ning. (2014). Ronald H. Coase, December 29, 1910-September 2, 2013. *Man and the Economy*, 1(1), 125-140.

Williamson, Oliver E. (1963). Selling Expense as a Barrier to Entry. *Quarterly Journal of Economics*, 77(1, Feb), 112-128.

Williamson, Oliver E. (1964). *The Economics of Discretionary Behavior: Managerial Objectives in a Theory of the Firm.* Englewood Cliffs NJ: Prentice-Hall.

Williamson, Oliver E. (1967). Hierarchical Control and Optimum Firm Size. *Journal of Political Economy*, 75, 123-138.

Williamson, Oliver E. (1968). Economies as an Antitrust Defense: The Welfare Tradeoffs. *American Economic Review*, 58(1, Mar), 18–36.

Williamson, Oliver E. (1971). The Vertical Integration of Production: Market Failure Considerations. *American Economic Review*, 61, 112-113.

Williamson, Oliver E. (1975). *Markets and Hierarchies: Analysis and Antitrust Implications.* New York: Free Press.

Williamson, Oliver E. (1981). The Modern Corporation: Origins, Evolution, Attributes. *Journal of Economic Literature*, 19(4), 1537-1568.

Williamson, Oliver E. (1985). *The Economic Institutions of Capitalism: Firms, Markets, Relational Contracting.* New York: Free Press.

Williamson, Oliver E. (1986). *Economic Organization: Firms, Markets and Policy Control.* Brighton, Sussex: Wheatsheaf Books.

Williamson, Oliver E. (1990a). The Firm as a Nexus of Treaties: An Introduction. In Masahiko Aoki, Bo Gustafsson, & Oliver E. Williamson (Eds.),

*The Firm as a Nexus of Treaties* (pp. 1-25). Newbury Park CA: Sage Publications.

Williamson, Oliver E. (1993). Calculativeness, Trust, and Economic Organization. *Journal of Law & Economics*, 36(1, Part 2, Apr), 453-486.

Williamson, Oliver E. (1996a). *The Mechanisms of Governance*. New York: Oxford University Press.

Williamson, Oliver E. (1996b). Revisiting Legal Realism: The Law, Economics, and Organization Perspective. *Industrial & Corporate Change*, 383-420.

Williamson, Oliver E. (1996c). Transaction Cost Economics and the Carnegie Connection. *Journal of Economic Behavior & Organization*, 31, 149-155.

Williamson, Oliver E. (1998a). The Institutions of Governance. *American Economic Review*, 88(2, May), 75-79.

Williamson, Oliver E. (1998b). Transaction Cost Economics: How it Works, Where it is Headed. *De Economist*, 146(1), 23-58.

Williamson, Oliver E. (1999). Strategy Research: Governance and Competence Perspectives. *Strategic Management Journal*, 20(12), 1087-1108.

Williamson, Oliver E. (2000). The New Institutional Economics: Taking Stock, Looking Ahead. *Journal of Economic Literature*, 38(3 (September)), 595-613.

Williamson, Oliver E. (2005). Transaction Cost Economics: The Process of Theory Develop-ment. In Ken G. Smith & Michael Hitt (Eds.), *Great Minds in Management* (pp. 485-508). Oxford: Oxford University Press.

Williamson, Oliver E. (2008). Friedman (1953) and the Theory of the Firm. In Uskali Mäki (Ed.), *The Methodology of Positive Economics* (pp. 241-256). Cambridge: Cambridge University Press.

Williamson, Oliver E. (2010a). Transaction Cost Economics: An Overview. In Peter G. Klein & Michael E. Sykuta (Eds.), *Elgar Companion to Transaction Cost Economics* (pp. 8-26). Cheltenham: Edward Elgar.

Williamson, Oliver E. (2010b). Transaction Cost Economics: The Natural Progression. *Journal of Retailing*, 86(3), 215-226.

Williamson, Oliver E. (2010c). Transaction Cost Economics: The Origins. *Journal of Retailing*, 86(3), 227–231.

Williamson, Oliver E. (2015). Ronald Harry Coase: Institutional Economist and Institution Builder. *Journal of Institutional Economics*, 11(2), 221–226.

Williamson, Oliver E. (2016). The Transaction Cost Economics Project: Origins, Evolution, Utilization. In Claude Ménard & Elodie Bertrand (Eds.), *The Elgar Companion to Ronald H. Coase* (pp. 34-42). Cheltenham: Edward Elgar.

Williamson, Oliver E. (Ed.) (1990b). *Organization Theory: From Chester Barnard to the Present and Beyond*. New York: Oxford University Press.

Zannetos, Zenon S. (1965). Review. *Journal of Business*, 38(4, Oct), 421-424.

Dr. J.-C. Spender is Research Professor, Kozminski University, Warsaw, Poland. Email: jcspender@yahoo.com

*Kindai Management Review* Vol. 6, 2018 (ISSN: 2186-6961)

# Japan's Incentive System in Medical Care: Preliminary Research on Psychiatric and General Hospitals

## Masahiko Takaya

*Faculty of Medicine, Kindai University, Japan*

### Abstract

The aim of this study is to investigate the effect of incentives, which the Japanese government offers, on the behavior of each medical corporation or institution. This study will investigate what factors have an effect on the choices of each medical corporation or institution in official medical systems. First, the hierarchal system of incorporated hospitals is introduced, in terms of emergency medical care. To achieve "higher public interest" in medical care, the Japanese government has specified about 15 areas of medical care that would benefit from greater public interest. For example, it revised the Medical Care Act to establish the "Social Medical Corporation" system, while also putting in place the "Emergency-Designated Hospital" system, both of which include incentives. Researching behavior of each corporation, whether or not it changes its type of corporation, remains to be performed in the future.

**Keywords:** *incentive, social medical corporation, psychiatric hospital, general hospital, emergency, moral hazard*

### INTRODUCTION

The neoclassical, theoretical approach to analyzing medical care is not strong (Hodgson, 2008). However, Hodgson argued that information asymmetry and supplier-induced demand are not unique to health care systems. Now, approaches other than neoclassical, theoretical ones are required to analyze and research medical or health care systems. The new approaches should derive from or be based on present data analyses. Therefore, the current article will begin with present data analyses of Japanese medical care.

Japan has a unique medical system, or "Medical Corporation (*Iryou Houjin* in Japanese)" system (Website 1). This system started in 1950 and continues today, although it has been revised. Most medical corporations own equity, though the 5th revised Medical Care Act (*Iryou Hou* in Japanese) states that newly-established medical corporations cannot own equity (Website 2). This means that non-profit entities are strengthened in medical corporations.

On the other hand, while the public interest is important in medical care, it cannot be defined economically and should be considered in various ways (Takaya, 2015). Therefore, when we hear the term "public interest" in medical care, it can be interpreted in various ways, which causes confusion.

Takaya (2016a) showed that the separation of ownership and management has no effect on activity (or the public interest) of incorporated psychiatric medical institutions. Moreover, Takaya (2016b) indicated that an uneven distribution of incorporated psychiatric hospitals, whether or not they have a license to charge a psychiatric emergency hospitalization fee, exists perhaps because internal and external controls do not function effectively.

A license to charge a psychiatric emergency hospitalization fee is a strong incentive, because the fee is about 30,000 JPY/day, much higher than other sorts of fee in psychiatric medical care. On the other hand, being an emergency designated hospital, for incorporated general hospitals, is a strong incentive, because it is accompanied by subsidies. Moreover, the Social Medical Corporation (*Shakai Iryou Houjin* in Japanese) system began in April, 2007. The system offers advantages to authorized medical corporations, and the corporations are expected to take part in activities with high public interest, including emergency medical care, as stated by the Japanese Ministry of Health, Labour and Welfare (Website 3).

Previous studies by Takaya mainly investigated psychiatric hospitals, because psychiatric hospitals do not have as much complicated medical technology as general hospitals. Therefore, the "Psychiatric Hospital Model" can offer a research prototype for other hospitals (Takaya, 2016a).

The aim of this study is to investigate the effect of incentives, which the Japanese government offers, on the behavior of each medical corporation or institution. It will investigate what factors affect each medical corporation or institution's choices about official medical systems.

## METHOD

First, "Medical Corporation" system in Japan is showed in Figure 1. Most private hospitals in Japan are run by medical coporations. Each medical corporation runs one or more hospitals, and often also medical clinic or nursing homes. The current study focuses only on hospitals (Figure 1).

Second, this study prepares the following Schema (Figure 2). In each step, ① to ④ in Figure 2, each hospital chooses whether or not to move to the next step. If the hospital wants to progress to the next step, it is obliged to perform high-public-interest activities, designated by the Japanese government.

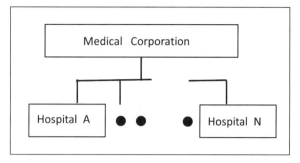

**Figure 1: "Medical Corporation" System in Japan**
Source: Author

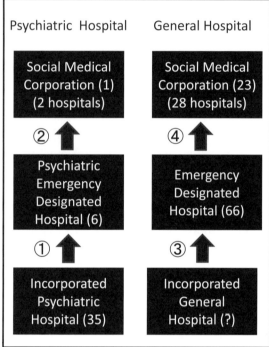

**Figure 2: The Public-Interest Hierarchy in Medical Care: Medical Corporations in Osaka Prefecture**

Source: Author; Numerical characters in parentheses indicate the numbers of the corresponding hospital types. "Psychiatric Emergency Designated Hospital" means a hospital that is allowed to charge a psychiatric emergency hospitalization fee. The definitions of "Psychiatric Hospital" and "General Hospital" in this study are described in the main text. The other terms are explained in the main text.

Third, this study will examine both incorporated psychiatric hospitals and incorporated emergency-designated hospitals in Osaka prefecture.

## Table 1: Psychiatric Hospitals run by medical corporations in Osaka Prefecture

| Number | Name of hospital (Abbreviation) | Medical Area | Social Medical Corporation | Governance Type | Regular Doctors | Irregular Doctors | Pychiatric Beds | Psychiatric Emergency Beds | Allowance of Psychiatric Emergency Hospitalization Fee |
|---|---|---|---|---|---|---|---|---|---|
| 1 | SAWA | A | 1 | N | 22 | 17 | 455 | 114 | 1 |
| 2 | AINOHA | A | 0 | Y | 9 | 27 | 606 | 0 | 0 |
| 3 | ESAKA | A | 0 | Y | 8 | 14 | 360 | 0 | 0 |
| 4 | MINO | A | 0 | Y | 9 | 17 | 345 | 0 | 0 |
| 5 | OZONE | A | 0 | Y | 16 | 14 | 557 | 0 | 0 |
| 6 | ORENJI | B | 0 | Y | 3 | 22 | 240 | 0 | 0 |
| 7 | KOAI | B | 0 | N | 9 | 14 | 221 | 0 | 0 |
| 8 | IBARAGI | B | 0 | Y | 9 | 8 | 350 | 0 | 0 |
| 9 | SHINABU | B | 0 | Y | 8 | 8 | 273 | 0 | 0 |
| 10 | NEYAGAWA | C | 0 | N | 10 | 20 | 267 | 60 | 1 |
| 12 | KOKUBU | D | 0 | Y | 10 | 9 | 201 | 48 | 1 |
| 13 | SAKAMOTO | D | 0 | Y | 15 | 25 | 546 | 0 | 0 |
| 14 | YAO | D | 0 | Y | 14 | 12 | 468 | 0 | 0 |
| 15 | YOSHIMURA | E | 0 | N | 6 | 5 | 222 | 0 | 0 |
| 16 | SAYAMA | E | 0 | N | 8 | 15 | 279 | 0 | 0 |
| 17 | TANPI | E | 0 | Y | 13 | 14 | 310 | 0 | 0 |
| 18 | KANAOKA | F | 0 | Y | 10 | 13 | 486 | 0 | 0 |
| 19 | MIKUNI | F | 0 | Y | 5 | 9 | 144 | 0 | 0 |
| 20 | HANNAN | F | 0 | Y | 52 | 13 | 690 | 168 | 1 |
| 21 | MIHARA | F | 0 | Y | 6 | 30 | 562 | 0 | 0 |
| 22 | MIZUMA | G | 0 | N | 9 | 30 | 541 | 0 | 0 |
| 23 | KIJIMA | G | 0 | Y | 15 | 12 | 492 | 0 | 0 |
| 24 | SAKANE | G | 0 | N | 3 | 7 | 150 | 0 | 0 |
| 25 | SHICHI | G | 0 | N | 14 | 22 | 640 | 48 | 1 |
| 26 | KAIZUKA | G | 0 | N | 8 | 14 | 406 | 0 | 0 |
| 27 | KUMEDA | G | 0 | N | 8 | 20 | 494 | 0 | 0 |
| 28 | SHINSEI | G | 0 | Y | 3 | 11 | 148 | 0 | 0 |
| 29 | KANSAI | G | 0 | Y | 2 | 10 | 192 | 0 | 0 |
| 30 | KOKOROA | G | 0 | Y | 11 | 6 | 450 | 0 | 0 |
| 31 | IZUMI | G | 0 | Y | 6 | 13 | 206 | 0 | 0 |
| 32 | KAEDE | G | 0 | Y | 4 | 12 | 150 | 0 | 0 |
| 33 | KISEN | G | 0 | Y | 3 | 11 | 260 | 0 | 0 |
| 34 | HAMADERA | G | 0 | Y | 21 | 9 | 749 | 0 | 0 |
| 35 | HOKUTO | H | 1 | N | 6 | 15 | 50 | 50 | 1 |

Source: Data are derived from the homepage of each hospital and the following URLs:
(a) Osaka Association of Psychiatric Hospitals: http://www.daiseikyo.or.jp/
(b) Kinki Regional Bureau of Health and Welfare: https://kouseikyoku.mhlw.go.jp/kinki/
(c) Japanese Association for Emergency Psychiatry: http://www.jaep.jp/
(d) Osaka Prefectural Government: http://www.pref.osaka.lg.jp/iryo/keikaku/keikaku2013to2017.html
(1) Numbers are assigned to each hospital randomly.
(2) "Name of Hospital (Abbreviation)" is defined at the author's discretion, relating to each hospital's full name.
(3) The letters A to H in "Medical Area" correspond to those in Takaya (2016b).
(4) The number 1 in "Social Medical Corporation" means that each hospital is run by a Social Medical Corporation. The number 0 means that it is not.
(5) The letters Y or N in "Governance Type" means that ownership and management are separate in each hospital, or not.
(6) Numbers assigned to each row named "Regular Doctors" and "Irregular Doctors" mean the number of "Regular Doctors" and "Irregular Doctors" hired by each hospital.
(7) Numbers assigned to each row named "Psychiatric Beds" and "Psychiatric Emergency Beds" mean numbers of "Psychiatric Beds" and "Psychiatric Emergency Beds" that each hospital either rents or owns.
(8) The letters 1 or 0 in "Allowance of Psychiatric Emergency Hospitalization Fee" means that each hospital is allowed to charge a psychiatric emergency hospitalization fee, or not.

**Table 2: Emergency-Designated Hospitals in Osaka Prefecture**

| Number | Name of hospital (Abbreviation) | Medical Areas | Social Medical Corporation | Governance Type | Regular DR | Irregular DR | General Hospital Beds | Chronic Stage Beds |
|---|---|---|---|---|---|---|---|---|
| 1 | IKEDAKAISEI | A | 0 | N | 6 | 35 | 97 | 0 |
| 2 | UEDA | A | 0 | N | 7 | 38 | 94 | 0 |
| 3 | KANSAIME | A | 1 | N | 24 | 36 | 225 | 0 |
| 4 | SUITATOKU | A | 0 | Y | 32 | 125 | 265 | 100 |
| 5 | KOYUKAI | B | 0 | N | 12 | 46 | 169 | 109 |
| 6 | TAKATSUKI | B | 1 | Y | 184 | 0 | 447 | 0 |
| 7 | DAIICHITOWA | B | 0 | N | 42 | 66 | 243 | 0 |
| 8 | HOKUSETSU | B | 1 | N | 58 | 67 | 217 | 0 |
| 9 | MIDORI | B | 1 | Y | 35 | 21 | 329 | 0 |
| 10 | MORIGUCHIIKU | C | 1 | Y | 34 | 98 | 199 | 0 |
| 11 | MORIGUCHIKEI | C | 0 | N | 47 | 21 | 185 | 0 |
| 12 | KAYASHIMAIKU | C | 1 | Y | 33 | 47 | 140 | 0 |
| 13 | SETSUNANSOU | C | 0 | N | 20 | 54 | 303 | 0 |
| 14 | KAMIYAMA | C | 1 | Y | 21 | 73 | 189 | 0 |
| 15 | NEYAGAWAIKU | C | 1 | Y | 19 | 15 | 103 | 0 |
| 16 | FUJIMOTO | C | 0 | N | 17 | 42 | 98 | 0 |
| 17 | KYORITSU | C | 0 | Y | 6 | 24 | 50 | 0 |
| 18 | KORIGAOKA | C | 0 | Y | 10 | 39 | 171 | 0 |
| 19 | SATO | C | 1 | Y | 23 | 70 | 120 | 0 |
| 20 | HIGASHIKORI | C | 0 | Y | 9 | 57 | 60 | 0 |
| 21 | KATANO | C | 1 | Y | 26 | 81 | 173 | 0 |
| 22 | NAWASHO | C | 1 | Y | 24 | 73 | 228 | 0 |
| 23 | DAITO | C | 0 | Y | 20 | 62 | 117 | 0 |
| 24 | NOZAKITOKU | C | 0 | Y | 44 | 64 | 218 | 0 |
| 25 | IKEDA | D | 0 | Y | 14 | 24 | 139 | 60 |
| 26 | ISHIKIRI | D | 0 | Y | 96 | 63 | 331 | 0 |
| 27 | WAKAKUSA | D | 1 | Y | 50 | 91 | 230 | 0 |
| 28 | YAOSOU | D | 1 | N | 24 | 20 | 301 | 0 |
| 29 | YAOTOKU | D | 0 | Y | 75 | 103 | 415 | 0 |
| 30 | SHIROYAMA | E | 0 | N | 54 | 71 | 299 | 0 |
| 31 | TAKAMURA | E | 0 | Y | 9 | 49 | 120 | 55 |
| 32 | FUJIMOTO | E | 0 | N | 7 | 22 | 117 | 60 |
| 33 | MATSUBARATOKU | E | 0 | Y | 26 | 127 | 189 | 0 |
| 34 | MEIJI | E | 1 | Y | 24 | 27 | 120 | 276 |
| 35 | TERAMOTO | E | 0 | N | 21 | 29 | 160 | 0 |
| 36 | SEIKEI | F | 1 | Y | 56 | 38 | 286 | 50 |
| 37 | BABA | F | 1 | N | 54 | 114 | 300 | 0 |
| 38 | BERU | F | 1 | Y | 129 | 3 | 477 | 0 |
| 39 | HOWA | F | 0 | N | 5 | 5 | 60 | 59 |

| | | | | | | | | |
|---|---|---|---|---|---|---|---|---|
| 40 | MINAMISA | F | 0 | N | 12 | 20 | 153 | 0 |
| 41 | FUCHU | G | 1 | Y | 125 | 25 | 380 | 0 |
| 42 | KISHIWADATOKU | G | 0 | Y | 108 | 103 | 341 | 0 |
| 43 | FUJII | G | 0 | Y | 8 | 14 | 95 | 0 |
| 44 | KAWASAKI | G | 1 | Y | 11 | 39 | 47 | 82 |
| 45 | KANO | H | 1 | N | 26 | 30 | 243 | 53 |
| 46 | YUKIOKA | H | 1 | N | 20 | 68 | 235 | 112 |
| 47 | MEISEI | H | 1 | Y | 9 | 40 | 195 | 0 |
| 48 | KITAOSAKA | H | 1 | Y | 5 | 44 | 77 | 0 |
| 49 | FUKUSHIMA | H | 0 | N | 4 | 36 | 97 | 0 |
| 50 | FUJITATE | H | 0 | Y | 5 | 15 | 52 | 45 |
| 51 | MATSUMOTO | H | 0 | Y | 13 | 17 | 199 | 0 |
| 52 | ONOKINEN | H | 1 | Y | 27 | 83 | 250 | 0 |
| 53 | TANE | H | 1 | Y | 89 | 55 | 304 | 0 |
| 54 | HIGASHINARI | H | 0 | N | 6 | 24 | 55 | 0 |
| 55 | IKUNOCHUO | H | 0 | N | 6 | 10 | 60 | 88 |
| 56 | JOTO | H | 0 | Y | 20 | 93 | 233 | 0 |
| 57 | MORINOMIYA | H | 1 | N | 45 | 60 | 355 | 0 |
| 58 | ABIKO | H | 0 | Y | 10 | 73 | 135 | 0 |
| 59 | NANKO | H | 1 | N | 6 | 45 | 64 | 0 |
| 60 | MINAMIOSAKA | H | 1 | Y | 57 | 24 | 400 | 0 |
| 61 | MORIMOTO | H | 0 | Y | 64 | 11 | 329 | 0 |
| 62 | NAGAYOSHI | H | 0 | Y | 23 | 53 | 192 | 0 |
| 63 | KYORIN | H | 0 | Y | 4 | 14 | 99 | 0 |
| 64 | SHION | H | 0 | Y | 7 | 43 | 60 | 0 |
| 65 | DAIWA | H | 0 | Y | 10 | 0 | 143 | 0 |
| 66 | DAISAN | H | 0 | N | 15 | 32 | 266 | 0 |

Source: Data are derived from the homepage of each hospital and the following URLs:

(a) Osaka Medical Facilities Information System: https://www.mfis.pref.osaka.jp/qq27scripts/qq/fm27qrinsm_in.asp

(b) Kinki Regional Bureau of Health and Welfare: https://kouseikyoku.mhlw.go.jp/kinki/

(1), (2), (3), (4), (5), and (6) are the same as those described in Table 1.

(7) Numbers assigned to each row named "General Hospital Beds" and "Chronic Stage Beds" mean numbers of "General Hospital Beds" and "Chronic Stage Beds" that each hospital either rents or owns.

Masahiko Takaya

*Subjects*

Osaka prefecture has eight secondary medical areas, as referred to in Takaya (2016b). 49 private psychiatric hospitals in Osaka are listed on the homepage of the Osaka association of psychiatric hospitals. This study deals with hospitals with psychiatric beds only. According to this criterion, 35 psychiatric hospitals are selected (Table 1). The letter assigned to each hospital in Table 1 corresponds to the letter representing each medical area described in Takaya (2016b). Table 1 is a modified version of the corresponding Table in Takaya (2016b) and comprises incorporated psychiatric hospitals in Osaka.

Osaka prefecture designates 256 hospitals as emergency-designated hospitals. Of the 256 hospitals in Osaka, the 66 emergency-designated hospitals that can accept patients for both general internal medicine and general surgery, 24 hours per day all year round, are shown in Figure 2 and Table 2. The list of incorporated general hospitals is not available, because general hospital cannot be defined precisely. They are now usually considered providing internal, surgical, and other medicine. On the other hand, "General Hospital" in Japan used to be hospitals that provide internal medicine, surgery, obstetrics and gynecology, ophthalmology, otolaryngology, and possibly other forms of medicine. However, the Medical Care Act in 1996 abolished "General hospital" system in the Japanese legal system. Now, many hospitals show "general hospital" in their English names. This is very confusing. For clarification, this study considers all emergency-designated hospitals that provide at least both internal medicine and surgery, 24 hours per day all year round, as "general hospital".

*Statistical Analysis*

Statistical analysis in this study was performed using the software jmp 10 (SAS Institute Inc., Cary, NC, USA).

RESULTS

*A) Incorporated Psychiatric Hospitals*

Japanese Ministry of Health, Labour and Welfare states that psychiatric emergency medical activity is one of the medical activities with high public interest (Website 3). Therefore, hospitals which are allowed to charge a psychiatric emergency hospitalization fee, or have psychiatric emergency beds, can be considered to be contributable to the world. Now, I examine what factors have an effect on "Psychiatric Emergency Beds" in Table 1.

About ① in Figure 2

(1) The statistical analysis was performed using Table1, in the following way.

- **Method:**
  least squares method
- Dependent variable:
  Psychiatric Emergency Beds
- Independent variables:
  Governance Type, Regular Doctors, Irregular Doc-

**Table 3: Verification of Multicollinearity for (1): Parameter Estimates (p-value) (r)**

|  | Governance Type | Regular Doctors | Irregular doctors | Psychiatric Beds |
|---|---|---|---|---|
| Governance Type |  | −0.0248<br>p (0.6242)<br>r (0.0825) | 0.0570<br>p (0.3146)<br>r (0.1546) | −0.0014<br>p (0.5071)<br>r (0.1025) |
| Regular Doctors |  |  | 0.0274<br>p (0.9095)<br>r (0.0202) | 0.0308<br>p (<.0001)<br>r (0.6295) |
| Irregular doctors |  |  |  | 0.0153<br>p (0.0128)<br>r (0.4225) |
| Psychiatric Beds |  |  |  |  |

Note: The left row indicates dependent variables, while the top column independent variables.

### Table 4: Least Squares Method for (1): r = 0.8940

|  | Estimate | p-value |
|---|---|---|
| Governance Type | 7.206 | 0.0410 |
| Regular Doctors | 4.802 | <.0001 |
| Irregular doctors | 1.390 | 0.0222 |
| Psychiatric Beds | −0.121 | <.0001 |

tors, Psychiatric beds

In the current article, criteria for multicollinearity is as follows: multiple correlation coefficient is more than 0.8 (r > 0.8).

(2) The statistical analysis in Table 1 was performed as follows:

- **Method:**
  Logistic regression analysis
- Dependent variable:
  Allowance of Psychiatric Emergency Hospitalization Fee
- Independent variables:
  Governance Type, Regular Doctors, Irregular Doctors, Psychiatric beds

### Table 5: Wald Test for (2): r=0.7629

|  | Estimate | p-value |
|---|---|---|
| Governance Type | −1.5275 | 0.1494 |
| Regular Doctors | −0.7820 | 0.0868 |
| Irregular doctors | −0.1473 | 0.3479 |
| Psychiatric Beds | 0.0163 | 0.0490 |

### Table 6: Likelihood Ratio Test for (2): r=0.7629

|  | Chi-square | p-value |
|---|---|---|
| Governance Type | 2.9578 | 0.0855 |
| Regular Doctors | 14.5099 | 0.0001 |
| Irregular doctors | 0.9359 | 0.3333 |
| Psychiatric Beds | 6.3597 | 0.0117 |

About ② in Figure 2

Hospitals number 1 and 35 in Table 1 are run by the same social medical corporation. The others are run by medical corporations. Therefore, the statistical analysis for ② in Figure 2 might be useless.

The results (mean ± s.d.) of statistical analysis only are shown as follows:

|  | Regular Doctors | Irregular Doctors | Psychiatric Beds | Psychiatric Emergency Beds |
|---|---|---|---|---|
| SMC (+) | 14.0±11.3 | 16.0±1.4 | 252.5±286.4 | 82.0±45.3 |
| SMC (−) | 21.5±20.4 | 16.0±6.1 | 449.5±251.1 | 81.0±58.3 |

SMC (+) and (−) mean hospitals which are certified social medical corporation, and not, respectively.

## B) Incorporated General Hospitals

The Japanese Ministry of Health, Labor and Welfare states that emergency medical care is one of the medical activities with a high public interest (Website 3).

About ③ in Figure 2

As mentioned above, general hospitals have various departments and too difficult to analyze statistically. This study reserves statistical analysis for future studies, when a better data set is available.

About ④ in Figure 2

It is possible to analyze the data in Table2 statistically, unlike in case ②. Multicollinearity can be observed between the number of regular doctors and general hospital beds (Table 7). Therefore, "General Hospital Beds" is excluded from the following analysis.

- **Method:**
  Logistic regression analysis
- Dependent variable:
  Social Medical Corporation
- Independent variables:
  Governance Type, Regular Doctors, Irregular Doctors, Chronic Stage Beds

The results of this analysis is shown in Table 8 and Table 9.

## Table 7: Verification of Multicollinearity Parameter Estimates (p-value) (r)

| | GT | RD | ID | GB | CB |
|---|---|---|---|---|---|
| GT | | −0.0182<br>p (0.0961)<br>r (0.2686) | −0.0103<br>p (0.2460)<br>r (0.4050) | −0.0020<br>p (0.4098)<br>r (0.2846) | 0.0020<br>p (0.7134)<br>r (0.3873) |
| RD | | | 0.0790<br>p (0.5737)<br>r (0.0703) | 0.2576<br>p<0.0001<br>r (0.8055) | −0.1258<br>p (0.1984)<br>r (0.5071) |
| ID | | | | 0.0556<br>p (0.1171)<br>r (0.4784) | −0.0601<br>r (0.4929)<br>p (0.0074) |
| GB | | | | | −0.4643<br>p (0.1278)<br>r (0.1894) |
| CD | | | | | |

Note: The left row indicates dependent variables, while the top column indicates independent variables.
Governance Type: GT, Regular Doctors: RD, Irregular Doctors: ID, General Hospital Beds: GB, Chronic Stage Beds: CB

## Table 8: Wald Test: r = 0.2902

| | Estimate | p-value |
|---|---|---|
| Governance Type | 0.1698 | 0.5454 |
| Regular Doctors | −0.0206 | 0.0360 |
| Irregular doctors | −0.0022 | 0.7998 |
| Chronic Stage Beds | −0.00569 | 0.3643 |

## Table 9: Likelihood Ratio Test: r = 0.2902

| | Chi-square | p-value |
|---|---|---|
| Governance Type | 0.3679 | 0.5441 |
| Regular Doctors | 5.8012 | 0.0160 |
| Irregular doctors | 0.0642 | 0.8000 |
| Chronic Stage Beds | 0.8933 | 0.3446 |

### C) Summary of results

First, the number of beds used to charge a psychiatric emergency hospitalization fee is significantly related to the number of doctors regularly hired in incorporated psychiatric hospitals. Although the causal relationship is not clear, the larger number of doctors regularly hired in a hospital suggests that the hospital has high potential and activity. Moreover, it shows that the hospital is attractive for psychiatrists, perhaps because of employment condition and carrier formation.

Second, whether or not a medical corpotration that runs an emergency-designated hospital is legally a social medical corporation is not significantly related with any available factors.

### DISCUSSION

A psychiatric emergency hospitalization fee is about 30,000 JPY/day, while acute psychiatric and chronic psychiatric hospitalization fees are about 20,000 JPY/day and about 10,000 JPY/day, respec-tively. Therefore, an allowance to charge psychiatric emergency hospitalization fees is a strong incentive for psychiatric hospitals. On the other hand, requirements for the allowance are very steep. For example, (1) the ratio of nurses in a ward to the number of beds cannot be less than 1/10, (2) the number of regularly hired psychiatric social workers in a ward cannot be less than two, (3) the number of mental health-designated doctors regularly hired for a ward and for the hospital is cannot be less than 1 and 5, respectively. (5) Isolation rooms must occupy more than half of all the beds in a ward (Website 4). This means that running a ward imposes large fixed costs. The application for an allowance may depend on the following:

(Expected revenue) −(Fixed and variable costs) $\geqq 0$

This is very simple model, at a glance. Expected revenue depends on the number of patients meeting the criteria, which can be estimated from the number of patients live in and around the secondary medical area where each hospital is located.

Variable costs can also be estimated, according to the number of patients. However, the total number of patients in a secondary medical area is constant at least in the short run. Therefore, getting an allowance in the medical field is competitive.

Designation of emergency hospitals by the Osaka prefectural government depends on the following criteria: (1) not less than two designated beds for each advocating department, (2) 24-hour-a-day emergency care all year round, (3) not less than two regularly-hired doctors for each department participating the system, and (4) a certain level of acceptance records. (Website 5). Emergency-designated hospitals are provided with subsidies. For example, the Osaka prefectural government has announced that the lower of either 30,000 JPY/case ×number of cases, or the labor cost for maintaining an emergency system in each institution will be provided to the institution (Website 6). Therefore, subsidies no lower than a fixed labor cost are provided. This designation of an emergency hospital system (for general hospitals) is not the same as psychiatric emergency-designated hospital systems. While the former has a subsidy system, the latter does not. This indicates an asymmetry in Japanese medical emergency system. Moral hazard might be caused in the designation of emergency hospital system, which accompany subsidies.

The Social Medical Corporation system in Japan was enforced in April, 2007, based on a revision in 2006 of the Medical Care Act (Website 7). The Social Medical Corporation is classified as one particular type of medical corporations. The aim of the Social Medical Corporation system is to offer higher public-interest facilities, while keeping a non-profit system in medicine. However, some profit is allowed, which provides large incentive. At the same time, a social medical corporation is not allowed to own equity. This may be a barrier to the convergence of a medical corporation with a social medical corporation. Most medical corporations running so-called emergency-designated psychiatric hospitals and emergency-designated hospitals have decided not to merge with social medical corporations (or institutions), as shown in Figure 2. There are 283 social medical corporations (as of July, 1, 2017) in Japan, 37 in Hokkaido prefecture and 36 in Osaka prefecture (Website 8). Twenty-eight general hospitals (28/66=42.4%) (Table 2) are run by 23 social medical corporations (Website 8). Tokyo has only 15 social medical corporations, which is relatively few considering its population. Aomori, Iwate, Miyagi, Akita, Yamagata, Ibaragi, Ishikawa, Yamaguchi, Tokushima, Kochi, and Saga prefectures each have only two social medical corporations (Website 8). Each of Gunma, Yamanashi, and Shiga prefectures has only one (Website 8). This shows the uneven distribution of social medical corporations in Japan, suggesting an uneven distribution of public interest. However, when considering the public interest in medical care, it is important to pay attention to the number of public hospitals and specific function hospitals, as well as social medical corporations.

A social medical corporation system is based on the ideal that private hospitals, instead of public hospitals, are responsible for high public-interest medical fields. This approach attains efficiency of management. In other words, incentive systems that accompany social medical corporation systems derive from the notion of "equal fitting." This is perhaps very clear to everyone. Theoretical approaches using economical models, suggest that the profits of rural public hospitals are lower than those of urban hospitals (Aiura & Sanjo, 2010). The article suggests that social medical hospitals are more necessary in rural areas than in urban areas. However, as described above, this is not the case.

Emergent medical care has little common with the latest medical technologies or with very expensive drugs. Rather, it is characterized by hard-working employees, who use the usual, modern "high technologies." This fact was not considered in previous studies, such as that by Ikegami & Cambell, 1999, who discussed fee-revision processes and stated that Japanese balancing principles inhibit rapid change, such as recommending low introductory fees for new, high-tech procedures. They treated health care reform in Japan in terms of its political economy. However, nowadays their methods are not sufficient for investigating the dynamic incentive systems that involve organizational changes of medical corporations.

The driving force to change the organization of medical corporations cannot be examined easily. Instead, simple models may be useful for prelimi-

Constant cost: $C_i$

Variable cost: $V_i$

Profit: $P_i$

Equity: $E_i$

Incentive: $I_i$

State A ($V_1$, $C_1$, $P_1$, $E_1$, 0)

↓

State B ($V_2$, $C_2$, $P_2$, 0, $I_2$)

[ $V_1 < V_2$, $C_1 < C_2$, $P_1 < P_2$ ]

**Figure 3: The Model of Shifting to Social Medical Corporation**

Source: Author. In this model, "State A" and "State B" indicate "Medical corporation running Emergency-Designated Hospital" and "Social Emergency Corporation," respectively.

nary research. Now, the convergence of medical corporations running emergency designated-hospitals with social medical corporations can be modeled in a simple way. Symplified factors that could influence a decision to merge with social medical corporations are described below.

Figure 3 shows that if a medical corporation prefers "State B" to "State A," it may convert to a social medical one. However, the conditions for this conversion are not revealed. The preference of each emergency designated hospital needs to be investigated, to facilitate the social medical corporation system.

The relationship between ownership and productivity of hospitals is introduced in the literature (Blank & Eggink, 2014), as follows. For-profit hospitals are more productive, while their quality is the reverse (Eggleston & Shen, 2011). Other studies found that there is no difference in cost efficiency between private and publicly-owned hospitals, but private hospitals shows higher profit efficiency tha publicly owned ones (Herr, Schmitz, & Augurzky). This current article deals with non-profit but private hospitals and investigates the effect of for-profit factors built into the new "Social Medical Corpora-

tion" system, to benefit the public interest. Though Japan's medical-care system is perhaps unique in the world, it has not been carefully investigated. The research of decision-making of each corporation, whether or not it decides to choose another style of corporation, remains to be performed in the future, both in theoretical and empirical ways.

REFERENCES

Aiura, Hiroshi, and Yasuo Sanjo (2010). Privatization of Local Public Hospitals: Effect on Budget, Medical Service Quality, and Social Welfare. *International Journal of Health Care Finance and Economics*. 10, 275-299.

Blank, Jos L.T. and Evelien Eggink (2014). The Impact of Policy on Hospital Productivity: A Time Series Analysis of Dutch Hospitals. *Health Care Management Science*. 17: 139-149.

Eggleston, Karen, and Yu-Chu Shen (2011). Soft Budget Constraints and Ownership: Empirical Evidence from US Hospitals. *Economics Letters*. 110: 7-11.

Hodgson, Geoffrey M (2008). An Institutional and Evolutionary Perspective on Health Economics. *Cambridge Journal of Economics*. 32, 235-256.

Herr, Annika, Hendrik Schmitz, and Boris Augurzky (2011). Profit Efficiency and ownership of German Hospitals. *Health Economics*. 20, 660-674.

Ikegami, Naoki, and Creighton Campbell (1999). Health Care Reform in Japan: The Virtues of Muddling Through. *Health Affairs*. 18 (3), 56-75.

Takaya, Masahiko (2015). On Evolution of Hospital System in Japan and Public Interest of Japanese Hospitals -Especially on Regular Hospitals and on Training for Specialists -. *Journal of Association for Research on NPOBP*. 17, 107-120.

Takaya, Masahiko (2016a). The Relationship between Forms of Governance and Activities in Incorporated Medical Institutions – Preliminary Research for Empirical Analyses of Psychiatric Hospitals. *Journal of Association for Research on NPOBP*. 18, 39-49.

Takaya, Masahiko (2016b). Effects of Incorporated Psychiatric Institutions' Internal and External

Control on Their Local Distributions and Hierarchical Formation: Case of Osaka. *Journal of Japanese Management*. 1 (1), 1-14.

Last view date of the following Websites: 15th of October 18, 2017

Website 1: The Medical Care Act. http://law.e-gov.go.jp/htmldata/S23/S23HO205.html

Website 2: Ministry of Health, Labour and Welfare. http://www.mhlw.go.jp/shingi/2007/11/dl/s1105-2b.pdf

Website 3: Ministry of Health, Labour and Welfare. http://www.mhlw.go.jp/topics/bukyoku/isei/igyou/igyoukeiei/kentoukai/8kai/7.pdf

Website 4: Ministry of Health, Labour and Welfare. http://www.mhlw.go.jp/shingi/2009/03/dl/s0326-8c.pdf

Website 5: Osaka prefectural government. http://www.pref.osaka.lg.jp/attach/3071/00155935/03_hc_2ji_manual.pdf

Website 6: Osaka prefectural government. http://www.pref.osaka.lg.jp/attach/3071/00207897/01_youkou. pdf

Website 7: Ministry of Health, Labour and Welfare. http://www.mhlw.go.jp/stf/seisakunitsuite/bunya/Kenkou_iryou/iryou/igyou/about_nintei.html

Website 8: Ministry of Health, Labour and Welfare. http://www.mhlw.go.jp/file/06-Seisaku-jouhou-10800000-Iseikyoku/0000172900.pdf

Dr. Masahiko Takaya is Lecturer of the Faculty of Medicine at Kindai University, Osaka, Japan.
Email: takaya@med.kindai.ac.jp

*Kindai Management Review* Vol. 6, 2018 (ISSN: 2186-6961)

# Creativity, Innovation and Organizational Performance: Does HRM Bind Them Together?

## Joseph Heller
*Bar-Ilan University, Israel*

## Jacob Weisberg
*Bar-Ilan University, Israel*

### Abstract

The relationships between creativity-innovation and firm performance are not at all new, but still call for thorough investigation. This paper combines insights from strategic human resource management and organizational behavior to examine how Human Resource Management can facilitate creativity and innovation, thus also bolstering firm performance. Specifically, we argue that commitment-based human resource practices enhance creativity itself, but also support the transformation of creativity into innovation by generating a social climate that advances knowledge sharing behavior. This paper contributes to the literature by delineating the mechanisms through which Human Resource Management influences key organizational resources, thus better honing the creativity-innovation-performance relationship. In today's dynamic economic reality, these conclusions can help managers improve employee performance and hence that of their firms.

**Keywords:** *creativity, knowledge sharing, innovation, performance, HRM*

### 1. INTRODUCTION

The relationship between creativity-innovation and organizational performance is not new but requires an in-depth understanding of the role of Human Resource Management (HRM) in bringing them together. This paper presents a comprehensive summary and integration of much past literature in the fields of creativity, innovation and human resource management into a simplifying model.

The prime role of HRM is often depicted as enabling and facilitating different work-related components to achieve higher performance. In this view, creativity can be developed into applicable utilities; i.e., innovation, and contribute to firms'

success in terms of better performance in the form of higher profits, lower production costs, more efficient working procedures, and better relationships with customers. The problem with this premise is that although this association is well documented, much less is known about how it operates, the ways in which creativity be transformed into innovation and the mediators involved. How can creativity be facilitated? How can creativity become innovation? How do both of them affect firm performance? These questions are still valid even after years of rigorous research. Here, we address these important issues by exploring the underlying processes. In so doing we respond to the call to combine insights from Organizational Behavior (OB) and organizational strategy to unveil the psychological micro-foundations of strategy (Ployhart and Hale, 2014). It was only recently that OB has made inroads into organizational strategy, and there is a need to further advance this approach, especially in the case of the complex relationship between creativity/innovation and performance.

Specifically, we explore how creativity can be utilized by a firm to improve its performance by taking an OB perspective on the Resource Based View (RBV), a more up-to-date approach that focuses on advancing organizational human capital and social exchange theory, thus emphasizing the psychological effects of the social environment. We demonstrate how creativity, innovation and performance are related and suggest ways that HRM practices can be used to develop employees' creativity to create a suitable climate that can alleviate the impact of obstacles to the transformation of creativity into innovation.

Numerous studies have shown that a firm's knowledge base gains from employees' new ideas (creativity) to promote innovation (Nonaka & Takeuchi, 1995). In other words, employees' creativity is the cornerstone for innovation. We argue that HRM practices; i.e., high performance/commitment (Huselid, 1995) play a major role in extending employees' knowledge and improving their skills. This directly impacts creativity (human capital), and also indirectly promoting Knowledge Sharing behavior (KS) (social capital), which we believe is a prime facilitator of innovation.

The social interaction process inherent to KS facilitates the transformation of creativity (a new idea) into innovation (implementation of that idea), but KS behavior depends on employees' willingness to give of their knowledge to others. By employing commitment-based HRM practices that foster a social climate of cooperation, firms can motivate employees to share their knowledge.

In the following sections we present some fundamental themes from the OB and HRM literature that support our arguments. We conclude this paper with important insights and suggestions for future research and implications for management.

## 2. HUMAN CAPITAL AND THE RESOURCE BASED VIEW (RBV)

Human capital is an example of how OB has influenced research on organizational performance, a field that was mainly studied by strategic management experts. In the last two decades, human capital has become an important and valuable strategic resource (Wright, MacMahan, and Mcwilliams, 1994, 2001). It is extremely important to organizations and has consistently been viewed as a driver of performance (Crook, Combs, Todd, Woehr, & Ketchen, 2011). The fact that a firm cannot own human capital, which is an intangible asset, which makes its management more complex, has attracted strategy scholars (Ployhart & Hale, 2014).

Human capital usually refers to the knowledge, skills and abilities (KSAs) embodied in people (Coff, 2002). KSAs include employees' education, training and experiences (Hambrick & Mason, 1984). Ployhart & Moliterno (2011) developed a multilevel model of human capital resource emergence which explicitly states that human capital resources originate from individuals' characteristics. Their model explains how individual knowledge, skill, ability, and other characteristics (KSAOs) contribute to the formation of human capital resources. The process of human capital emergence is modeled as comprising two facets. . The first has to do with the complexity of the task, which determines the extent to which employees need to interact and coordinate their behavior. Task complexity can range from including relatively independent employees to being completely interdependent. When coordination demands are high, the likelihood that human capital resources will emerge from KSAOs is higher. Second, is it assumed that emergence-enabling states are social contextual factors that support or hinder employees' interactions. These states can be behavioral (e.g., backing up behaviors), cognitive (e.g., transactive memory), and affective (e.g., cohesion, trust). Even if a task demands interaction, without these enablers human capital will not emerge.

The Resource Based View (RBV) supplies the theoretical explanation why high quality human capital can lead to superior performance. Several scholars have contributed to this framework but the most prominent is Barney (1991) who pointed out that firm resources can be considered as enablers of strategy. Resources may be tangible (e.g., financial) or intangible (e.g., human capital). Resources that are rare, valuable, inimitable, and non- substitutable can be sources of sustainable competitive advantage. Valuable resources must be in short supply and semi permanently tied to the organization to provide long- lasting above average performance. If not, competitors can acquire resources that perform the same function and the advantage will be lost (Peteraf, 1993). Factors that can promote inimitability include social complexity (e.g., resources based on interactions between employees), causal ambiguity (e.g., uncertainty with regard to the creation of resources), and path dependency (e.g., historical factors that influence a firm's current state) (Barney, 1991; Dierickx & Cool, 1989).

The knowledge based view that emerged from RBV posits that the knowledge embedded in human capital not only meets the criteria for these types of resources but also ultimately is the only source of competitive advantage (cf. Grant, 1996). Felin & Hesterly (2007) suggested that knowledge resources are firm-specific due to the fact that they are tied to specific people and processes within a firm. Wright et al. (1994) noted that in order to constitute a source of competitive edge, the human capital pool must have both high levels of skill and the motivation to exhibit productive behavior.

As a further development of the RBV, mostly due to the inroads of psychology into strategy, it is well-established today that improved firm performance and sustained competitive advantage are the outcome of a combination of human capital, strategically relevant employees' behaviors, and appropriate HRM practices. These latter support the development of KSAs and aid in aligning the human capital pool with the firm's strategic objectives (Dunford, Snell, & Wright, 2002).

What the current RBV conceptualization suggests is that firm performance is not just an aggregate of actions of individuals, but rather the result of several core competencies including human capital, social capital (internal or external relationships), and organizational capital (i.e., processes, policies, technologies) that create knowledge (Snell, Youndt, & Wright, 1996). These "knowledge repositories"

complement and affect one another (Youndt & Snell, 2001). Thus for a firm to achieve its desired competitive advantage, it must take into account the interplay among these three components.

RBV was instrumental to the development of the strategic human resource management (SHRM) field because it shifted the focus of strategy research from factors outside the firm to internal resources as the medium for competitive edge (Hoskinsson, Hitt, Wan, & Yiu, 1999). This positioned human resources at the core, thus solidifying the importance of the HRM function.

SHRM is somewhat difficult to define, but there is a general consensus that it is:

*"...the pattern of planned human resource (HR) deployments and activities intended to enable an organization to achieve its goals."* (Wright & McMahan, 1992, p. 298).

That is to say, SHRM focuses on HRM practices that firms develop and how they align them to support their strategy. In the following section, we deal with HRM practices.

## 3. COMMITMENT- BASED HR PRACTICES

### 3.1 The contingency approach

The literature on SHRM deals with ways to enhance desirable organizational outcomes (Jiang, Lepak, Hu, & Baer, 2012). A well-known perspective is the contingency approach (Jackson, Schuler, & Rivero, 1989) which argues that organizations use HRM practices (also known as high performance/commitment work systems) to encourage employees' behavior to facilitate goal attainment (Becker & Huselid, 1998). The firm selects HRM practices that fit its goals (employee cooperation or efficiency). Their success is contingent on having employees behave in ways that foster attainment of firm's objectives (Becker & Huselid, 1998).

### 3.2 Commitment-based HR practices

It is believed that although HRM practices are highly varied, they can be categorized into several sub-dimensions (Jiang et al., 2012). One such categorization distinguishes between transaction based

HRM practices and commitment based HRM practices. Transaction based practices emphasize individual short term exchange relationships; commitment based practices focus on long term investment in employees and maintaining an organizational atmosphere that strengthen employees' commitment to their workplace (Tsui, Pearce, Porter, & Hite, 1995). In the SHRM line of research these practices are called the high performance/investment HRM approach. This approach underscores firms' will to create new and unique in-house knowledge and skills, and facilitate employees' motivation and discretion (Lawler, 1992).

The specific practices that form a commitment based approach may vary, but generally include training programs and performance appraisals that emphasize the development of firm- specific knowledge, team work, and long term growth, compensation practices that align employee motivation with group-organization objectives, selection practices that assess employees' suitability to the firm rather than to a specific job (Tsui, Pearce, Porter, & Tripoli, 1997; Delery & Doty, 1996).

Studies have shown that there is a positive relationship between commitment based practices and firm performance in diversified organizations (e.g., Youndt, Snell, Dean, & Lepak, 1996; Batt, 2002). High commitment HRM practices have profound effects on performance outcomes in terms of higher productivity and quality, a lower turnover rates, and a lower scrap rate (MacDuffie, 1995). Through these practices, employees feel that the firm invests highly in them, their motivation to contribute is increased, and they are more willing to aid the firm in achieving its strategic goals (Rousseau, 1995).

Taken together, we believe that commitment-based HRM practices play a pivotal role in both the quest for valuable, rare and hard to replace human capital and in creating the conditions for a cooperative workplace environment in which the value of the existing human capital potential can be realized. In the following sections, we show how these practices can impact two of the most fundamental resources of a firm: creativity and innovation.

## 4. CREATIVITY AND COMMITMENT-BASED PRACTICES

### 4.1 Definition of Creativity

In the field of OB, several researchers have suggested definitions of creativity. For instance, Farid, El-Sharkawy, & Austin (1993) suggested that creativity is the production of new and useful ideas, whereas Brennan & Dooley (2005) emphasized the originality of creativity and claimed that creativity is a combination of elasticity, originality and thought sensitivity that allow the individual or a team to think outside of the box. West (2002) focused on the place where creativity occurs: inside the individual. He claims that:

*"...creativity is a cognitive process in which events occur within the person"* (p.11).

Amabile (2000) put forward the dominant definition, which constitutes a conceptual integration of the three definitions above. She suggested that creativity is:

*"...the production of novel and useful ideas by individuals or teams of individuals...where the idea is appropriate, useful and actionable"* (p. 80).

Of what we know about creativity, it is a process of thinking and producing new and useful ideas (Amabile, 2000).

### 4.2 Commitment-based practices impact on creativity

Commitment-based HRM practices are assumed to relate directly and positively to creativity. These practices can improve the quality of human capital by expanding employees' knowledge and by motivating them to have a sense of autonomy, thus enabling them to become more effective at creating new ideas and solving problems (Jiang et al., 2012). Specific commitment-based practices can impact creativity through:

1. Selection – which can augment human capital by hiring talented and creative people who have the necessary skills the firm needs (Jimenez-Jimeneza

& Sanz-vallea, 2008)

2. Training – which facilitates learning in firms and helps to build a better knowledge pool by enhancing employees' knowledge and skills that are needed for creative thought processes and task domain expertise (Mumford, 2000)

3. Performance appraisal – appraisal that includes clear feedback and mistake toleration that helps convey precise information to employees on the disparities between their performance and the desired goals (Jaing et al., 2012) and also signals to employees that the firm expects them to engage in learning (Nonaka, 1994), thus prompting employees to work more creatively

4. Reward systems – which push employees to make an extra effort and attracts creative people to the firm (Jiang et al., 2012)

5. Job design – which can contribute to employees' creativity by increasing their intrinsic motivation (Shalley & Gilson, 2004). Jobs that are characterized by autonomy and the opportunity to pursue one's own ideas, job enrichment, etc, cause employees to be intrinsically motivated by focusing on the challenge of the job , job satisfaction and enjoyment more than on external demands (Shalley & Gilson, 2004; Oldham & Cummings, 1996). In light of these arguments, we propose:

*Proposition 1. Commitment-based HRM practices enhance creativity.*

## 5. DEFINITION OF INNOVATION AS DISTINCT FROM CREATIVITY

### 5.1 Definition of Innovation

For an idea to be defined as innovative and not as creative, it needs to be developed and transformed into a product, process or service, and be commercialized (Popadiuk & Choo, 2006). Afuah (1998) classified innovation into three categories: 1. Technological – knowledge of components, linkages between components, methods, processes and techniques that go into a product or service; 2. Market – new knowledge embodied in distribution channels, product, applications, as well as customer expectations, preferences, needs, and wants; 3. Administrative – innovations that pertain to the organizational structure and administrative processes.

### 5.2 Creativity-Innovation: Similarities and Differences

Even though there are considerable differences between creativity and innovation, some use the terms interchangeably (Man, 2001). The three main differences according to West et al. (2004), Amabile (2000), and Mathisen et al. (2008) are:

1. The nature of the process – West et al. (2004) refer to creativity as a cognitive process, and to innovation as a social process;

2. The element of implementation – Innovation includes an element of implementation, creativity does not;

3. Unit of analysis – Mathisen et al. (2008), Amabile (1988) and Staw (1990) indicate that creative performance refers to products and ideas at the individual or team levels. Innovation is the successful implementation of these products at the organizational level.

In spite of their differences, creativity and innovation are related and affect an organization's ability to reach future goals. Empirical support for their relationship can be found in several studies that have employed individual factors such as predictors of innovation (e.g., Pirola-Merlo & Mann, 2004; West & Anderson, 1996). In light of the above, we propose that:

*Proposition 2. Creativity relates positively to innovation.*

## 6. THE ROLE OF KNOWLEDGE SHARING IN THE LINK BETWEEN CREATIVITY AND INNOVATION

### 6.1 Definition of Knowledge sharing

There are different definitions of knowledge sharing; here it is defined as a social interaction involving the exchange of employee knowledge, experiences and skills through a department or organization (Lin, 2007). According to Van den Hooff & Van Weenen (2004), knowledge sharing is a bi-dimensional process that involves knowledge collection and knowledge donation. Knowledge collection is a process of consultation with others that is intended to encourage them to share their personal intellectual capital. Knowledge donation is a process in which individuals give their personal intellectual capital to others. Knowledge sharing occurs between employees, at the group or organizational levels.

## 6.2 Types of knowledge

Based on Polanyi (1958, 1966), Nonaka (1994) differentiated explicit from tacit knowledge:

1. Sharing explicit knowledge can be promoted by information technology whereas tacit knowledge is subject to social interaction
2. Explicit knowledge is often in documentary form and is transferred by technology, unlike tacit knowledge that is embedded in social ties; its transfer is varied, but is usually done by direct contact and observation of behavior
3. Explicit knowledge can be reduced to writing easily. It is impersonal by nature, obtained through education and formal practice, and is usually in the form of reports and documents, etc. (Holste & Fields, 2010). Tacit knowledge is personal (i.e., abilities, developed skills, etc.) and cannot easily be reduced to writing
4. Tacit knowledge is acquired by learning through life experience, experimentation and learning by doing (Mascitelli, 2000). This knowledge is described as local, and is strongly rooted in the context in which it developed (Holste & Fields, 2010). Explicit knowledge is not acquired by learning or experience, and is not bound to context.

## 6.3 Social exchange theory as the basis of knowledge sharing

One key way to conceptualize the relationship between an organization and its employees is based on the social psychology perspective of Social Exchange Theory (Blau, 1964). Social Exchange theory has been shown to account for non-contractual interactions between people in a vast number of domains ranging from market relations, work relations and love (Blau, 1964) to team knowledge sharing (Cummings, 2004). The theory posits that people donate to others in a manner commensurate to what others give to them (Reychav & Weisberg, 2010). The theory sees the "donations" people give to an organization as elements in a mutual arrangement (Gouldner, 1960). Mutual agreements take place when an individual performs an act that benefits some other individual, group or organization. This gesture is made without a specific monetary contract guaranteeing that it will be rewarded (King & Marks, 2008). The person who makes the gesture does so because s/he believes that it will be rewarded in the future, although the exact time and nature of the reward is unknown and unimportant (Van der Vegt & Janssen, 2003). In social exchanges, unlike economic ones, the possible outcomes of behavior are based on the belief that the relationship will be conducted according to previous behavior (King & Marks, 2008). Numerous studies have emphasized the positive outcomes of social exchange in organizations (e.g., Allen et al., 2003; King & Marks, 2008; Liao & Chuang, 2004).

## 6.4 Knowledge sharing as a mediator between creativity and innovation

There is a general consensus that creativity is a necessary but not sufficient prerequisite for innovation (Amabile, 2012). The innovation process builds upon knowledge sharing and is affected by group dynamics and organizational support (e.g., West, 2002; Agrell & Gustafson, 1996). The process starts with individuals who come up with an idea or recognize an organizational problem (Farr & Ford, 1990). These individuals decide whether or not to share knowledge and suggest their novel ideas to the group for further discussion and development (Agrell & Gustafson, 1996). Kogut & Zander (1992), as well as Nahapiet & Ghoshal (1998) argued that the process of knowledge sharing helps create valuable knowledge within firms by connecting previously unconnected knowledge and ideas or recombining existing knowledge into novel knowledge.

According to Basadur & Gelade (2006), thinking organizations strive for constant innovation; they continuously seek out new opportunities to use their knowledge. Basadur & Gelade (2006) strongly emphasize that only knowledge management in the sense of active sharing of knowledge can promote organizational learning and innovativeness. They indicate that:

> "...availability of information is not sufficient. If efficiency, flexibility, and adaptability are to be increased, that information must be put to use." (p.46).

It is not the mere existence of the knowledge that solves crises or promotes the company but rather knowing how to use it and wanting to do so.

Summarizing this section, for creativity to be exploited for the benefit of the group and the organization as a whole, it needs to be shared and put to use. Thus, we propose that:

> *Proposition 3. Knowledge sharing mediates the relationship between creativity and innovation.*

## 7. COMMITMENT-BASED PRACTICES AS FACILITATORS OF INNOVATION

Commitment-based HRM practices lay the foundation for organizations' innovative capability. Meta-analyses of RBV have shown that HRM policies are not limited to their direct effects on employee competencies and skills. They have a more comprehensive role in weaving the knowledge and skills of employees together (Snell, Youndt, & Wright, 1996). Subramaniam & Youndt (2005) indicated that:

> "...unless individual knowledge is networked, shared, and channeled through relationships, it provides little benefit to organizations in terms of innovative capabilities." (p. 459).

The literature indicates that a commitment-based HRM system is a powerful innovation- facilitating tool in particular through the reinforcement of social ties (Collins & Clark, 2003). Collins & Smith (2006) indicated that commitment-based HRM practices can affect firm performance indirectly by fostering a social climate that motivates employees to share their creative knowledge, and by so doing, transform it to an implementable asset; i.e., innovation. Finally, HRM practices that signal employees that the organization cares about them and wants to invest in them are likely to lead to a similar stance on the part of employees towards the organization and the manifestation of out-role performance such as knowledge sharing (Allen, Shore, & Griffeth, 2003).

## 8. DEFINITION OF SOCIAL CLIMATE AND ROLE

### 8.1 Definition of social climate

A social climate is the product of the shared perceptions of employees in an organization regarding formal and informal policies, procedures, and practices (Schneider, Ehrhart, & Macey, 2013). Collins & Smith (2006) defined social climate as:

> "...the collective set of norms, values, and beliefs that express employees' views of how they interact with one another while carrying out tasks for their firm" (p. 547).

In other words, the social climate of a firm refers to its employees' shared beliefs regarding the norms that guide their interactions when they work (Ashkanasy, Wilderom, & Peterson, 2000).

### 8.2 The role of social climate role as a mediator

Intra-firm contextual influences such as social climate are consistent with the notion prevalent in RBV which suggests that firms possess heterogeneous resources that drive competitive advantage (Barney, 1991). Numerous studies on social climate have supported the notion that it moderates the relationship between diversity and firm performance (Dass & Parker, 1999). In a similar manner, social climate has been examined as a mediator of the relationship between HRM policies and firm performance (e.g., Bowen & Ostroff, 2004). An important theme in the innovation field is that good social relationships between employees are necessary to innovation (Collins & Smith, 2006). Burt (1997) stated that:

> "...while human capital is surely necessary to success, it is useless without the social capital of opportunities in which to apply it". (p. 339).

According to the RBV, human capital, although very important, has only limited value in the absence of social capital. Coleman (1988) noted that social capital has an important influence on the creation of human capital.

Takeuchi, Lepak, Wang, & Takeuchi (2007) emphasized the importance of the combination of human capital and social capital for achieving organizational goals. These authors conducted a study on a sample of Japanese firms and found that human capital and social exchange mediated the relationship between high commitment/performance systems and firm performance.

Based on Kang et al. (2007), we suggest that commitment-based practices can help create a social climate characterized by cooperation and consisting of cohesion, trust and perceived organizational support (POS). This climate encourages employees to focus on the best interests of the firm rather than on their own objectives, thus fostering knowledge sharing among employees. Cohesion, for instance, facilitates the formation of strong, close ties between employees that motivate them to share their unique, valuable knowledge with their colleagues and organization (Reagans, Zuckerman, & McEvily, 2004). In addition, a work environment that emphasizes trust and mutual dependence tends to reinforce a sense of collectivity (Zhou, Hong, & Liu, 2013). This should lead to more freely transferred knowledge (Moran, 2005) and also guarantees that in time, team members can create communication codes and protocols that improve the communication and ease the transfer of knowledge (Nahapiet & Ghoshal, 1998). All of the above can facilitate knowledge sharing and by so doing promote innovation. In the following sections we discuss exactly how commitment-based HRM practices affect each one of the components forming the social climate and how in turn they can facilitate knowledge sharing.

## 9. COMMITMENT-BASED PRACTICES ROLE IN CREATING A CLIMATE OF COOPERATION

### 9.1 Definition of Cohesion

Over the years several definitions have been put forward for the 'elusive' concept of cohesion (Mullen & Cooper, 1994). Despite differing opinions, there is a general consensus that cohesion is a group level variable (Gully, Devine, & Whitney, 1995) as defined by Festinger (1968):

*"...the total field of forces that acts on members to remain in the group"* (p. 185).

Initially, researchers referred to cohesion as a unidimensional concept (Seashore, 1954), but more recent definitions include both task and social components as part of the shift towards a multidimensional conceptualization (Cota, Evans, Dion, Kilik, & Longman 1995). The well- accepted multidimensional definition Carron, Brawley, & Widmeyer (1998) includes the following dimensions:

1. Individual attraction to group-task: Team members' perceptions of their involvement in a group task
2. Group integration-task: Team members' perceptions of the similarity, closeness and bonding that exists in the group, in the context of a collective task
3. Individual attraction to group-social: Team members' perceptions of their acceptance by the group and their social interaction with the group
4. Group integration-social: Team members' perceptions of closeness and similarity in the group, in a social context.

### 9.2 Commitment-based HRM practices and cohesion

We suggest that the implementation of commitment-based HRM practices of team work and group-based compensation can have a complementary effect. An emphasis on the team work paradigm can facilitate the consolidation of team members' social ties and a sense of belonging (Hulsheger, Anderson, & Salgado, 2009), thus leading to social cohesion, whereas a group based compensation agenda can strengthen team members' commitment to work together and encourage them to focus on team success and achieving shared goals and objectives rather than on individual aspirations as a means to obtain desired rewards (DeMatteo, Eby, &

Sundstrom, 1998). It may also minimize the occurrence of social loafing (Sheppard, 1993) and favorize the task component of cohesion.

### 9.3 Definition of trust

Trust is a psychological construct relating to the experiential outcome of interactions between people's values, attitudes, mood and emotions (Jones & George, 1998). It is the willingness of a party to be vulnerable to the actions of another party based on the expectation that the other will not misuse this act (Mayer, Davis & Schoorman, 1995). According to Schoorman, Mayer, & Davis (2007), trust is based on these components:

1. Ability – The trustor's belief that the trustee is capable and skilled
2. Benevolence – The intention to do good for the other
3. Integrity – The trustor's belief that the trustee is guided by values of fairness.

Although each component is distinct, total trust necessitates the existence of all. In addition, the trustor's ability to believe in the other is mandatory. Hence, people can differ in their ability to trust others (Schoorman et al., 2007). We believe that commitment-based HRM practices can facilitate a social climate of trust.

### 9.4 Commitment-based HRM practices and trust

Commitment-based HRM practices such as team work and group based compensation can facilitate a climate of trust between employees by aligning employees' actions with the team's or firm's objectives and insuring that everyone contributes, thus reducing social loafing (Lawler, Mohrman, & Ledford, 1995). An emphasis on training, development, and job rotation also contributes to employee interaction and better acquaintanceship.

### 9.5 Definition of Perceived Organizational Support (POS)

According to Organizational Support Theory (OST) (Eisenberger et al., 1986, 1990), employees tend to ascribe humanlike characteristics to an organization and see it as a subject with the ability to act. The organization is perceived as responsible for the way organizational jobholders treat employees (Eisenberger et al., 1986). Employees develop high levels of Perceived Organizational Support (POS) when the organization is attentive to their well-being and values their contribution by giving rewards, better working conditions, maintaining procedural justice, etc.

### 9.6 Commitment-based HRM practices and POS

We believe that commitment-based HRM practices of performance appraisal that focus on employee development, training and development programs, as well as incentive practices (compensation and rewards), communicate to employees that they are appreciated and valued, thus causing them to perceive the organization in a positive manner and act in ways that benefit it. In a similar manner, Allen et al. (2003) showed that HRM practices emphasizing growth opportunities, fairness of rewards, and participation in decision making contribute to employees' sense of perceived support from the firm. Summing up, we propose:

*Proposition 4a-c. Commitment-based HRM practices promote a social climate consisting of cohesion, trust, and POS.*

## 10. THE SOCIAL CLIMATE FACILITATES KNOWLEDGE SHARING

### 10.1 Cohesion and knowledge sharing

When cohesion is high, employees are likely to cooperate with one another and cease to compete, thus enhancing their tendency to share knowledge (Szulanski, 1996). In addition, when cohesion exists, individuals experience a positive psychological state. This leads to perceiving things in a positive way and may increase the propensity for pro-social behavior (George & Brief, 1992). Increased cohesion is expected to lead to a greater willingness on the part of team members to help each other and demonstrate altruistic behavior; i.e., Organizational Citizenship Behavior (OCB) such as knowledge sharing. Thus, we propose

*Proposition 5. Cohesion relates positively to knowledge sharing.*

## 10.2 Trust and knowledge sharing

Trust lays the foundation for effective social exchange (Blau, 1964), and can influence knowledge sharing. Social exchange depends to a great extent upon trust, because it involves undefined commitments that cannot be forced (there is no written contract). When trust is high, knowledge sharing should be enhanced because mutual trust between employees enhances a person's belief that the current exchange will lead to later reciprocation (Coleman, 1990). Trust finds expression in knowledge sharing because knowledge seekers must let themselves be vulnerable to colleagues, for instance by acknowledging their lack of knowledge in a specific domain (Gray, 2001). Further, they need to trust colleagues to supply credible and beneficial information (Gray, 2001). Similarly, knowledge donors need to believe that the information will be used properly. Thus, we propose:

*Proposition 6. Trust relates positively to knowledge sharing.*

## 10.3 POS and knowledge sharing

Organizational support indirectly affects employee attitudes and behaviors through the creation of a sense of commitment which results in reciprocity. When employees feel supported, they develop a greater global sense of commitment to the organization. Employees feel obligated to reciprocate by helping the organization reach its goals (Eisenberger et al., 2001). Organizations depend on the creation of new ideas that arise from sharing and the application of knowledge in one domain through implementation in another, a process that is facilitated by knowledge sharing (Bartol, Liu, Zeng, & Wu, 2009). Knowledge sharing is usually an act of choice and is a beneficial behavior, not a formal job requirement (Lin, 2010). Research supports the notion that organizational support contributes to these kinds of behaviors (Podsakoff et al., 2000). Thus, we propose:

*Proposition 7. POS relates positively to knowledge sharing.*
*Proposition 8a-c. A social climate consisting of cohesion, trust, and POS is likely to mediate the relationship between commitment-based*

*HRM practices and knowledge sharing.*

## 11. INNOVATION AND PERFORMANCE

Innovation can be evaluated in terms of its effects on organizational outcomes. Previous studies have shown that innovation exploited in an organizational setting can contribute to performance improvement (Artz et al., 2010; Shalley, Gilson, & Blum, 2000; Zimmerman & Darnold, 2009), and that innovative firms outperform non-innovative firms in terms of productivity and growth (e.g., Hall & Mairesse, 1995; De Clercq et al., 2011). We focus here on intra-organizational performance as a proximal indicator of a firm's utilization of its resources. High quality human capital was found to relate strongly to this type of performance in a recent meta-analysis (Crook et al., 2011). For example, in a longitudinal study Roberts (1999) examined the pharmaceutical industry in the US and found that the innovation capability of a firm had a positive effect on its profits. Cho & Pucik (2005) examined the relationship between innovativeness, quality, growth, profitability and market value at the firm level in the US finance industry and showed that innovation contributes to the growth and profitability of an organization. Similarly, Atalay, Anafarta, & Sarvan (2013) found that technological innovation (product and process innovation) had a significant and positive impact on intra-organizational performance in a sample of top level managers of 113 firms operating in the Turkish automotive industry. Thus, we propose:

*Proposition 9. Innovation relates positively to firm performance*

## 12. PROPOSED RESEARCH MODEL

Above, we reviewed the underlying direct and indirect HRM practices to account for the association between creativity-innovation and firm performance. We also examined the elements that affect the relationships between creativity and innovation. We discussed high commitment HRM practices (selection and training, performance appraisal, reward system, job design and team work), social climate (cohesion, trust, POS), the nature of KS and

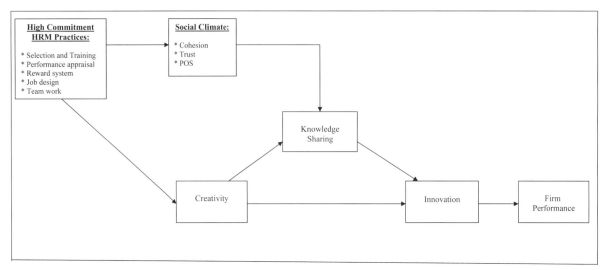

Figure 1: Conceptual Model of the Association between Creativity and Innovation and Firm Performance

knowledge sharing as a mediator between creativity and innovation.

Below, we propose a multivariate theoretical model comprised of these elements to predict firm performance.

## 13. SUMMARY AND IMPLICATIONS FOR RESEARCH AND PRACTICE

Despite considerable evidence supporting the existence of positive relationships between creativity, innovation and firm performance, much is still unknown. The basic questions raised by Morgeson & Hoffman (1999) and later Ployhart & Hale (2014) still remains valid; namely how do resources at one level contribute to the formation of resources at other levels? As we see it, not enough theory and research have been devoted to the emergence of firm performance from creativity. This may be due to the absence of intersections between the macro (strategy) and micro (OB) literatures. In this paper, we incorporated a combination of RBV and organizational behavior view to shed light on this important issue. We presented a model (Figure 1) which delineates the mechanisms through which HRM practices can improve firm performance. Specifically, we claim that a specific bundle of practices dubbed commitment-based HRM practices (i.e., selection and training, performance appraisals, reward system, job design and team work) impact firm performance through the following processes by: 1. directly enhancing creativity; 2. promoting a social climate supportive of knowledge sharing (which is crucial for innovation). When the innovative capability of a firm improves, so does its performance.

We reiterated the importance of the social environment in an organization. As scholars have indicated, context shapes the nature of the elements, processes, and systems that reside within it (Ployhart & Hale, 2014). Therefore, to exploit the full potential of a highly skilled workforce, social capital is mandatory.

We believe that the proposed model captures the reciprocal relationships between structures and functions of resources at different levels. It shows that a meaningful understanding of workplace phenomena requires integrative approaches that combine multiple levels (Kozlowski & Klein, 2000). With that in mind, it is also clear that much research is still needed. This work provides a foundation for the role of HRM in future research on creativity, innovation and performance.

Here we focused on commitment-based practices. We suggest that future research should examine the effects of other types or bundles of HRM practices on knowledge sharing and innovative process as a whole (Jiang et al., 2012). It is possible that other bundles of practices may exert different effects on creativity and on knowledge sharing, which are undoubtedly important to discover.

It is also recommended to examine the proposed model empirically. In this regard, comparing samples of employees from different sectors could be of value. It is important to bear in mind that what we suggested here may apply more successfully to high tech firms. This is because the type of employees who form the backbone of hi tech firms, and therefore are crucial to generating superior human capital and achieving competitive advantage are knowledge workers; i.e., scientists, engineers etc. (Grant, 1996). Clearly firms' innovative capability and improved performance are based on their employees' knowledge and willingness to share it. Knowledge workers hold the key to this kind of rare, valuable, and inimitable knowledge (Appleyard & Braun, 2002).

We believe that the practical implications of our model may be considerable. We stress the importance of a fully integrated, strategically aligned HRM system, an underdeveloped function in many workplaces (Lawler & Boudreau, 2009). Further, our model provides managers and HRM practitioners with the means to improve HRM interventions. Effective implementation of the proposed HRM practices can exert an enormous influence over both human and social capital which, are so important to firms' innovative capabilities (Collins & Smith, 2006). These interventions can improve the knowledge and skills of employees, while also shaping an organizational climate that motivates employees to contribute more (Grant & Berry, 2011). In today's challenging economic reality, succeeding on this task may prove decisive.

## 14. CONCLUSION

In this paper we aimed to provide a better understanding of the creativity-innovation-performance chain. We incorporated insights from different domains to depict a multi-stage mechanism that highlights the important role of HRM practices in advancing firm performance. We also believe that the implementation of our suggestions can bolster HRM practitioners' and managers' efforts to achieve success and prosperity in organizations.

## REFERENCES

Afuah, A. (1998). *Innovation management: Strategies, implementation, and profits.* New York: Oxford University Press.

Agrell, A., & Gustafson, R. (1996). Innovation and creativity in work groups. In M. A. West (Ed.), *Handbook of work group psychology.* 314-343. London: Wiley.

Allen, D. G., Shore, L. M. & Griffeth, R. W. (2003). The role of perceived organizational support and supportive human resource practices in the turnover process. *Journal of Management.* 29, 99–118.

Amabile, T. M. (1988). A model of creativity and innovation in organizations. In B.M. Staw & L. L. Cummings (Eds.), *Research in organizational behavior.* 10, 123-167. Greenwich, CT: JAI Press.

Amabile, T. M. (2000). Stimulate Creativity by Fueling Passion. In E. A. Locke (Ed.), *Basic Principles of Organizational Behavior: A Handbook*, Oxford: Blackwell Publishers.

Appleyard, M. M., & Brown, C. (2001). Employment practices and semiconductor manufacturing experience. *Industrial Relations.* 40, 436–471.

Artz, K. W., Norman, P. M., Hatfield, D. E., & Cardinal, L. B. (2010). A longitudinal study of the impact of R&D, patents, and product innovation on firm performance. *Journal of Product Innovation Management.* 27, 725-740.

Ashkanasy, N. M., Wilderom, C. P. M., & Peterson, M. F. (2000). Introduction. In N. Ashkanasy, C. P. M. Wilderom, & M. F. Peterson (Eds.), *Handbook of organizational culture and climate.* 1–18. Thousand Oaks, CA: Sage.

Barney, J. B. (2001). Resource-based theories of competitive advantage: A ten year retrospective on the resource-based view. *Journal of Management.* 27, 643-650.

Bartol, K. M., Liu, W., Zeng, X., & Wu, K. (2009). Social Exchange and knowledge sharing among knowledge workers: The moderating role of perceived job security. *Management and Organization Review.* 5, 223-240.

Bartol, K. M., & Srivastava, A. (2002). Encouraging knowledge sharing: The role of organizational reward systems. *Journal of Leadership and Organization Studies*, 9, 64-76.

Basadur, M. & Gelade, G. A. (2006). The role of knowledge management in the innovation process. *Creativity and Innovation Management*. 15, 45-62.

Batt, R. (2002). Managing customer services: Human resource practices, quit rates, and sales growth. *Academy of Management Journal*. 45, 587–597.

Batt, R., & Golvin, A. J. S. (2011). An employment systems approach to turnover: HR practices, quits, dismissals, and performance. *Academy of Management Journal*. 54, 695-717.

Becker, B. E., & Huselid, M. A. (1998). High performance work systems and firm performance: A synthesis of research and managerial implications. In G. R. Ferris (Ed.), *Research in personnel and human resources management*. 16, 53–101. Greenwich, CT: JAI Press.

Blau, P. (1964). *Exchange and power in social life*. New Brunswick, NJ: Wiley.

Boxall, P., & Purcell, J. (2008). *Strategy and human resource management*. Basingstoke, U.K: Palgrave Macmillan.

Brennan, A., Dooley, L. (2005). Networked creativity: A structured management framework for timulating innovation. *Technovation*. 25, 1388-1399.

Buller, P. F., & McEvoy, G. M. (2012). Strategy, human resource management and performance: Sharpening line of sight. *Human Resource Management Review*. 22, 43-56.

Burt, R. S. (1997). The contingent value of social capital. *Administrative Science Quarterly*. 42, 339–365.

Caldwell, F. (2004). *Enterprises are challenged to benefit from 'Grass-Roots' KM*. Gartner, Inc. Research Report.

Camelo-Ordaz, C., Garcia-Cruz, J., Sousa-Ginel, E. & Valle-Cabrera, R. (2011). The influence of human resource management on knowledge sharing and innovation in Spain: The mediating role of affective commitment. *The International Journal of Human Resource Management*. 22, 1440-1461.

Carless, S. A., De-Paola, C. (2000). The measurement of cohesion in work teams. *Small Group Research*. 31, 71-88.

Carron, A.V., Brawley, L.R. & Widmeyer, W.N. (1998). Measurement of cohesion in sport and exercise. In J.L. Duda (Ed.), *Advances in Sport and Exercise Psychology Measurement*. 213-226. Morgantown, WV: Fitness Information Technology.

Coleman, J. S. (1990). *Foundations of social theory*. Cambridge, MA: Harvard University Press.

Collins, C. J., & Clark, K. D. (2003). Strategic human resource practices, top management team social networks, and firm performance: The role of human resource practices in creating organizational competitive advantage. *Academy of Management Journal*. 46, 740–751.

Collins, C. J. & Smith, K. G. (2006). Knowledge exchange and combination: The role of human resource practices in the performance of hi-technology firms. *Academy of Management Journal*. 49, 544-560.

Cota, A., Evans, C. R., Dion, K. L., Kilik, L., & Longman, R. S. (1995). The structure of group cohesion. *Personality and Social Psychology Bulletin*. 21, 572–580.

Crook, T. R., Combs, J. G., Todd, S. Y., Woehr, D. J., & Ketchen, D. J. (2011). Does human capital matter? A meta analysis of the relationship between human capital and firm performance. *Journal of Applied Psychology*. 96, 443-456.

Cummings, J. N. (2004). Work Groups, structural diversity, and knowledge sharing in a global organization. *Management Science*. 50, 352-364.

Damanpour, F. (1988). Innovation type, radicalness, and the adoption process. *Communication Research*. 15, 545-567.

Damanpour, F., Gopalakrishnan, S. (1998). Theories of organizational structure and innovation adoption: The role of environmental change. *Journal of Engineering and Technology Management*, 15, 1-24.

Davenport, T. H., & Prusak, L. (1998). *Working knowledge: How organizations manage what they know*. Cambridge, MA: Harvard Business School Press.

De Clercq, D., Thongpapanl, N., & Dimov, D. (2011). The moderating role of organizational context on the relationship between innovation and firm performance. *IEEE Transactions on Engineering Management.* 58, 431-444.

Delery, J. E., & Doty, D. H. (1996). Modes of theorizing in strategic human resource management: Tests of universalistic, contingency, and configurational performance predictions. *Academy of Management Journal.* 39, 802-835.

Delery, J. E., & Shaw, J. D. (2001). The strategic management of people in work organizations: Review, synthesis, and extension. In G. R. Ferris (Ed.), *Research in personnel and human resource management.* 20, 167-197. Stamford, CT: JAL.

DeMatteo, J. S., Eby, L. T., & Sundstrom, E. (1998). Team based rewards: Current empirical evidence and directions for future research. In B. M. Staw and L.L. Cummings (Eds.), *Research in organizational behavior.* 141-183. Stamford, CT: JAI Press.

Dunford, B. B., Snell, S. A., & Wright, P. M. (2002). *Human resources and the resource based view of the firm* (CAHRS Working Paper #01-03). Ithaca, NY: Cornell University, School of Industrial and Labor Relations, center for Advanced Human Resource Studies. http://digitalcommons.ilr.cornell.edu/cahrswp/66/

Eisenberger, R., Armeli, S., Rexwinkel, B., Lynch, P. D., & Rhoades, L. (2001). Reciprocation of perceived organizational support. *Journal of Applied Psychology.* 86, 42-51.

Eisenberger, R., Fasolo, P., & Davis-LaMastro, V. (1990). Perceived organizational support and employee diligence, commitment, and innovation. *Journal of Applied Psychology.* 75, 51-59.

Eisenberger, R., Huntington, R., Hutchison, S., & Sowa, D. (1986). Perceived organizational support. *Journal of Applied Psychology.* 71, 500-507.

Farr, J. L., & Ford, C. M. (1990). Individual innovation. In M. A. West & J. L. Farr (Eds.), *Innovation and creativity in work: Psychological and organizational strategies.* 63-80. London: Wiley.

Festinger, L. (1968). Informal social communication. In D. Cartwright, & A. Zander (Eds.), *Group dynamics research and theory.* 182–191. Evanston, IL: Row, Peterson.

Fulmer, I. S., Gerhart, B., & Scott, K. S. (2003). Are the 100 best better? An empirical investigation of the relationship between being a "great place

to work" and firm performance. *Personnel Psychology.* 56, 965– 993.

George, J. M., & Brief, A. P. (1992). Feeling good-doing good: A conceptual analysis of the mood at work-organizational spontaneity relationship. *Psychological Bulletin*, 112, 310-329.

Gouldner, A. (1960). The norm of reciprocity. *American Sociological Review.* 25, 161-178.

Grant, R. M. (1996). Prospering in dynamically-competitive environments: Organizational capability as knowledge integration. *Organization Science.* 7, 375–387.

Grant, A. M. & Berry, J. W. (2011). The necessity of others is the mother of invention: Intrinsic and prosocial motivations, perspective taking, and creativity. *Academy of Management Journal.* 54, 73-96.

Gray, P. H. (2001). The impact of knowledge repositories on power and control in the workplace. *Information Technology and People.* 14, 368-384.

Guesta, D., & Conway, N. (2011). The impact of HR practices, HR effectiveness and a "strong HR system" on organizational outcomes: A stakeholder perspective. *International Journal of Human Resource Management.* 22, 1686–1702.

Gully, S. M., Devine, D. S., & Whitney, D. J. (1995). A meta-analysis of cohesion and performance: Effects of level of analysis and task interdependence. *Small Group Research.* 26, 497–520.

Hall, B. H. & Mairesse, J. (1995). Exploring the relationship between R&D and productivity in French manufacturing firms. *Journal of Econometrics.* 65, 263-293.

Holste, J. S. & Fields, D. (2010). Trust and tacit knowledge sharing and use. *Journal of Knowledge Management.* 14, 128-140.

Hulsheger, U. R., Anderson, N., & Salgado, J. F. (2009). Team-level predictors of innovation at work: A comprehensive meta-analysis spanning three decades of research. *Journal of Applied Psychology.* 94, 1128-1145.

Huselid, M. A. (1995). The impact of human resource management practices on turnover, productivity, and corporate financial performance. *Academy of Management Journal.* 38, 635–672.

Jackson, S. E., Schüler, R. S., & Rivero, J. (1989).

Organizational characteristics as predictors of personnel practices. *Personnel Psychology*. 42, 727-786.

Jiang, K., Lepak, D. P., Hu, J., & Baer, J. C. (2012). How does human resource management influence organizational outcomes? A meta-analytic investigation of mediating mechanisms. *Academy of Management Journal*. 55, 1264-1294.

Jimenez-Jimeneza, D., & Sanz-Vallea, R. (2008). Could HRM support organizational innovation? *International Journal of Human Resource Management*. 19, 1208–1221.

Kang, S., Morris, S. S., & Snell, S. A. (2007). Relational archetypes, organizational learning, and value creation: Extending the human resource architecture. *Academy of Management Review*, 32, 236–256.

King, W. R., Marks, P. V. (2008). Motivating knowledge sharing through a knowledge management system. *The International Journal of Management Science*. 36, 131-146.

Kozlowski, S. W. J. (1987). Technological innovation and strategic human resource management: Facing the challenge of change. *Human Resource Planning*. 10, 69–79.

Kozlowski, S. W. J., & Klein, K. J. (2000). A multilevel approach to theory and research in organizations: Contextual, temporal, and emergent processes. In K. J. Klein & S. W. J. Kozlowski (Eds.), *Multilevel theory, research and methods in organizations: Foundations, extensions, and new directions* (pp. 3-90). San Francisco, CA: Jossey-Bass.

Kuvaas, B. (2008). An exploration of how the employee-organization relationship affects the linkage between perception of developmental human resource practices and employee outcomes. *Journal of Management Studies*, 45, 1–25.

Lawler, E. E. (1992). *The ultimate advantage: Creating the high-involvement organization*. San Francisco, CA: Jossey-Bass.

Lawler, E. E. & Boudreau, J. W. (2009). What makes HR a strategic partner? *People & Strategy*. 32, 14-22.

Lawler, E. E., III., Mohrman, S. A., & Ledford, G. E. (1995). *Creating high performance organizations: Practices and results in the Fortune 1000*. San

Francisco, CA: Jossey-Bass.

Lepak, D. P., & Snell, S. A. (1999). The human resource architecture: Toward a theory of human capital allocation and development. *Academy of Management Review*. 24, 31–48.

Lepak, D. P. & Snell, S. A. (2002). Examining the human resource architecture: The relationships among human capital, employment, and human resource configurations. *Journal of Management*. 28, 517-543.

Liao, H., & Chuang, A. (2004). A multilevel investigation of factors influencing employee service performance and customer outcomes. *Academy of Management Journal*. 47, 41-58.

Lin, C. P. (2007). To share or not to share: Modeling tacit knowledge sharing, its mediators and antecedents. *Journal of Business Ethics*. 70, 411-428.

Lin, H. F. (2007). Knowledge sharing and firm innovation capability: An Empirical study. *International Journal of Manpower*. 28, 315-332.

Lin, L. H. (2011). Electronic human resource management and organizational innovation: The roles of information technology and virtual organizational structure. *The International Journal of Human Resource Management*. 22, 235–257.

Liu, Y. & Phillips, J. S. (2011). Examining the antecedents of knowledge sharing in facilitating team innovativeness from a multilevel perspective. *International Journal of Information Management*. 31, 44-52.

MacDuffie, J. P. (1995). Human resource bundles and manufacturing performance: Organizational logic and flexible production systems in the world auto industry. *Industrial and Labor Relations Review*. 48, 197-221.

Man, J. (2001). Creating innovation. *Work Study*. 50, 229-233.

Mascitelli, R. (2000). From experience: Harnessing tacit knowledge to achieve breakthrough innovation. *Journal of Product Innovation Management*. 17, 179-193.

Mathisen, G. E., Martinsen, O., Einarsen, S. (2008). The relationship between creative personality composition, innovative team climate, and team innovativeness: An input-process-output perspective. *The Journal of Creative Behavior*. 42,

13-31.

Mayer, R. C., Davis, J. H. & Schoorman, F. D. (1995). An integrative model of organizational trust. *Academy of Management Review*. 20, 709-734.

Moran, P. (2005). Structural vs. relational embeddedness: Social capital and managerial performance. *Strategic Management Journal*. 26, 1129–1151.

Mullen, B., & Cooper, C. (1994). The relation between group cohesiveness and performance: An integration. *Psychological Bulletin*. 115, 210–227.

Mumford, M. D. (2000). Managing creative people: Strategies and tactics for innovation. *Human Resource Management Review*. 10, 313–351.

Nahapiet, J., & Ghoshal, S. (1998). Social capital, intellectual capital, and the organizational advantage. *Academy of Management Review*. 23, 242–266.

Nonaka, I. (1994). A dynamic theory of organizational knowledge creation. *Organization Science*. 5, 14-37.

Nonaka, I. & Takeuchi, H. (1995). *The knowledge creating company: How Japanese companies create the dynamics of innovation*. New York: Oxford University Press.

Oldham, G. R., Cummings, A. (1996). Employee creativity: Personal and contextual factors at work. *Academy of Management Journal*. 39, 607-634.

Organ, D. W. (1988). A restatement of the satisfaction-performance hypothesis. *Journal of Management*. 14, 547-557.

Paauwe, J. (2009). HRM and performance: Achievements, methodological issues and prospects. *Journal of Management Studies*. 46, 129-142.

Pelled, L. H., Eisenhardt, K. M., Xin, K. R. (1999). Exploring the black box: An analysis of work group diversity, conflict, and performance. *Administrative Science Quarterly*. 44, 1-28.

Ployhart, R. E. & Hale, D. (2014). The fascinating psychological microfoundations of strategy and competitive advantage. Annual Review of *Organizational Psychology and Organizational Behavior*. 1, 145-172.

Podsakoff, P. M., MacKenzie, S. B., Lee, J. Y., Podsakoff, N. P. (2003). Common method biases in behavioral research: A critical review of the literature and recommended remedies. *Journal of Applied Psychology*. 88, 879-903.

Podsakoff, P. M., MacKenzie, S. B., Paine, J. B., & Bachrach, D. G. (2000). Organizational citizenship behaviors: A critical review of the theoretical and empirical literature and suggestions for future research. *Journal of Management*. 26, 513-563.

Polanyi, M. (1958). *Personal knowledge: Towards a post-critical philosophy*. Chicago, IL: University of Chicago Press.

Polanyi, M. (1966). *The Tacit Dimension*. Garden City, NY: Doubleday.

Popadiuk, S. & Choo, C. W. (2006). Innovation and knowledge creation: How are these Concepts related? *International Journal of Information Management*. 26, 302-312.

Pirola-Merlo, A. & Mann, L. (2004). The relationship between individual creativity and team creativity: Aggregating across people and time. *Journal of Organizational Behavior*. 25, 235-257.

Cho, H. & Pucik, V. (2005). Relationship between innovativeness, quality, growth, profitability, and market value. *Strategic Management Journal*. 26, 555-570.

Reychav, I. & Weisberg, J. (2010). Bridging intention and behavior of knowledge sharing. *Journal of Knowledge Management*. 14, 285-300.

Reagans, R., Zuckerman, E., & McEvily, B. (2004). How to make the team: Social networks vs. demography as criteria for designing effective teams. *Administrative Science Quarterly*. 49, 101–133.

Roberts, P. W. (1999). Product innovation, product-market competition and persistent profitability in the U.S. pharmaceutical industry. *Strategic Management Journal*. 20, 655-670.

Rousseau, D. M. (1995). P*sychological contracts in organizations: Understanding written and unwritten agreements*. Thousand Oaks, CA: Sage.

Schneider, B., Ehrhart, M. G., & Macey, W. H. (2013). Organizational climate and culture. *The Annual Review of Psychology*. 64, 361-388.

Seashore, S. (1954). *Group cohesiveness in the industrial work group*. Ann Arbor, MI: Survey Research Center.

Shalley, C. E., Gilson, L. L., & Blum, T. C. (2000). Matching creativity requirements and the work environment: Effects on satisfaction and intentions to leave. *Academy of Management Journal.* 43, 215-223.

Shaw, J. D., Gupta, N., & Delery, J. E. (2005). Alternative conceptualizations of the relationship between voluntary turnover and organizational performance. *Academy of Management Journal.* 48, 50-68.

Sheppard, J. A. (1993). Productivity loss in performance groups: A motivation analysis. *Psychological Bulletin.* 113, 67-81.

Shipton, H., West, M., Dawson, J., Birdi, K., & Patterson, M. (2006). HRM as a predictor of innovation. *Human Resource Management Journal.* 16, 3-27.

Srivastava, A., Bartol, K. M. & Locke, E. A. (2006). Empowering leadership in management teams: Effects on knowledge sharing, efficacy, and team performance. *Academy of Management Journal.* 49, 1239-1251.

Staw, B. M. (1990). An evolutionary approach to creativity and innovation. In M. A. West & J. L. Farr (Eds.), *Innovation and creativity at work.* 287-308. Chichester, UK: Wiley.

Subramaniam, M., & Youndt, M. A. (2005). The influence of intellectual capital on the types of innovative capabilities. *Academy of Management Journal.* 48, 450-463.

Szulanski, G. (1996). Exploring internal stickiness: Impediments to the transfer of best practice within the firm. *Strategic Management Journal.* 17, 27-43.

Tajfel, H. (1978). *Differentiation between social groups: Studies in the social psychology of intergroup relations.* London: Academic Press.

Takeuchi, R., Chen, G. & Lepak, D. (2009). Through the looking glass of a social system: Cross-level effects of high-performance work systems on employees' attitudes. *Personnel Psychology.* 62, 1–29.

Tsui, A. S., Pearce, J. L., Porter, L. W., & Hite, J. P. (1995). Choice of employee-organization relationship: Influence of external and internal organizational factors. In G. R. Ferris (Ed.), *Research in personnel and human resource management.* 13, 117–151. Greenwich, CT: JAI

Press.

Tsui, A. S., Pearce, J. L., Porter, L. W., & Tripoli, A. M. (1997). Alternative approaches to the employee-organization relationship: Does investment in employees pay off? *Academy of Management Journal.* 40, 1089–1121.

Van de Ven, A. H. (1986). Central problems in the management of innovation. *Management Science.* 32, 590–607.

Van Den Hooff, B. & Van Weenen, F. D. L. (2004). Committed to share: Commitment and CMC use as antecedents of knowledge sharing. *Knowledge and Process Management.* 11, 13-24.

Van der Vegt, G. S. & Janssen, O. (2003). Joint impact of interdependence and group diversity on innovation. *Journal of Management.* 29, 729-751.

West, M. A. (2002). Sparkling fountains or stagnant ponds: An integrative model of creativity and innovation implementation in work groups. *Applied Psychology: An International Review.* 51, 355-424.

West, M. A. & Anderson, N. R. (1996). Innovation in top management teams. *Journal of Applied Psychology.* 81, 680-693.

West, M. A., Hirst, G., Richter, A. & Shipton, H. (2004). Twelve steps to heaven: Successfully managing change through developing innovative teams. *European Journal of Work and Organizational Psychology.* 13, 269-299.

Widmeyer, W. N., Brawley, L. R., & Carron, A. V. (1985). *The measurement of cohesion in sport teams: The Group Environment Questionnaire.* London, Ontario: Sports Dynamics.

Williams, K., O'Reilly, C. (1998). Forty years of diversity research: A review. In B. M. Staw and L.L. Cummings (Eds.), *Research in organizational behavior.* 77-140. Stamford, CT: JAI Press.

Wright, P. M., Dunford, B. B., & Snell, S. A. (2001). Human resources and the resource based view of the firm. *Journal of Management.* 27, 701-721.

Wright, P. M., & McMahan, G. G. (1992). Theoretical perspectives for strategic human resource management. *Journal of Management.* 18, 295-320.

Wu, P. C. & Chaturvedi, S. (2009). The role of procedural justice and power distance in the relationship between high performance work systems and employee attitudes: A multilevel perspective. *Journal of Management.* 35, 1228–47.

Yang, J. T. (2007). The impact of knowledge sharing on organizational learning and effectiveness. *Journal of Knowledge Management.* 11, 83-90.

Yang, S. C. & Farn, C. K. (2009). Social capital, behavioral control, and tacit knowledge sharing - a multi-informant design. *International Journal of Information Management.* 29, 210–218.

Youndt, M. A., Snell, S. A., Dean, J. W., & Lepak, D. P. (1996). Human resource management, manufacturing strategy, and performance. *Academy of Management Journal,* 39, 836–866.

Zacharatos, A., Barling, J., & Iverson, R. D. (2005). High performance work systems and occupational safety. *Journal of Applied Psychology.* 90, 77-93.

Zhou, Y., Hong, Y., & Liu, J. (2013). Internal commitment or external collaboration? The impact of human resource management systems on firm innovation and performance. *Human Resource Management.* 52, 263-288.

Zimmerman, R. D. & Darnold, T. C. (2009). The impact of job performance on employee turnover intentions and the voluntary turnover process: A meta-analysis and path model. *Personnel Review.* 38, 142-158.

---

Dr. Joseph Heller is a psychologist and a lecturer at Bar-Ilan's Business School, Ramat Gan, 5290002, Israel. E-mail: josef_he@walla.com

Dr. Jacob Weisberg is Professor Emeritus of Management at Bar-Ilan University, Ramat Gan, 5290002, Israel. Email: Jacob.Weisberg@biu.ac.il

*Kindai Management Review* Vol. 6, 2018 (ISSN: 2186-6961)

# Creative Industries: Managers' Perceived Creativity and Innovation Practices

## Fernando Cardoso de Sousa

*University of the Algarve. Campus de Gambelas, Portugal*

## Florbela Nunes

*University of Evora. Colégio do Espírito Santo, Portugal*

## Ileana Pardal Monteiro

*University of the Algarve. Campus de Gambelas, Portugal*

## Abstract

This article aims to demonstrate that the relationship between entrepreneurs' perceived attitudes to creativity and business innovation practices is stronger in the case of creative industries. A sample of 454 managers of micro and medium-sized companies (94 belonging to creative industries) was surveyed, using an inventory of innovative business practices, and the scale of attitudes towards creativity. The results, derived from a linear regression model (two factors for the scale of attitudes – leadership and autonomy – and for the inventory of business practices – business and strategy) confirmed the proposition by revealing the influence of the creative attitudes of managers on the company's innovative practices, fundamentally on strategy, especially in the creative industries segment. The innovative manager appeared as a disciplined individual, driven to collaborating with the employees. Because the creative industries include a wide range of businesses, from the public sponsored companies to the growing digital sector, further evidence is necessary to situate the managers who correspond to the interesting characterization found.

**Keywords:** *Creativity, Innovation, Creative Management, Creative Industries, Cultural Industries*

## INTRODUCTION

Following the statements of Coakes and Smith (2007), only innovation can allow a company to continue to optimize the introduction of original products at the right time, in the right market, and with the right distribution network. In turn, Tucker (2008) states that the only thing that separates the company from the competition are the ideas, knowledge, commitment and skills of innovation of employees. So, being innovation the general rule in organizations, creativity becomes not only desired but sought, with companies striving to incorporate it into their culture. Thus, the organizational strategies are increasingly focusing on creativity that, in general, is associated with the innovation practices (Keogh & McAdam, 2004). Creativity thus supports a corporate culture that encourages innovative expression, with a strong relationship with entrepreneurship (Drucker, 1985). In turn, the attitudes of entrepreneurs towards creativity influence the type of leadership exercised, and various authors (e.g. Cummings & O'Connell, 1978; Howell & Avolio, 1993; Woodman, Sawyer & Griffin, 1993), point to the influence of leadership on organizational innovation, which McAdam and Keogh (2004) found having a positive effect on micro and small enterprises. This influence between leadership and innovation is seen more often in the so-called "creative industries" (Bilton, 2007) because of the collaborative nature of a business activity connected to art and technology.

Thus, given that in the Portuguese business context one can get examples of such industries, this article aims at demonstrating that the influence of creative attitudes on innovative business practices is evident when considering entrepreneurs running micro-enterprises, and small and medium companies (SMEs), whose activities fall in what is meant by creative industries. Because of this influence, after describing approaches to creative industries, creativity and innovation, and their insertion in a model closer to this type of industry, the article discusses the attitudes of management in the face of creativity and its role in company innovation. After this presentation, the investigation is described, ending with a discussion of the results and conclusions.

## CREATIVE INDUSTRIES

The notion of creative industry is associated with economic and social changes that displace the focus of industrial activities to those related with knowledge. It emerged in the early 1990s in Australia, assuming greater importance when integrated in the policies defined in the United Kingdom, the DCMS (*Department of Culture, Media and Sports*), in 1997. Although having its roots in a range of very old activities, the term "creative industry" only came into existence with the advent of digital technology. Its antecedent "cultural industry" became common since Theodor Adorno and Max Horkheimer mentioned it in their essay "The culture industry: Enlightenment as mass deception", in 1947. The most striking innovation of this terminology, set by the DCMS, was its identification with a "new economy", driven by digital technologies, and closely related with "information" or "knowledge economy". It was the exploitation of intellectual property rights that was seen to provide the

crucial link, positioning the creative industries at the forefront of economic competitiveness. The inclusion of appropriate software made the statistics look more impressive and fundamental for the creation of the creative industries as an object of policy (O'Connor, 2010). As a consequence, one key objective of these policies was to get the sector recognize itself precisely as a sector, which may well make us think that the creative industries are not an "industry" at all, but part of the innovation system of the economy.

Associated with economic growth revitalization, "creative industries" is a concept that varies from country to country, turning it almost impossible to make comparisons (Newbigin, 2014). However, it always includes activities in which creativity is incorporated into the core of the business, being simultaneously "art, science and business" (Henry, 2007). These industries include a wide range of activities with a common characteristic: they rely heavily on imagination and individual creativity and, according to Hartley (2005), are associated with skill and talent. Nevertheless, not every job is creative and many outside of its scope are. According with Newbigin (2014), the number of jobs in the non-creative industries is probably greater than in the creative ones.

The DCMS believe that the creative industry is in production and distribution circuits of goods and services that use creativity and intellectual capital as raw materials, as focused by Howkins (2001), connecting the creative industries to value attribution to knowledge, work and intellectual property.

The emergence of the knowledge society (Castells, 2000) is oriented to an economy based on the individual and his intellectual resources, together with information and knowledge exchange capacity, in contrast with an economy centered on the intensive use of capital and work, and oriented to mass production. In a post-materialistic society the interests no longer revolve around the satisfaction of basic needs but around the aesthetic, intellectual, life quality and participation needs, carried out with autonomy.

This change is associated with a discourse about the change in values, disruptions and innovation (Howkins, 2001). In fact, the current trend focuses on the individual and reflects changes in terms of values, personal preferences, lifestyles and consumption patterns, different and apart from traditional behaviors. The change that puts creativity and innovation as a central element of the organizations is an individual and collective one, being critical to the organizations' development, performance and competitiveness (Mumford, 2012). Similarly, Howkins (2001) associates the creative industries to the "imperatives" of originality, with a focus on creativity and innovation, a creative economy, and presenting ways of turning ideas into money.

The year 2008 also represents a milestone, when UNESCO (United Nations Educational, Scientific and Cultural Organization) (UNESCO, 2008) established the creative economy as a way to boost economic growth, representing an alternative for development, especially for being based on creativity and able to use cultural and social characteristics of each country/region as an advantage for the development and production of unique and competitive goods and services.

In general terms, the benefits of the creative economy can be found in four levels: (a) job creation, exportation, social inclusion and cultural diversity; (b) intertwining of economy, culture and social aspects with technology, intellectual property and tourism objectives; (c) economic system based on knowledge, developing links between elements of macro and micro economy; and (d) development of innovation through multidisciplinary policies. At the same time, support policies by governments become important to enable creative businesses, which have grown over time. Creative industries also reflect small under-capitalized companies that, although providing jobs at twice the rate of the economy as a whole, deal with individuals taking a succession of different jobs, many of which are based on one-off short term projects (Carr, 2009).

We are witnessing an integrated and consistent vision which calls for the growing importance of the creative economy and affirms its value and benefits for growth and socio-economic development (Caves, 2001; Florida, 2002; Bendassolli, Kirschbaum, & Cunha, 2009; UNESCO, 2010; DCMS, 2012). This line highlights four components considered inseparable from the disruptive nature of the creative industries:

-   Creativity is the central element, necessary and essential for production.
-   Coupled with different resources management, the convergence between arts, business and technology is cultivated.
-   The generation of innovative content can be translated into salable products.
-   The economic value is based on the cultural and intellectual property.

This phenomenon has in common the ability to generate and trade ideas with "significant value", and Throsby (2004) identifies a set of dimensions to this value:

Aesthetic - reflects beauty, harmony and form.
Spiritual - seeks spiritual meaning shared by all human beings, including understanding, insight and awareness.
Social - creates links between individuals, fostering an environment in which the relationships and identities can thrive.
History - ensures clarity and a sense of continuity with the present.
Symbolic - gives meaning and symbolic value, which will be broadcast by work to the consumer.
Authenticity - stresses the fact that a work of art represents reality, is original and unique.

Indeed, the creative industries represent the economic areas that, in the early years of the twenty-first century, have assumed greater importance, giving place to the growth of central sectors to success and economic development (Fleming, 2008; Henry, 2007). Taking the UK as an example, the creative industries can help transform some cities, as is the case of Manchester and Glasgow, being London a case of higher economic and social weight. Nevertheless, these industries also face the challenge of longer-term growth, together with the improvement of their business models. As some authors (Carr, 2009) indicate, they lack the adoption of business models common in other sectors of the economy.

In Portugal, the dissemination and promotion of the creative economy is a strategic objective and, in accordance with paragraph 8 of the Technologi-

*Creative Industries: Managers' Perceived Creativity ans Innovation Practices*

cal Plan Coordination Unit (2005), sectors included in the creative industry concept are: advertising, architecture, art and antiques market, design, fashion, audiovisual productions, educational software and leisure, music, performing arts and entertainment, broadcast through television, radio and internet, writing and publishing, and can include other economic activities involving cutting-edge technologies, such as research in life sciences or engineering. The cultural heritage, tourism and museums are also identified as being close to the creative industries.

The macroeconomic study of Mateus (2010), on the development of a cluster of creative industries, linking innovation to the creative industries and their concentration, responds to the challenge of mapping a region. At the same time, it is also an example of the opportunity to propose a new development paradigm that joins culture and economy, recognizing that creativity, knowledge, innovation and access to information are the engines of development in the global world.

## CREATIVITY AND INNOVATION

As Woodman & Schoenfeld (1990) recall, the term *creativity* can be seen either as a social concept, expressed by people's implicit theories, or as a theoretical construct, developed by researchers in the field. Considering the theoretical definitions, and after carefully analysing the propositions evidenced by Kasof (1995), it is possible to conclude that the construction of creativity was (and still is) used in scientific literature to designate something perceived by others. Stein (1953) maintains that, "creativity is a process that results in novelty which is accepted as useful, tenable, or satisfying by a significant group of others at some point in time." Amabile (1983) states that, "a product or response is creative to the extent that appropriate observers independently agree it is creative. ...and it can also be regarded as the process by which something so judged is produced." These examples illustrate what may be designated as "hetero-attributed creativity", something pertaining to the communication process.

As the product of that communication process, creativity appears connected to what is perceived as

new by someone other than its originator, or as the putting to use of an idea (Kanter, 1983; West & Farr, 1990), in the domains of production, adoption, implementation, diffusion, or commercialisation of creations (Rogers, 1983; Spence, 1994). In these cases, creativity is seen as innovation.

As explained in Sousa (2008), creativity seems then to acquire its full meaning as a process of communication between the creator (or the product) and the judges or audience (hetero-attributed), or between the creator and the product (self-attributed). Innovation seems to be more appropriate to designate the resulting attribution made by the audience *a propos* the product. As a consequence, hetero-attributed creativity can only be measured through socio-cultural judgements, and is therefore context-dependent. Quoting Csikszentmihalyi (1991), "creativity is located in neither the creator nor the creative product but rather in the interaction between the creator and the field's gatekeeper who selectively retains or rejects original products."

As to innovation, Ghoshal and Bartlett (1987) classify it into broadly two categories: those that see innovation as the final product—the idea, practice, or material artifact that has been invented or that is regarded as novel independent of its adoption or non-adoption—and those who see it as a process, which proceeds from the conceptualization of a new idea to a solution of the problem and then to the actual utilization of a new item of economic or social value. However this distinction between creativity (undoubtedly the source of the whole process), and innovation is a minor issue in the corporate context, since the most important question turns out to be with regards to the system that allows putting the ideas into practice. Therefore, for every creative act producing an idea or a product, a social act is required to promote it in the organization and that is the reason why real innovation in companies is always a team effort (Woodman, Sawyer, & Griffin, 1993). Every innovation starts with an initial idea but needs a system to expand the individual creativity and install it at the group level. This group will need to solve a wide variety of problems resulting from the adoption, dissemination and implementation of this product.

As Burns & Stalker (1996) explained, if innovation does not necessarily need creativity to emerge, for it can be reached by introducing new techniques or technologies, it cannot be ignored during the adaptation process required to succeed in the market. Innovation for the sake of innovation can even be harmful to the enterprise, as happened when Coca-Cola tried a different flavor, or it could happen if McDonald's changed its production chain.

Individual creativity seems always to be the starting point, because it may exist even in the absence of innovation. As to innovation (Kilbourne & Woodman, 1999) it depends on a wide number of variables besides creativity, such as autonomy, the available information, the reward system, education or training, the system of authority, participation in decision-making, or the team cohesion.

## ATTITUDES AND CREATIVE MANAGEMENT

The construct of "attitude" was formulated by Allport (1935; 810) to designate a *mental and neural state of readiness, organized through experience, exerting a directive and dynamic influence upon the individual's response to all objects and situations with which it is related, activating affective, cognitive and behavioral processes*. Some researchers noted that these three parts are deeply intertwined, thus preferring to adopt a single dimension, defining attitude as a *summary evaluation of an object of thought* (Vogel & Wänke, 2016). In the present work we adopt the latter definition, speaking of attitudes as an evaluation towards a presented social object – in this case, creativity.

The discussion regarding whether such evaluations must be stable and consistent over time, retrieved from long term memory, following the "file-drawer model" (Wilson & Hodges, 1990), or if it may form on temporary or recent information as in the "attitude as construction perspective", in such a way that context is likely to influence individual's attitudes. Allport's seminal work has established attitude formation as a process of organization and sense making of experiences, thus influencing individual behavior. Following the author's work, we may state that information towards present or past behavior may determine the construction of an attitude.

In organizational context, Basadur and Basadur (2012) explain that attitudes towards creativity play a function of adaptation to the environment and may relate to the search of original and valuable strategies of reality interpretation, which promotes innovative practices. Management plays a fundamental role in analyzing the context, identifying problems and searching for corresponding solutions in a way that builds a creative attitude. And Goodman (1995) used the term of management's *creative response* to refer to the way managers give structure to the organizational context, manages team's autonomy in project development, and uses participatory processes. In addition, Gomes, Rodrigues, and Veloso (2015) show the importance of managers' role in bundling the contextual factors that help to create a system in which creativity and innovation become embedded in the organizational culture.

A manager's creative attitude is strongly related to the search for opportunities and differentiated experiences (Florida, 2002), as creativity is the result of hard work and profound knowledge in the domain one is working in. Research focused on creative industries and the management of creative people showed some tensions and paradoxes, as did the need for freedom and total devotion to the art, together with the need to manage the business in very organized terms (Eikhof & Haunschild, 2006). These tensions also emerged in Armstrong and Page's (2015) research, aiming at identifying leadership and management of creative people in United Kingdom's creative industries, showing five major tensions of the creative leader. Firstly, the tension between *commercial constraints* – centered on the effort to commercialize the products and on restrictions to experimentation – and *creative freedom* – focused on the creation and experimentation requiring few restrictions. Secondly, management roles fear failure and do not appreciate new experiences, preferring to *stick to the tried and tested*, versus the *appetite for risk*, which drives the creative leader to try new solutions, new products and develop new talents. A third tension refers to *competition* opposed to *collaboration* – competition which imposes secrecy to protect the ideas, the intellectual property keeping business under control and collaboration indispensable to creativity, helping to develop new ideas and maintain openness to others and new opportunities. A fourth tension deals with *automation*, granting faster results and cost reduction, versus *craft skills*, which uses technology to develop creative processes. Finally, time horizon; *long-term*, dealing with strategy, people management and talent development, and *short-term*, experimenting, improving and project management. The leaders, in Armstrong and Page's (2015) research, highlight the importance of mentors or role models helping them to develop the attitudes suitable to creative industries and creative people.

These considerations allow us to establish the proposition stating that managers' attitude towards creativity and managerial innovation practices is stronger in the creative industry sector, as we try to demonstrate in the following section.

## METHOD

To study the research question, a multiple linear regression analysis, with *stepwise* selection of variables, was used to obtain a parsimonious model that allowed to make predictions about the dependent variables.

### Subjects

The study was carried out using an opportunity sample consisting of 454 subjects, responsible for micro and SMEs in Portugal. Managers in the sample were predominantly male, representing 71% of respondents. Aged between 23 and 84 years (mean 44), the majority (59%) had higher qualifications and more than 25% had completed secondary education. About half (42%) of the subjects had an entrepreneurial experience higher than 10 years and the vast majority (84%) had previous professional experience (average 6 years).

In the study, micro and small companies were predominant: 61% had fewer than 10 employees and 33% between 10 and 49; only the remaining 6% were medium-sized enterprises, hiring more than 50 people. These companies were headquartered mainly in the North and Centre (30% and 29%, respectively), from Lisbon and Tagus Valley, while the South had the remaining 30%.

Considering the sectors included in the concept of "creative industry", a segment composed of 94 managers was selected. This segment was respon-

sible for companies with consulting activities, media and advertising, social support services and education, crafts, art, recreation and leisure. It represented 21% of the sample described, being similar in terms of gender, previous experience, size, and geographical distribution, in relation to the total sample. Managers of this segment constituted, however, a younger group, with a mean age of 41 years and with a lower level of education, where only 38% had a grade school of higher education and about half (53%) had completed secondary education. Business experience was also lower, as only about a third (34%) was manager for over 10 years.

### Instrument

The data collection was carried out with questionnaires consisting of an inventory and a scale. The inventory was intended to identify innovative business practices and, in its preparation, the structure and application form contents of the SME Innovation Network COTEC Portugal (Business Association for Innovation), were considered. The general objectives of COTEC's inventory are to promote public recognition of a group of SMEs by their attitude and innovative activity. This form was adapted to our target population and resulted in an instrument addressing four themes, or dimensions of cross-business innovation:

1. Conditions: involving the strategic aspects susceptible to influence entrepreneurial attitudes and behaviors towards innovation, which includes culture, leadership and business strategy.
2. Resources: refers to the contribution of different types of organizational resources to ensure more dynamic and better innovation performance, involving human capital, skills and foreign relations.
3. Processes: concerns the most relevant organizational processes for innovative dynamics of the organization, and its performance in terms of innovation. It involves the management of IDI activities, learning and results.
4. Results: ascertains to what extent conditions, resources and process-oriented innovation translates themselves into results. This

involves the financial and operational aspects, the market and society.

The inventory of innovative business practices consisted of a total of 20 binary questions with dichotomous answers (yes / no). The collection of items took into account the objectives of the original instrument and what was intended with its adaptation, which aimed to verify the existence of certain behaviors, assigning a code for expression of a given characteristic and, the other, the absence of that feature.

This instrument was submitted to the validation of COTEC Portugal, where the person in charge of the SME Innovation Network, responded positively to the adjustments made, having suggested changes in its use. The association was also informed that the inventory would be used along with the scale.

The scale was designed to identify creative attitudes by self-perception. Its development came from the creative investment theory, from Sternberg and Lubart (1991; 1996), which refers to the confluence of different sources of investment in creativity that interact with each other, consisting of six dimensions that describe:

1. Intelligence: points out the theoretical and practical ability to redefine problems, analyze and recognize good ideas and persuade the value of one's own ideas. It involves synthetic capabilities, analytical and practical-contextual.
2. Cognitive styles: relates to the way of thinking and how the person exploits and uses the intelligence. It involves the legislative styles, executive and judicial.
3. Knowledge: concerns explicit or tacit knowledge, acquired by books and documents, and by practice, respectively.
4. Personality: involves the set of features that characterize the individual. It includes aspects such as the willingness to take risks, trust in oneself, tolerance for ambiguity, courage to express new ideas, perseverance and self-esteem.
5. Motivation: refers to the driving force of creative performance. An oriented task determines the passion and concentration,

and energy at work.
6. Environmental context: refers to the environment in interaction with the individual, which facilitates creative expression. It involves aspects such as family, school, organizations and society, contributing, directly or indirectly, to creative expression.

The scale consisted of 36 questions, and the answer to the items was carried out using a four-point Likert-type matrix, expressed in terms of agreement: 1- strongly disagree, 2 - disagree, 3 – agree, and 4 - totally agree. We opted for a forced scale in which the average option neither agreed nor disagreed, so that the respondents had to avoid central tendency. The items were written in the positive, for the sake of clarity and simplicity, across the six dimensions, with a total of nine items for each dimension.

Confirmation of the metric characteristics of the instruments was ensured by a pilot study with 180 entrepreneurs who subsequently joined the sample. The descriptive analysis of the results of responses to the instruments showed a normal distribution, mean, standard deviation, minimum and maximum for each item.

In order to identify a smaller number of variables, by reducing the complexity of the analysis, we chose the factor analysis of the instruments, using the extraction of the principal components with varimax rotation. The inventory of business practices, after eliminating 10 items, resulted in two factors, explaining 48% of the variance, with Factor 1 - *Performance* (prestige and image, development of the business sector and the creation of skilled employment) with an coefficient alpha 0.75, and Factor 2 - *Strategy* (employee participation, goal setting, human resources management, external cooperation and management, and evaluation of activities), with a coefficient of 0.67. The composition of each factor is shown in Table 1.

As shown in Table 2, from the range of creative attitudes resulted factors with a coefficient alpha of 0.85, for factor 1, and 0.79, for factor 2, obtained after deleting 11 items. The study of dimensionality allowed the definition of two factors with eigenvalues greater than 1, which explained 48% of the variance:

*Creative Industries: Managers' Perceived Creativity ans Innovation Practices*

**Table 1: Saturations of Each Item of Inventory of Innovative Business Practices, After Varimax Rotation, and Respective Percentage of Explained Variance**

| Items | Factors (% explained variance) | |
|---|---|---|
| | Performance (26%) | Strategy (22%) |
| The innovation activities have a positive contribution to financial performance. | ,68 | ,07 |
| The human capital has a positive contribution to financial performance. | ,61 | ,15 |
| The innovation activity contributes to the prestige and good image. | ,84 | ,15 |
| The innovation activity has a positive impact on their activity sector. | ,79 | ,07 |
| The innovation activity has a positive impact in terms of skilled job creation. | ,56 | ,12 |
| It has a clear and shared innovation strategy, involving workers in its definition. | ,19 | ,66 |
| It has an innovation strategy translated into an action plan with medium and long term goals. | ,09 | ,72 |
| It has a human resource management policy geared to innovation. | ,06 | ,51 |
| It develops systematic cooperation actions in innovation with external entities | ,05 | ,60 |
| It offers process management and evaluation of innovation activities. | ,22 | ,73 |

**Table 2: Saturations of Each Item of the Scale Attitudes Towards Creativity, After Varimax Rotation, and Respective Percentage of Explained Variance**

| Items | Factors (% explained variance) | |
|---|---|---|
| | Leadership (29%) | Autonomy (19%) |
| I seek new solutions to respond to old problems. | ,57 | ,08 |
| I easily identify good ideas or projects. | ,56 | ,18 |
| I easily expose ideas and projects. | ,51 | ,35 |
| I mobilize others to follow my ideas. | ,64 | ,03 |
| I value the skills of my staff. | ,63 | ,14 |
| I share the idea that are learned every day. | ,63 | ,09 |
| If necessary, I change my routines. | ,70 | ,13 |
| I adapt myself easily to new environments. | ,75 | ,08 |
| I am able to express my ideas, even in unfavorable circumstances | ,63 | ,30 |
| Usually I don't give up in the face of difficulties. | ,65 | ,26 |
| I organize daily activities in a clear way. | ,01 | ,79 |
| I set goals to improve my performance. | ,17 | ,75 |
| I dedicate myself to work with method and rigor. | ,05 | ,79 |
| I seek to implement clear projects. | ,38 | ,63 |
| I concentrate easily on the tasks ahead. | ,42 | ,54 |

- Leadership - defined by imaginative capacity, capacity assessment, exposure fluidity, mobilization of the other, valuing the other, humility, flexibility, adaptability, security and persistence.
- Autonomy - defined by organizational skills, self-assessment, dedication to work, objectivity and ability to concentrate.

This resulted in two instruments, with two factors each, but with different scales (dichotomous for innovation practices and seven points to attitudes towards creativity), and with few effects of collinearity (significant regression coefficients and correlations between factors of different instruments with less than 0.2), which, along with the internal consistency of the factors, came in support of its validity.

Fernando Cardoso de Sousa, Florbela Nunes and Ileana Pardal Monteiro

**Table 3: Values of Explained Variance (R2), and Regression Coefficient (B), and Respective Significance of the Variables "Autonomy" and "Leadership", in Each of the Factors of "Innovation Practices" (N=454).**

| Factors (Creative Attitudes) | | Factors (Innovation Practices) | |
|---|---|---|---|
| | | Performance | Strategy |
| | $R^2$ | .03(**) | .07 (**) |
| Leadership | β | .13 (**) | .12 (*) |
| Autonomy | β | .07 | .18 (**) |

(**) Significant to p<.01; (*) Significant to p<.05

**Table 4: Values of Explained Variance (R2), Regression Coefficient (B), and Respective Significance of the Variables "Autonomy" And "Leadership", in Each of the Factors of "Innovation Practices" for Creative Industries (N=94).**

| Factors (Creative Attitudes) | | Factors (Innovation Practices) | |
|---|---|---|---|
| | | Performance | Strategy |
| | $R^2$ | .05 (*) | .14 (**) |
| Leadership | β | .25 (*) | .19 |
| Autonomy | β | -.10 | .26 (*) |

(**) Significant to p<.01; (*) Significant to p<.05

PROCEDURE

As mentioned above, the data collection was carried out with a questionnaire consisting of two parts: an inventory of innovative business practices and an auto-perception range of creative attitudes.

About 3,250 Portuguese companies - Micro and SME - based in Portugal, were contacted, regardless of the industry. This process resulted in 454 valid responses (14% of the target population), obtained electronically. As to ethical considerations, the first concern was with the establishment of an agreement with the organizations involved in this research.

RESULTS

Considering the research question of this investigation (*What is the relationship between the creative attitudes of entrepreneurs and their innovative business practices?*), we looked to answer it by means of a multiple linear regression, having the business practices' dependent variables (performance and strategy factors) as a function of the independent variable creative attitudes (factors leadership and autonomy).

The results generally showed the influence of creative attitudes on innovative business practices, verifying that managers' leadership and autonomy influenced their strategy and performance. As indicated in Table 3, and taking performance as the dependent variable, the model explained a significant variance percentage (3%), where Leadership is responsible for this variability, having Autonomy been deleted. Taking strategy as a dependent variable, it was found that the explained variance increased (7%) due to the autonomy factor, but still with both factors identified as predictors.

It was observed that the attitude towards leadership influenced the performance indices and the attitude towards the autonomy (the strategy indices). Finally it was examined till what extent the segment of creative industries differed in the linear regression, and the results are shown in Table 4. In the analysis of this group - 94 managers - it was found that the relationship was strengthened, in particular the attitudes towards creativity and strategy, responsible for 14% of the variance, which placed the perception of autonomy as a key predictor of strategy. Also, with greater intensity than in the global sample (5% of the explained variance), the perception of leadership as a predictor of performance.

Thus, 35% of the managers who were part of the sample allowed the execution of a significant linear regression model, and the relationship of the influence between the variables was bigger compared with the initial regression model.

In addition, it should be noted that the variables of personal development and context, and the gender, age and education, did not show statistical significance, by contrast with previous experience, business concentration and the business sector of creative industries.

It was concluded that there was a set of mediators that related creativity and innovation, operating at a multilevel (individual, team and organizational), influenced by individual character variables and organizational context.

## DISCUSSION

The main results of this investigation came from a linear regression model that revealed the existence of an influence relationship in the variables under study, between attitudes towards creativity and innovation practices in the business context. This relationship is based on the specificity of the influence of the creative attitudes of managers on the company's innovative practices, fundamentally on the strategy. The segment of the creative industries has shown an increasing variance as compared to the initial sample, indicating a dependency between innovative business practices and creative attitudes in an environment conditioned by the context of a particular type of activity.

Thus, we concluded that the breakthrough capacity is influenced by a number of characteristics (e.g. intelligence, personality or motivation), wherein the medium in which it operates, and with which it interacts, also influences innovative orientation. Working in the creative medium seems to favor and stimulate active and creative attitudes and, consequently, the implementation of relevant practices in terms of business innovation. Leadership is assumed as one of the factors that affect innovation, in a line of thought also advocated by Mumford (2012), who mentions the importance of leadership in motivating employees to foster innovation. Indeed, leadership is stated as a determinant of innovation, being the creative leader responsible for business impact and performance (Cummings & O'Connell, 1978; Woodman, Sawyer, & Griffin,

1993), along with a leading role of creating and maintaining a favorable climate for the creation and sharing of ideas (Robinson, 2001).

Attitudes were worth of a special interest, in face of the importance of the organization and the dedication to work, objectivity and ability to concentrate on practices that result in employee participation, goal setting, human resources management, external cooperation and evaluation activities. There seems to be a real sense of discipline, delivery and humility that determines much of the collaborative attitude in company management. If this seems to be more a marked feature in creative industries, it may be due, not only to a greater specialization and skills of employees, but to the need for greater perseverance and delivery to obtain favorable results in line with what was already identified by Eikhof and Haunschild (2006). The idea that transpires here is that the innovative manager is, above all, a disciplined individual, driven to share decisions with employees. Discipline, persistence and collaboration arise here as the keywords of innovation in companies, especially in the creative industries.

As to the limitations of this study, we found that although the instruments used have revealed good metric qualities, regarding the explanatory power of the items and their grouping factors, consistency was not very significant (Cronbach's alpha was less than 0.70 in the case of Factor 2, Inventory). Another limitation had to do with the fact that the sample was one of opportunity, not enabling to generalize results to similar groups. Also, it should be noted that the studies mentioned, although related to the theme that we tried to develop, giving it sustainability and heuristic value, hinder comparative analysis and systematization of knowledge related to the creative industries. In fact, it may happen that what we designated by "creative industries" provided a list of companies that have little to do with one another, and while some continue to depend upon subsidies, turning its business model less relevant, others reflect all the desirable characteristics of the modern economy. These ones may well be related with the new digital businesses, which have been taking over all others, in terms of development (Newbigin, 2009). If it is the case, we have no way of providing data to support it, as it would require a new investigation.

In view of the conclusions and the limitations

presented, and considering the emerging predictive model, we suggest further research to explain how more and better teachings may be withdrawn from innovative companies, from any industrial sector, and how they can take advantage of the creativity of employees. The link between innovation and the observation of a strict work discipline by management is also of research value.

## REFERENCES

Allport, G. (1992). Attitudes. In C. Murchison (Ed.). *Handbook of social psychology*. Worcester Mass: Clark University Press.

Amabile, T. (1983). *The social psychology of creativity*. New York: Springer-Verlag.

Armstrong, A. & Page, N. (2015). *Creativity and constraint: Leadership and management in the UK creative industries*. Hertfordshire: Ashridge Business School.

Basadur, M.S., e Basadur, T. (2012). Attitudes and creativity. In M. Runko e S. Pritzker (Eds.), *Encyclopedia of Creativity* (2nd Ed.). New York: Elsevier.

Bendassolli, P., Jr, T.W., Kirschbaum, C. & Cunha, M.P (2009). Industrias criativas: Definição, limites e possibilidades. Retrieved in 31 July, 2016 from: http://www.scielo.br/pdf/rae/v49n1/v49n1a03.pdf.

Bilton, C. (2007). *Management and creativity: From creative industries to creative management*. Oxford: Blackwell Publishing.

Burns, T. & Stalker, G. (1996). *The management of innovation*. New York: Oxford University Press.

Carr, J. (2009). Creative industries, creative workers and the creative economy: a review of selected recent literature. Scottish Government Social Research Retrived from http://www.gov.scot/Publications/2009/10/29154630/0

Castells, Manuel. (2002). *A Era da Informação: Economia, sociedade e cultura* (Vol. 1). Lisboa: Fundação Calouste Gulbenkian.

Caves, R. (2001). *Creative Industries: Contracts between art and commerce*. Cambridge NY: Harvard University Press.

Cebon, P., Newton, P. & Noble, P. (1999). Innovation in organizations: Towards a framework for indicator development. *Melbourne Business School Working Paper* #99-9, September.

Coakes, E. e Smith, P. (2007). Developing communities of innovation by identifying innovation champions. *The International Journal of Knowledge and Organizational Learning Management*, 14 (1), 74-85.

Csikszentmihalyi, M. (1991). Society, culture and person: a systems view of creativity. In R. J. Sternberg (Ed.). *The nature of creativity: Contemporary psychological perspectives* (325-340). Cambridge, NY: Cambridge University Press.

Cummings, L.L. e O'Connell, M.J. (1978). Organizational innovation. *Journal of Business Research*, 6, 33-50.

DCMS (2012). Creative industries facts and figures. Retirado, em 23 de Agosto, 2012, de http://www.culture.gov.uk/what_we_do/creative_industries/default.aspx.

Drucker, P. (1985). *Innovation and entrepreneurship: Practice and principles*. New York: Harper e Row.

Eikhof, D. R. e Haunschild, A. (2006). Lifestyle Meets Market: Bohemian Entrepreneurs in Creative Industries. *Creativity and Innovation Management*. 15 (3), 234-241.

Fleming, T. (Ed.) (2008). *Estudo macroeconómico: Desenvolvimento de um cluster de indústrias criativas na região norte*. Porto: Fundação de Serralves.

Florida, R. (2002). *The rise of the creative class*. New York: Basic Books.

Goodman, M. (1995). *Creative management*. New York: Prentice Hall.

Gomes, J., Rodrigues, F. & Veloso, A. (2015). Creativity at work: The role of context. In H. Shipton, P. Budhwar, P. Sparrow, P. & A. Brown (Eds.), *Human Resource Management, Innovation and Performance* (282-297). London, Palgrave Macmillan.

Hartley, J. (2005). *Creative Industries*. London: Blackwell.

Henry, C. (2007). *Entrepreneurship in the creative industries: An international perspective*. Cheltenham: Edward Elgar, Ltd.

Howell, J.M., e Avolio, B.J. (1993). Transformational leadership, transactional leadership, locus of control and support for innovation: Key predictors of consolidated business unit performance. *Journal of Applied Psychology*, 78, 891-902.

Howkins, J. (2001). *The creative economy: How people make money from ideas*. London: Allen Lane.

Kanter, R. (1983). *The change masters*. New York: Simon & Schuster.

Kasof, J. (1995). Explaining creativity: The attributional perspective. *Creativity Research Journal*, 8, 311-365.

Kilbourne, L. M., & Woodman, R. W. (1999). Barriers to organizational creativity. In R. E. Purser & A. Montuori (Eds.), *Social creativity* (Vol. 2). Cresskill, NJ: Hampton Press, Inc.

Mateus, A. (2010). *Sector cultural e criativo em Portugal*. Lisboa: Ministério da Cultura.

McAdam, R. e Keogh, W. (2004). Transitioning towards creativity and innovation measurement in SMEs. *Creativity and Innovation Management*. 13 (2), 126-139.

Mumford, M. (Ed.) (2012). *Handbook of organizational creativity*. USA: Academic Press.

Newbigin, J. (2014). What is the creative economy. The British Council. Retrieved from https://creativeconomy.britishcouncil.org/guide/what-creative-economy/

O'Connor, J. (2010). The cultural and creative industries : A literature review [2nd ed.]. Newcastle: Creativity, Culture and Education. Retrieved from http://eprints.qut.edu.au/43835/

Robinson, K. (2001). *Out of our minds: Learning to be creative*. UK: Capstone Publishing, Ltd.

Rogers, E. M. (1983) *Diffusion of innovations* (3rd Ed.). New York: The Free Press.

Sousa, F. (2008). Still the elusive definition of creativity. *International Journal of Psychology: A Biopsychosocial Approach*. 2, 55-82.

Sousa, F., Pellissier, R. & Monteiro, I. (2012). Creativity, innovation and collaborative organizations. *The International Journal of Organizational Innovation*. 5, 1, 26-65.

Spence, W. R. (1994). *Innovation: The communication of change in ideas, practices and products*. London: Chapman e Hall.

Stein, M. I. (1953). Creativity and culture. *The journal of psychology*. 36, 311-322.

Sternberg, R. J., e Lubart, T. (1996). Investing in creativity. *American Psychologist*. 51, 677-688.

Throsby, D. (2004). *Economics and culture*. Cambridge University

Tucker, R. B. (2008). *Driving growth through innovation*. San Francisco-Berret-Khoeler Publishers

UNESCO (2008). *Creative economy: Report 2008*. Nova York: United Nation.

UNESCO (2010). *Creative economy: Report 2010*. Nova York: United Nation

Vogel, T. & Wänke, M. (2016). *Attitudes and attitude change*. London: Routledge Taylor & Francis Group.

Wilson, T. D. & Hodges, S. D. (1992). Attitudes as temporary constructions. In L.L. Martin & A. Tesser (Eds.). *The construction of social judgements* (pp. 37-65). Hillsdale, N.J.: Erlbaum.

West, M. A. & Farr, J. L. (1990). Innovation at work. In M. A. West & J.L. Farr (Eds.), *Innovation and creativity at work: Psychological and organizational strategies* (pp. 3-15). Chichester: Wiley & Sons.

Wilson, T. D. & Hodges, S. D. (1992). Attitudes as temporary constructions. In L.L. Martin & A. Tesser (Eds.). *The construction of social judgements* (pp. 37-65). Hillsdale, N.J.: Erlbaum.

Woodman, R. W., & Schoenfeldt, T. (1989). Individual differences in creativity: An interactionist perspective. In Glover, J. A., Ronning, R. R & Reynolds, C. R. (Eds.). *Handbook of Creativity* (77-93). New York: Plenum Press.

Woodman, R. W., Sawyer, J. E., & Griffin, R. W. (1993). Toward a theory of organizational creativity. *Academy of Management Review*. 18, 2, 293-321.

---

Dr. Fernando Cardoso de Sousa is researcher at Research Centre for Spatial and Organizational Dynamics, University of the Algarve, Portugal. Email: cardoso_sousa@hotmail.com

Dr. Florbela Nunes is service worker of the IEFP, Colégio do Espírito Santo, University of Evora, Portugal. Email: florbela.nunes@iefp.pt

Dr. Ileana Pardal Monteiro is researcher at Research Centre for Spatial and Organizational Dynamics, University of the Algarve, Portugal. Email: ileanamonteiro@hotmail.com

*Kindai Management Review* Vol. 6, 2018 (ISSN: 2186-6961)

# The Early Investment Ecosystem for Start-ups in Canada, a Preliminary Study

**Kenneth A. Grant**

*Ted Rogers School of Management, Ryerson University, Canada*

**Divya Padmanaban**

*National Angel Capital Organisation, Canada*

**Amr El-Kebbi**

*Ted Rogers School of Management, Ryerson University, Canada*

### Abstract

The concept of the entrepreneurial ecosystem is relatively new and has seen quite limited research activity, particularly on the early stages of a startup's life. This empirical study examines the early investment ecosystem in Canada through the perspectives of 113 of its key players, drawing on input from 10 incubators, 17 accelerators, 24 angel investor groups, 8 venture capitalists and 54 entrepreneurs). In addition, the characteristics of some 170 Angel investment deals are examined as are the investment/approval funnels of both angel groups and VCs. The relationships between the players in the ecosystem are examined, with commonalities and significant differences identified. Using Storey's (1998) framework for entrepreneurial evaluation the study addresses his three monitoring stages—participation levels, the opinions of participants and the assessment of the usefulness of assistance provided to entrepreneurs by the other players in the ecosystem with a particular focus on potential high-growth start-ups. The findings should be of use to entrepreneurs, policymakers and other researchers interested in the interaction between ecosystem players and in gaining an understanding of a national investment ecosystem.

**Keywords:** *Entrepreneurial Ecosystem, Incubators, Accelerators, Angel Investors, VCs, Start-ups*

### INTRODUCTION

Since Schumpeter's early view of economies being impacted by entrepreneur-driven disruption (Schumpeter, 1934) academics have used varied perspectives in examining the phenomenon, with some taking the economic/market perspective, others focusing on the entrepreneur as an individual and, perhaps more recently, those taking a process view (Landstrom, 2005). Over the last decade,

increasing interest is being given to the concept of an *entrepreneurial ecosystem*. As Ketikidis et al point out, entrepreneurship "can only thrive if equipped with a well-developed ecosystem, with coordination between all relevant stakeholders" (Ketikidis et al., 2017) for entrepreneurial activity, however in direct comparison with the united states, its closest neighbour and most significant trading partner, it is seen as lacking in many areas.

In comparison to most nations, Canada is generally seen as a supportive country for entrepreneurial activity (Global Entrepreneurship Monitor, 2018). However, in direct comparison with the United States, its closest neighbour and most significant trading partner, it is seen as lacking in many areas.

## BACKGROUND DISCUSSION

As Stam (2015) notes, this concept of an entrepreneurial ecosystem is relatively recent and there is no widely shared definition. He further argues that, "the entrepreneurial ecosystem approach speaks directly to practitioners, but its causal depth and evidence base is rather limited." Isenberg is frequently cited as an early proponent, suggesting, "In an era when microfinance for small-scale entrepreneurs has become mainstream, the re-allocation of resources to support high-potential entrepreneurs may seem elitist and inequitable. But especially if resources are limited, programs should try to focus first on ambitious, growth- oriented entrepreneurs who address large potential markets" (Isenberg, 2010). Additionally, attention in both research and policy development is focused on the VC element, which funds less than 1% of all startups.

### The Concept

Mason and Brown (2014) define the entrepreneurial ecosystem as "interconnected entrepreneurial actors (both potential and existing), entrepreneurial organisations (e.g. firms, venture, business angels, banks), institutions (e.g. universities, public sector agencies, financial bodies) and entrepreneurial processes (e.g. the business birthrate, numbers of high-growth firms, levels of 'blockbuster entrepreneurship ', number of serial entrepreneurs,

degree of sell-out mentality within firms and levels of entrepreneurial ambition) which formally and informally coalesce to connect, mediate and govern the performance within the local entrepreneurial environment" and that, "The availability of finance is a further critical feature of entrepreneurial ecosystems. Particularly important is a critical mass of seed and start-up investors to provide finance and hands on support."

Mack and Meyer (2016) suggest that, "Entrepreneurial ecosystems (EE) consist of interacting components, which foster new firm formation and associated regional entrepreneurial activities. However they express concerns that much of the work on these entrepreneurial ecosystems focuses on documenting the presence of system components, and that there has ben very limited examination of the interdependencies between these entrepreneurial ecosystems' components and their evolutionary dynamics.

Stangler and Bell-Masterson (2015) discuss methods of measuring the entrepreneurial ecosystem, identifying a wide range of approaches to such measurement. They propose a high level set of measures addressing density, fluidity, connectivity and diversity and suggest that this is best done, not as a snapshot but over time. Hechavarria and Ingram (2014) also suggest that measures of entrepreneurial activity are very important in evaluating an entrepreneurial ecosystem.

Table 1 summarises these different authors views of the key characteristics/components of the Etrepreneurial Ecosystem.

### The Investment Ecosystem

While, as discussed above, the entrepreneurial ecosystem includes several elements, funding chal-

### Table 1: Suggested Characteristics/Components of the Entrepreneurial Ecosystem

| Author | Characteristics/Components |
|---|---|
| Isenberg (2011) | Policy, Finance, Culture, Support, Human capital and Markets |
| Spigel (2017) | Cultural (supportive culture, histories of entrepreneurship), Social (worker talent, investment capital, networks, mentors), Material (policy and governance, universities, support services, physical infrastructure, open markets) |
| Stam (2015) | Networks, Leadership, Finance, Talent, Knowledge, Support services and intermediaries, Formal institutions, Culture, Physical infrastructure, Demand |
| World Economic Forum (2013) | Accessible markets, Human capital/workforce , Funding & finance, Support systems/mentors, Government & regulatory framework Education & training Major universities as catalysts Cultural support |

lenges are seen as a major impediment for entrepreneurs. Obviously, early stage financing can come from a variety of sources, typically: The founders; family and friends; government loans and grants; financial institutions, crowdfunding platforms; incubators and accelerators, angel investors; and venture capitalists

Certainly, entrepreneurs and their potential investors have different needs, but the needs of these different stakeholders must be satisfied in a win-win relationship. This relationship is often influenced by other players, including government, universities and incubators/accelerators, who are sometimes investors themselves but, more often, are involved in other roles. For example, Lerner (2010) recognises the importance of the government supporting the complete entrepreneurial ecosystem beyond simply providing investment capital, suggesting that, "in many cases government officials hand out money without thinking about barriers other than money that entrepreneurs face".

In a recent paper, Spigel (2017), while recognising that, "Entrepreneurial ecosystems have become a popular tool in the study of the geography of high-growth entrepreneurship" suggests that "research on ecosystems is underdeveloped and under- theorized." Spigel further identifies 1) A need for "theoretical frameworks to understand the processes through which ecosystems emerge, change, and influence the activities of entrepreneurial actors," suggesting that 2) "identifying the attributes of entrepreneurial ecosystems and their relationships is the first part of a much broader research agenda" and that 3) "researchers must develop metrics that can be used to identify the presence of the ecosystem attributes."

This paper is a preliminary effort to address the second and third of Spigel's challenges in a Canadian context, with a particular focus on potentially high-growth start-ups.

## THE CANADIAN ENTREPRENEURIAL ECOSYSTEM

Similar to other developed economies, the Canadian entrepreneurial ecosystem has several participants such as start-ups, industry clusters, Canadian federal and regional governments, investors and supporting environments, and educational institutions. Industry clusters provide the ecosystem with suppliers and customers for the new ventures. Government, with its various levels (federal, provincial, and municipal), influences the ecosystem through its ability to regulate and fund (Pitelis, 2012). Investors financing the new start-ups include banks, angel investors, venture capitalists, crowdfunding, and loving individuals, i.e. friends and family (Harris et al., 2014). Supporting environments can include: incubators, accelerators, and other entrepreneurship programs that support entrepreneurs create and develop their start-ups throughout the entrepreneurial process to become a sustainable business (Tang, 2008) as well as educational institutions, such as universities, which have various roles in supporting the creation of new start-ups. Canada has a well developed system, with participation rates superior to most jeep thing 30 countries, but is often seen as significantly lagging with respect to US rates of participation, investment and returns.

### Key Players in the Investment Ecosystem

#### Incubators & Accelerators
Incubators and accelerators act as temporary protective environments for new start-ups, helping them overcome early challenges throughout the opportunity development process (Aernoudt, 2004, Patton and Marlow, 2011, Peters et al., 2004). While incubators and accelerators can be defined, based on their functionality, this paper allows them to self-classify. The main objective of incubators/accelerators is to prepare new start-ups to successfully stand alone as quickly as possible by offering three categories of services: infrastructure, mentoring, and networking (Peters et al., 2004). Their contributions to the entrepreneurial ecosystem are supporting business start-ups, creating job opportunities, and producing innovative technology (Tamasy, 2007). The Canadian Centre for Digital Entrepreneurship and Economic Performance has identified some 140 incubators and accelerators in Canada (The Centre for Digital Entrepreneurship and Economic Performance, 2018).

#### Angel Investors
The largest source of equity capital for start-ups is

the informal market (Berger and Udell, 1998), which can be separated into friends and family members of entrepreneurs, typically one-off investors, and business angels.

Angel investors are typically high net-worth individuals who invest their own money in small firms (Wong et al., 2009). Angel investors are typically cashed out entrepreneurs, or wealthy businesspeople, and their motivations for investment vary among several considerations, such as generating profit, regional development, self-actualization, and affection toward the entrepreneurial process. However, since angels invest their own money, they tend to invest in start-ups that they consider to have high growth potential and that belong to industries relevant to the investors' previous experiences. In order to minimize their risks, angel investors tend to coordinate among each other when approaching new investments and form angel groups (Wong et al., 2009). Estimating the total level of angel investment is very difficult, with Riding (2008) claiming that "Collectively, it is understood that business angels invest more funds in more firms than does the formal venture capital industry, particularly with respect to early-stage enterprises. However, it is difficult to obtain precise estimates of business angel activity," citing the challenges of identifying individual angels and tracking their activities. NACO is the only organization that tracks angel investment in Canada, with its data being restricted to that provided by its member angel groups. It found that its members invested $134 million in 2015 (Silcoff, 2016), however some observers suggest the total annual Angel investment might exceed $1 billion per year. By comparison, the UNH Centre for Venture Research suggests that US angel investment in 2015 was, $24.5 billion indicating a much higher level of investment when compared to national GDP (UNH Center for Venture Research, 2016).

Venture Capitalists (VCs)

Venture Capitalists VCs are quite distinct from Angel Investors. While both provide private equity investment for (relatively) early stage start-ups, likely to have high growth potential, VCs are investment firms who run funds for others to invest in, in turn using these funds to take equity positions in high potential start-ups. Writng in Forbes Magazine, John Greathouse defined a VC as, "a professional investor who deploys third-party funds into relatively early-stage companies" (Greathouse, 2012). As Amita et al (1998) further suggest, "Venture capitalists operate in environments where their relative efficiency in selecting and monitoring investments gives them a comparative advantage over other investors" focussing on industries with high potential returns and start-ups that will likely have low costs related to selection and monitoring. Estimates for the level of VC investment in Canada vary, ranging from $1.7 billion to about $3 billion(BDC Capital, 2017, PwC Canada, 2016). This compares to estimates of about 60 billion for the United States (PwC, 2018). Thus, as with angel investment, this is about half the level of investment found in the United States, when adjusted for GDP.

The Entrepreneurs

At the centre of the ecosystem is the entrepreneur. For Howard Stevenson of Harvard Business School "entrepreneurship is the pursuit of opportunity beyond resources controlled" (Eisenmann, 2013), with most popular definitions of entrepreneur being variants of "a person who organizes and manages any enterprise, especially a business, usually with considerable initiative and risk" . Filion points out that "the range of entrepreneurial roles is increasing steadily, and now includes venture creators, technopreneurs, intrapreneurs, extrapreneurs, social entrepreneurs, the self-employed and many others" (Filion, 2011). In the context of this study, our target is seen as the individual responsible for an active Canadian start-up, who has experience of interactions with the other ecosystem key players –incubators, aceratios, angels and VCs.

*The Purpose of this Study*

Commissioned by the Canadian National Angel Capital Organisation (NACO) with the support of the Canadian Government's Mitacs[1] funding program, this study examines the Canadian early investment ecosystem through the eyes of its key players – incubators, accelerators, Angel investors, VCs and, of course, the start-ups themselves. This is intended to be the first of several studies, setting the baseline for future work and to be of use to academics, policy makers, investors, entrepreneurs and others interested in the Canadian ecosystem.

The study conforms to Storey's (1998) framework for entrepreneurial program evaluation addressing his three Monitoring Stages, addressing participation levels, the opinions of participants and the assessment of the usefulness of assistance provided. It dos not address his higher levels of formal Evaluation.

## METHODOLOGY

This research project is the first in a series of project drawing on secondary data available from the National Angel Capital Organisation and primary data collected in a series of surveys.

### The Research Questions

The overall objective of this project is to prepare an initial assessment of the Canadian Early Investment Ecosystem and the views and interactions of key players in that ecosystem. At the centre of the ecosystem is the start-up, with a focus on those with a potential for significant growth. Thus the other ecosystem participants considered are those with the most significant interactions with start-ups with high growth potential – incubators, accelerators, angel investors and venture capitalists. It is largely a descriptive study, intended to be the precursor to other more focused projects to follow.

The study investigates five research questions, which were developed in discussion with an advisory group of industry representatives and academics, assembled by NACO:

1. What services are provided to start-ups by incubators and accelerators, and which are (rated by respondents as) most important?
2. What services are provided to start-ups by Angel investor groups, and which are most important?
3. What services are provided to start-ups by venture capitalist firms, and which are most important?
4. Are these services/value-adds congruent with the requirements of the Canadian start-ups, as identified by the start-up participants

in the study
5. What are the strengths and weaknesses of the current early investment ecosystem in Canada, based on the findings?

### The Survey Instruments and Subject Groups

The research team had access to data collected by NACO from its Angel group members providing data on some 125 deals done by the Angel groups during 2015. In addition, the research team developed and administered four surveys, one for each subject group that, taken together, represent the early investment ecosystem:

- Incubators and accelerators
- Angel investor groups
- Venture capital firms
- Entrepreneurs with start-ups

Each survey includes specific ) valuions relevant to each of the four subject categories. Given the limited differences between accelerators and incubators, one survey instrument was used to target both of these groups.

- Accelerator/incubator survey questions examine: (1) general characteristics of the accelerator/incubator; (2) operational characteristics of the accelerator/incubator; and (3) extent and value of interactions between the accelerator/incubator and start-ups. NACO invited 28 accelerators and 12 incubators to complete the survey, with 17 accelerators and 10 incubators completing the survey (a response rate of 60% and 83% respectively).
- Angel group survey questions examine: (1) Angel group characteristics; and (2) data on Angel investments, including pre-investment, post-investment and exit information. NACO invited 40 Angel groups to complete the survey, with 24 completing Part One of the survey (response rate of 60%) and 15 completing both parts of the survey (37.5% response rate). The research also team had access to data collected by NACO from its Angel group members providing data on the deals done by the Angel groups during

2015.

- Venture capitalist (VC) survey questions examine: (1) VC firm characteristics; (2) extent and value of interactions between the VC firms and start-ups; (3) investee start-ups' exit information; and (4) extent and value of interactions between VC firms and incubators, accelerators and Angel groups. NACO invited 65 VC firms to complete the survey, with 8 completing the survey (a response rate of 13%).
- Start-up/entrepreneur survey questions examine: (1) start-up characteristics; (2) extent and value of interactions between start-ups and incubators and accelerators; and (3) start-up financing information. Start-ups were invited to participate in the study through a variety of sources that included emails from industry associations and advisors, with 54 completing the survey.
- Finally, all four surveys include questions that address the following themes: (1) the extent and basis of interactions between respondents and other players in the entrepreneurial ecosystem; (2) the selection criteria for choosing start-ups to support or fund; and (3) the perceived value and impact of support that start-ups receive from other players in the ecosystem.

The majority of questions asked for factors to be scored on a Likert scale or to be ranked on their relative level of importance. In developing the results for this paper, these were frequently converted to rankings or relative importance, using weighted analysis, grouping according to relative importance.

## FINDINGS

### *The Perspectives of Incubators and Accelerators*

For the purposes of this study, we had assumed that incubators aim to nurture the development of early-stage entrepreneurial companies, helping them survive and grow during the start-up period, when they are most vulnerable; whereas the accelerators aim to grow the size and value of a company as fast as possible, possibly in preparation for an initial round of funding. Respondent organizations were asked to self-identify as one or the other. Responses were received from 10 incubators and 17 accelerators.

In general, incubators had a slightly more local focus, with accelerators more likely to have a national scope. About half chose their business location based on personal location or links with supporting bodies.

Formal Relationships

Almost all the incubators (9 of 10) and accelerators (16 of 17) had formal relationships with other types of organization. Table 2 shows the relative frequency of relationships with different types of organization for both incubators and accelerators.

The majority of both incubators and accelerators had relationships with universities, syndicate partners, Angel groups and VCs, with a slightly different ranking between each. For incubators, universities and Angel groups were most frequent; whereas for accelerators, the most frequent were corporate partners and then universities.

Respondents were also asked to comment on

**Table 2: Relationships between Incubators/Accelerators and Other Ecosystem Members**

| Type of Organization | # Incubators with Relation | % Accelerators with Relation | # Accelerators with Relation | % Accelerators with Relation |
|---|---|---|---|---|
| Angel Groups | 8 | 89% | 11 | 69% |
| Venture Capital Firms | 6 | 67% | 12 | 75% |
| Universities | 8 | 89% | 14 | 88% |
| Corporate Partners | 6 | 67% | 15 | 94% |
| Other | 1 | 11% | 7 | 44% |
| None | 0 | 0% | 0 | 0% |

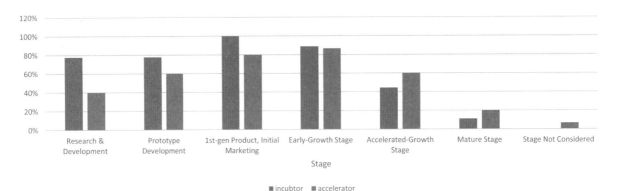

Figure 1: Incubators/Accelerators Interest in Start-ups By Stage

the value of the relationship with each of these partners. For incubators, universities were seen as the most important partners for sourcing and education, with Angels seen as most useful for syndication partnerships and for financing. Corporate partners were less often seen to have high value. Accelerators saw universities and VCs as the most important sourcing resource, with both corporate partners and universities being seen as the most significant education partners. Incubators and accelerators used a variety of techniqies to promote awareness of their firm and its services. Notably, the most mentioned was word of mouth, with pitch competitions being more popular with incubators and universities and government being slightly more popular with accelerators..

Interest in Specific Stages of Firm Evolution
Respondents were presented with a six-stage model of start-up evolution and were asked to select the stages of most interest to them. Their responses are shown in Figure 1.

Respondents did not have equal interest in all the stages, with only one respondent stating that stage was not a consideration for interest. For both accelerators and incubators, the highest levels of interest were in Stage 3 (first-generation product) and Stage 4 (early-growth). As might be expected, more incubators than accelerators had an interest in Stage 1 (R&D) and Stage 2 (prototype-development); however, both exhibited a lower interest in Stage 5 (accelerated- growth), and few were interested in mature businesses. However, these differences are still less than might be expected given the different expectations of incubators and accelerators.

Sources of Funding
Most participants received funding from multiple sources, typically two or three for incubators and three or four for accelerators. The most frequently received support was from federal and provincial governments, while universities were more likely to fund incubators than accelerators. Table 3 shows the relative importance of different funding sources.

Identification and Selection of Incubator/Accelerator Participants
All survey respondents used multiple sources of participant selection, an average of about four sources each. The most widely used method was online application, closely followed by hosted events. Alumni referrals were slightly more frequent than board referrals.

As shown in Table 4, the relative importance of selection criteria for participants was quite similar, with both incubators and accelerators ranking

Table 3: Sources of Funding for Incubators/Accelerators

|  | Incubator | Accelerator |
| --- | --- | --- |
| Provincial Government | 89% | 53% |
| Federal Government | 67% | 53% |
| Universities | 56% | 12% |
| VC/PE Firms | 44% | 35% |
| Other Larger Entity | 22% | 24% |
| Returns made from Investments | 44% | 24% |
| Non-Government Party | 44% | 59% |

*The Early Investment Ecosystem for Start-ups in Canada, a Preliminary Study*

## Table 4: Selection Criteria Used by Incubators/Accelerators

| | Incubator | | Accelerator |
|---|---|---|---|
| 1 | Innovation of product/service | 1 | Innovation of product/service |
| 2 | Management team qualification | 2 | Management team qualification |
| 3 | Customer traction | 3 | Business model |
| 4 | Business model | 4 | Product traction |
| 5 | Product traction | 5 | Revenue/Employee growth |
| 6 | Other | 6 | Management team size |
| 7 | Revenue/Employee growth | 7 | Other |
| 8 | Crowdfunding history | 8 | Crowdfunding history |
| 9 | Management team size | 9 | Customer traction |

the innovation of the product or service and the quality of the management team most highly, generally followed by the business model and product traction, with the most significant differences being the unimportance of customer traction for accelerators and of the management team size for incubators. Notably, crowdfunding history was unimportant for both. To the degree that management team size was considered, a single management team member was sufficient for most incubators, while two to three members were preferable for accelerators.

### Application and Acceptance Rates

In total, the incubators received 1,340 applications in 2014, of which they accepted 299, an acceptance rate of 22%. Accelerators received 2,510 applications and selected 410, an acceptance rate of 18%.

### Program Structure

The programs varied significantly in program length, with only about one-third of either incubators or accelerators having a standard period of participation for all participants. Length of participation ranged from about six to 24 months, with 24 months being the period most often reported.

The number of mentors/instructors/consultants available to start-ups varied widely, from two to more than 30. There were significant differences in the number of hours provided by incubators, with most providing between 10 and 75 hours and three reporting more than 300 hours provided. Accelerators provided between 35 and 75 hours, with two providing about 200 hours.

### Graduation and Funding Success

There was little consistency across participants on how they identified and evaluated successful graduation from their programs. Accelerators most often defined success as one or more of: receiving funding, acquiring a contract, or significant revenue/market share growth. For incubators, receiving funding and significant revenue/market share growth were the most common, with committee review and completing a set period in the program also being broadly used.

In terms of start-ups that did not graduate, about 25% of incubators would allow them to continue, with 31% of accelerators requiring re-application. (In four programs, all start-ups are viewed as graduates.) While not all participants provided data, collectively, incubators reported 156 graduates in 2014 and accelerators reported 167. Most incubators/accelerators reported that virtually all of their participants received some form of funding during their participation, with angels, VCs and governments being the most common.

In terms of typical first-round external funding, incubator participants fell into two groups: those seeking less than $100,000 and those seeking about $300,000. For accelerator participants, most were looking for around $300,000, with many reporting an ask above $500,000.

Overall, most incubators/accelerators expected 30 to 60% of companies to receive Angel/VC/Private Enterprise investment, with an average of around 45%.

### Services Provided

Table 5 shows the proportion of incubators/ accel-

The Institute for Creative Management and Innovation, Kindai University    83

Kenneth A. Grant, Divya Padmanaban and Amr El-Kebbi

**Table 5: Service Provided to Start-ups by Incubators/Accelerators**

|  | Incubator | Accelerator |
|---|---|---|
| Basic Facilities Support | 89% | 59% |
| Common External Service Providers | 89% | 82% |
| Access to Bank Loans, Loan Funds | 44% | 41% |
| Network/Community of Entrepreneurs | 100% | 100% |
| Business Mentoring/Training | 100% | 100% |
| Investor Introductions | 89% | 100% |
| Patent Support | 67% | 41% |
| Strategic Alliances | 89% | 76% |
| Assistance in Formulating Business Plans | 89% | 88% |
| Help in Improving Company's Sales Growth | 78% | 82% |
| Aid in Internationalizing Company's Operations | 56% | 65% |
| Financial Support | 67% | 53% |
| Pitch Competitions | 78% | 65% |
| Demo Days | 44% | 65% |
| Firm Specific Programs | 67% | 59% |
| Industry Sector Specific Programs | 56% | 53% |
| Alumni Network Post Graduation | 67% | 71% |
| Provide Feedback to Companies If They Are Not Selected Into the Program | 56% | 47% |

erators that provide each type of service. There was little difference between incubators and accelerators, except that accelerators were somewhat less likely to provide basic facilities or patent support. All provided access to networking and communities and to business mentoring. In terms of the relative importance of the services provided, there were some similarities but also significant differences

Figure 2 shows a comparison of the incubators and accelerators ranking of the services they provide, highlighting the areas of similarity and difference. Notably, each ranked business mentoring/training first, with access to a network/community of entrepreneurs and investor introductions also in the top four. The biggest difference was the importance of providing basic facilities, which incubators ranked highly and accelerators very low. They held inverse views on the relative importance of industry-specific and firm-specific programming.

Post-Program Interaction
Virtually all incubators and accelerators tracked the development of their start-ups post-graduation, with about half reporting ongoing mentorship activities, and about two-thirds providing alumni

events. Typically such events took place at intervals of between three months and a year. In terms of the perception of the importance of alumni services provided, both incubators and accelerators ranked investor introductions as the most important, followed by help in securing funding. Providing introductions to other alumni entrepreneurs was seen as substantially less important.

*The Perspectives of Angel Groups*

Twenty-four Angel groups provided details on how they are structured, how they approach investment activities, and with which organizations they most frequently work. They were also asked to describe their recent deals. The 24 Angel groups described some 125 deals that took place within the previous year. (Note: There were actually 109 unique deals because, in a few cases, more than one Angel group participated in the deal, with each participant reporting separately.)

The Angel groups had been in operation from one to sixteen years, with an average of around five years. Collectively they have funded 466 investments, 169 of these within the previous year. The study team were also able to access and integrate

*The Early Investment Ecosystem for Start-ups in Canada, a Preliminary Study*

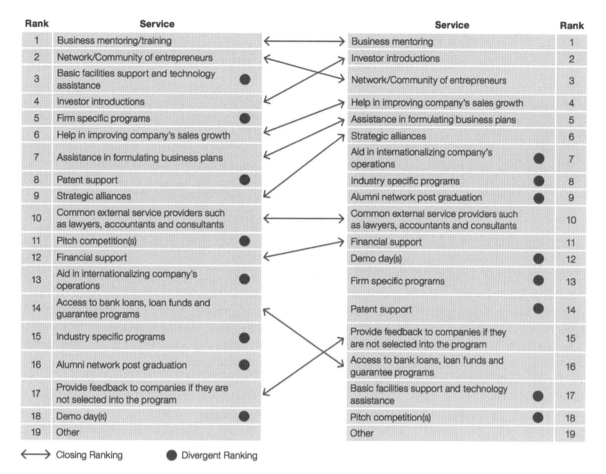

Figure 2: Relative Importance of Services Provided by Incubators/Accelerators

some data from NACO's 2014 Report on Angel Investing Activity in Canada and have integrated this material with the survey results.

*The Motivations of the Member Investors Within the Angel Group*

When asked about the motivational factors for the individual members of the angel group. Monetary motivation and passion rate very highly, with other factors being ranked substantially lower (strategic fit being the highest of these).

Formal Relationships With Other Ecosystem Participants

All but four respondents reported that they had formal relationships with other organizations. More than half had relationships with incubators and accelerators and about one-third had relationships with other angels and VCs and with universities

The primary value for angel group relationships with both incubators and accelerators was their use as a sourcing partner. This was confirmed by an analysis of the third-party contacts involved in investments actually made, where incubators and accelerators were, by far, the most likely source when third parties were involved. Only six had relationships with universities, primarily as a sourcing partner, with four mentioning education value.

Important Factors Used in the Evaluation of Investee Firms

Angel groups were asked to rank the importance of a number of characteristics of potential investee start-ups. As shown in Table 6, the most important factors related to prior entrepreneurial experience, with participation in incubator accelerators being of some importance, followed by industry awards and tax advantages. Interestingly, being environ-

## Table 6: The Factors Used by Angel Investors to Select Investee Start-ups

| Rank | Characteristics of Potential Investees |
|---|---|
| MOST IMPORTANT | |
| 1 | Past entrepreneurial experience |
| 2 | Serial entrepreneur |
| IMPORTANT | |
| 3 | Joined an incubator or accelerator program in the past |
| 4 | Obtained competitive research funding |
| 5 | Have tax advantage |
| 6 | Received industry award |
| LESS IMPORTANT | |
| 7 | Environmentally friendly |
| 8 | Have had crowdfunding history |

## Table 7: Angel Investors Ranking of the Services They Provide

| Rank | Characteristics of Potential Investees |
|---|---|
| MOST IMPORTANT | |
| 1 | Advice/Consultation |
| IMPORTANT | |
| 2 | Regular mentorship |
| 3 | Bring in new deals, business relations and contracts |
| 4 | Introduction to follow-on investors |
| 5 | Sit on the board of directors |
| 6 | Help in secure additional funding/co-investors |
| LESS IMPORTANT | |
| 7 | Join the company as a formal staff member |
| 8 | Other |

mentally friendly or having a history of crowdfunding were not seen as important. In the vast majority of cases, the due diligence was done by a member of the Angel group (about 90%), or a member of another Angel group (about 9%). Very little use was made of professional services firms such as consultants or accountants.

To a lesser degree, many incubators and accelerators are seen as providing value as a syndication partner, a co-investor and a source of education. A smaller number (nine) with relationships with venture capitalists did identify their usefulness as investment partners in some form (syndicate, co-investor, help in arranging financing). Similarly, when asked to rank the importance of specific screening criteria, the most important factor was the quality and track record of the management team; with product and market criteria, along with more specific investment criteria, clumped together as the next most important. The firm's background was seen as slightly less important.

Value Provided to the Investee Firms

The Angel groups were also asked to identify the most important value-add services they provided to the investee start-ups. The results are shown in Table 7. Perhaps not surprisingly, they ranked the majority of the choices quite highly. In particular, providing advice was ranked most highly, followed by mentorship (the difference between the two being the relative frequency and formality), with helping secure funding (both additional funding

and introduction to follow-on investors) also being seen as significant value-add. Interestingly, while providing board members was seen as an important service, providing staff members was seen as relatively unimportant.

Opportunities Reviewed and Investments Made by the Angel Firms

Sixteen of the respondent Angel groups provided information on their screening and investment activities over the last year. Collectively the groups reported having 2,112 applications in 2014, with 519 pitches being given, 185 being subjected to due diligence and 169 receiving investments. (Note: The number of Angel groups reporting in each category varied.) Figure 3 shows the relationship between opportunities considered, pitches/presentations received, due diligence carried out, and investments made.

To ensure consistency, this figure includes only those groups that provided data in all categories (nine of the original 16). Thus, about 23% of applicants were given the opportunity to make presentations, with about one-half of these proceeding to due diligence. Investments were made in almost 70% of those undergoing due diligence. Thus, about 8% of the original applicants received investment. In most cases (79%) the investment took the form of common shares. In total, the 16 Angels groups made 169 investments, with a total value of just over $60 million. The average investment was about $380,000, with the typical group making about 10

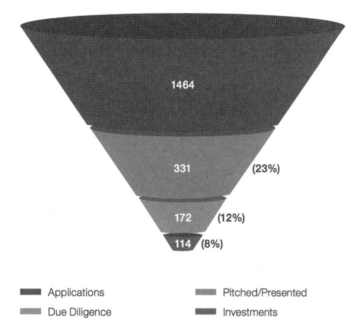

Figure 3: The Angel Investors' Investment Funnel

Table 8: Number of Deals per Group and Size of the Deals

| 1-5 deals | 6-10 deals | 11-15 deals | 16-20 deals | 20+ deals |
|---|---|---|---|---|
| 3 | 7 | 2 | 2 | 2 |

| Less than $1 million | $1-5 million | $5-10 million | Over $10 million |
|---|---|---|---|
| 6 | 8 | 1 | 1 |

investments. Table 8 shows the distribution of investments by Angel group and the range of the total investments.

An Examination of Specific Deals
Eighteen of the Angel groups provided details of the deals they carried out during 2014, and 125 deals were described. In some deals, more than one of the Angel groups were involved. In total these 125 deals involved some $83 million of investment. The level of detail provided in different sections of the survey varied widely. Where relevant, the number responding in a specific area is provided as part of the discussion. 76% of the deals were new deals, with 24% being follow-up investment. Employee information was provided for 33 of the companies, with employment ranging from three to 37, with an average of seven.

In making the first contact with the Angel group, about half of the firms (n=112) used email or other online approach, with another third using a third-party introduction. Incubators, accelerators and other Angel investors were the most common sources, with a much smaller portion coming from venture capitalists, industries, industry associations and government bodies. None were reported as coming from professional firms (consultants or accountants) or from social media sources.

In carrying out due diligence, the vast majority (87%) of groups used their own members to carry out the work, followed by the use of other Angel investors (9%). In only one case was a consulting or accounting firm involved. About 50% of the deals were with startups located in the province of Ontario, with British Columbia and Alberta being the next most likely.

The levels of investment varied considerably, as shown in Figure 4, from $15,000–2 million, with the average investment being some $271,000. However, the median investment was much lower, at

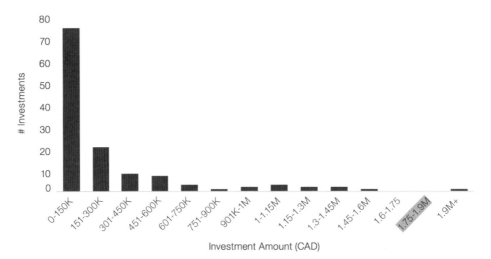

Figure 4: Levels of Investment by the Angel Investors

$122,500, as the skewed nature of the Figure 4 plot indicates. About one-third (52) of the deals had co-investors. These were split evenly between other Angel groups and individual investors, with very limited partnerships with other sources, although about 21% did have a combination of sources. Some participants provided details of their level of involvement with the investees' businesses (n=52). Most frequently this consisted of holding a board seat (35%) or acting as an advisor (27%). In a small number of cases, they provided management or industry introductions.

Participants also provided some details on their experience related to the primary industry of the investees' businesses (n=61), with the major experience spread across entrepreneurship in the industry, operating and management experience. In most cases, this was general experience in the same sector, with only six claiming core experience for the business. Only 12 of the Angel groups had a pre-planned exit strategy at the time of the deal, with most of them ex, and a generally productive relationshippecting a trade sale. Two expected a company buyback or an IPO. However, a higher number, 18, claim to have advised the entrepreneur about their exit expectations.

Finally, Angel groups were asked to indicate whether they supported some statements on the future of crowdfunding. Their responses suggest that, while Angels are somewhat conservative about the growth of crowdsourcing, they do see crowd-funding becoming a more important source of funds with a need for better and more flexible regulation, but not as a significant challenge to their own investment activities.

*The Perspectives of Venture Capitalists*

Of the eight venture capitalist firms providing responses, four had been in operation for between one and five years and three had over 15 years of existence. All but one had a national or international focus. Primarily, they chose their own business location for reasons of access to talent and local government policies. Only one mentioned that this was due to the residence location of the members. Each had a degree of industry focus, ranging from two to five industries; the frequency of each of these is shown in Table 9.

Investment Activities

The fund size of each venture capitalist firm is

Table 9: The Industries of Most Interest to Canadian VCs

| Sector | n |
|---|---|
| Information and Communication Technologies | 6 |
| Life Sciences | 5 |
| Clean Technologies | 4 |
| Manufacturing | 4 |
| Energy | 2 |
| Other | 4 |

*The Early Investment Ecosystem for Start-ups in Canada, a Preliminary Study*

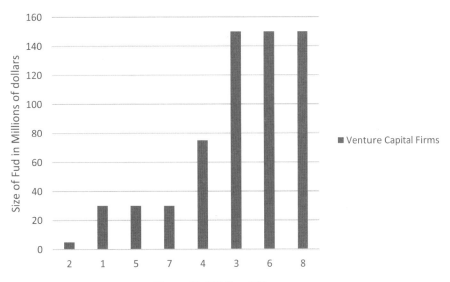

**Figure 5: VC Fund Size**

**Table 10: Canadian VCs Investment Interest By Stage**

| Stage and Rank | # VCs | % VCs |
|---|---|---|
| Research & Development - 1 | 2 | 25% |
| Prototype - 2 | 2 | 25% |
| 1st generation - 3 | 3 | 38% |
| Early-growth - 4 | 6 | 75% |
| Accelerated-growth - 5 | 4 | 50% |
| Mature - 6 | 1 | 13% |
| No - 7 | 1 | 13% |

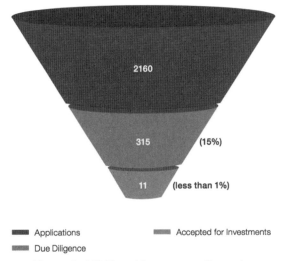

**Figure 6: VC Firms' Investment Funnel**

shown in Figure 5. The level of interest in each stage of business development is shown in Table 10, with the highest levels being in the early-growth and accelerated- growth stages.

All but one of the firms had some formal relationships with other organizations, the most mentioned being accelerators. Regardless of whether or not they had a formal relationship, all but one contacted incubators and accelerators in their regions to get exposure to the participating companies.

Six firms provided details of their application and acceptance rates. As shown in Figure 6, of 2,160 applications, 315 (15%) were chosen for due diligence and 11 accepted for investments, an acceptance rate of less than 1%. Of these, seven were first-time investments. In terms of investment levels per start-up, Table 11 shows the range of investments across the eight firms.

Six firms reported on the value of their investment activities during 2014, with total investments ranging from $2.5 million to $26 million (Table 12), with an average investment of $1.7 million per deal. All of the firms reported that they discussed exit expectations with the entrepreneurs of their firm's investee start-ups prior to investment, and four of the firms reported that they had successful exits in 2014 (a total of 6 exits – four M&A/ Trade Sales, one IPO and one Secondary purchase). Three of the venture capitalist firms indicated that, if the start-up's exit was not in their firm's best favour,

### Table 11: Typical Investment by VCs in a Start-up

| Investment Range | # Reporting |
|---|---|
| Up to $200,000 | 1 |
| $200,000 - 500,000 | 3 |
| $500,000 - 1 million | 0 |
| Over $1 million | 4 |

### Table 12: Total Investment by the VC Firms in a Year (2014)

| # of Investments | Total Value ($) | Average Value ($) |
|---|---|---|
| 2 | 2,500,000 | 1,250,000 |
| 12 | 5,500,000 | 458,333 |
| 8 | 12,000,000 | 1,500,000 |
| 12 | 15,000,000 | 1,250,000 |
| 6 | 24,000,000 | 4,000,000 |
| 10 | 26,000,000 | 2,600,000 |

### Table 13: VC Firms Start-up Investment Selection Criteria

| Rank | Criterion |
|---|---|
| HIGH | |
| 1 | Startup industry outlook |
| 2 | Management team qualifications |
| 3 | Product traction |
| 4 | Exit expectation (for both the VC fund and the investee firm |
| MEDIUM | |
| 5 | Business plan feasibility |
| 6 | Startup's existing competition |
| 7 | The fund's ability to guide the investee firm |
| 8 | Size of the deal |
| LOW | |
| 9 | Startup having received Angel investment(s) |
| 10 | Startup's participation in an accelerator program |
| 11 | Startup's participation in an incubator program |
| 12 | "Startup having received funding through a crowdfunding platform" |
| 13 | Other |

they required compensation from the investee start-up.

Five of the firms had co-invested or syndicated with Angel groups, and when they did, it sometimes had an impact on some aspects of the deal, with the most common Angel contribution being to increase

### Table 14: VC Firms Start-up Management Team Evaluation Criteria

| Rank | Criterion |
|---|---|
| HIGH | |
| 1 | Integrity and trustworthiness |
| 2 | Track record of the team |
| 3 | Good judgement |
| FAIRLY HIGH | |
| 4 | Efficient cooperation in the team |
| 5 | Social skills (presentation, negotiating, leadership) |
| 5 | High level of energy and strong passion |
| 7 | Complementary of each member's background and experience |
| LOW | |
| 8 | Management team size |

### Table 15: VC Firms Views of the Value of the Services They Provide

| Rank | Criterion |
|---|---|
| HIGH | |
| 1 | Help in securing additional funding/co-investors |
| 2 | Advice/Consultation |
| 2 | Introduction to follow-on investors |
| 4 | Regular mentorship |
| 5 | Bring in new deals, business relationships and contracts |
| 6 | Sit on the board of directors |
| LOW | |
| 7 | Provide feedback to companies if they are not selected for investment or into our program |
| 8 | Join the company as a formal staff member |

the investment amount.

Selection Criteria

Table 13 shows the relative importance of the various selection criteria for investment. Four areas stand out as of high importance – industry outlook, management team qualifications, product traction, and exit expectations. Factors such as the business plan or the size of the deal were seen as of medium importance, while those related to the prior history of the firm had low importance.

When further questioned about the management team qualifications, they ranked integrity, track record and judgement most highly; but,

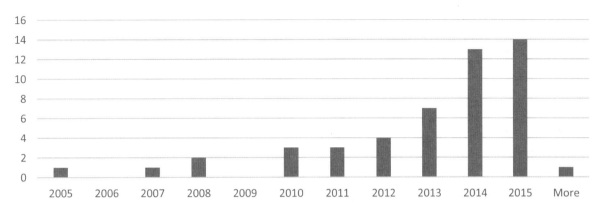

Figure 7: Year Start-Ups Were Established

**Table 16: Industry Sectors of the Start-ups Studied**

| Sector | # Companies | % |
|---|---|---|
| Information and Communication Technologies | 25 | 50% |
| Life Sciences | 6 | 12% |
| Services | 4 | 8% |
| Clean Tech | 3 | 6% |
| Energy | 1 | 2% |
| Manufacturing | 0 | 0% |
| Other | 11 | 22% |

except for the size of the management team, all of the criteria were seen as important as shown in Table 14.

When asked about the relative value of services provided to investees, most were seen as having high value. As Table 15 shows, only providing feedback to rejected companies and providing staff were seem as providing little value. On average, VCs met about 12 times with each investee start-up.

*The Perspectives of Entrepreneurs*

Organizations were recruited through a variety of means, primarily electronic. Requests for participation were done through a number of intermediaries who had access to early-stage entrepreneurs, including participants in a number of incubators and accelerators. Thus, the responses and industry sectors represented an opportunistic rather than a structured sample, likely with a bias towards start-ups with potentially high growth. In all, 54 responses from start-ups were received. Table 16 shows the industries represented, with ICT companies representing almost half of the participants. As Figure 7 demonstrates, most were established between 2013 and 2015.

Most start-ups reported having between zero to four full-time employees at the end of 2014, and a similar range of members of the management team. When asked for reasons for their choice of business location, the most important reasons given were:

- Ease of funding
- Access to talent
- Living nearby

*Relationships With Incubators*

Thirty-three start-ups, 61% of the total, had joined an incubator, typically taking from one to 12 months from application to acceptance. They spent significant time in the incubator, with 12 reporting being there for two years or more. Six reported that they had been turned down in their application to join an incubator and eight indicated a future intent to apply. The start-ups found the incubator through a variety of sources, with word of mouth and university affiliation being the most significant.

Most start-ups (about 84%) found a medium to high overall level of value from their interactions with incubators, with only five (16%) reporting little or no value. Table 17 shows the services judged to be of most value.

In terms of possible improvements to the incubators, 23 looked for more company-specific training, with some limited interest in a different program duration and larger programs.

## Table 17: Start-ups Assessment of the Areas of Most Value in Incubator Participation

| Rank | Criterion |
|---|---|
| HIGH VALUE | |
| 1 | Basic facilities support and technology assistance |
| 2 | Network/Community of entrepreneurs |
| 3 | Common external service providers such as lawyers, accountants and consultants |
| 4 | Industry-specific programs |
| SIGNIFICANT VALUE | |
| 5 | Firm-specific programs |
| 6 | Strategic alliances |
| 7 | Alumni network post-graduation |
| 8 | Business mentoring/training |
| 9 | Assistance in formulating business plans |
| 10 | Access to bank loans, loan funds and guarantee programs |
| 11 | Help in improving company's sales growth |
| 12 | Provide feedback to companies if they are not selected into the program |
| 13 | Aid in internationalizing company's operations |
| 14 | Investor introductions |
| LESS VALUE | |
| 14 | Demo day(s) |
| 16 | Pitch competition(s) |
| 17 | Patent support |
| 18 | Financial support |
| 19 | Other |

## Table 18: Reasons Start-ups Used Accelerators

| Rank | Criterion |
|---|---|
| HIGH VALUE | |
| 1 | Basic facilities support and technology assistance |
| 2 | Network/Community of entrepreneurs |
| 3 | Common external service providers such as lawyers, accountants and consultants |
| 4 | Industry-specific programs |
| SIGNIFICANT VALUE | |
| 5 | Firm-specific programs |
| 6 | Strategic alliances |
| 7 | Alumni network post-graduation |
| 8 | Business mentoring/training |
| 9 | Assistance in formulating business plans |
| 10 | Access to bank loans, loan funds and guarantee programs |
| 11 | Help in improving company's sales growth |
| 12 | Provide feedback to companies if they are not selected into the program |
| 13 | Aid in internationalizing company's operations |
| 14 | Investor introductions |
| LESS VALUE | |
| 14 | Demo day(s) |
| 16 | Pitch competition(s) |
| 17 | Patent support |
| 18 | Financial support |
| 19 | Other |

## Table 19: Start-ups Criteria Used to Select Accelerators

| Rank | Criterion |
|---|---|
| HIGH | |
| 1 | Industry relevance |
| 2 | Trusted referral |
| 3 | Location |
| MEDIUM | |
| 4 | Program length |
| 5 | Links to Angel |
| 6 | Reputation |
| LOWER | |
| 7 | Rolling acceptance |
| 8 | Financial aid |
| 9 | Other |

Relationships With Accelerators

Eleven businesses, 20% of the total, had relationships with accelerators. The time taken to join the accelerator was significantly faster than that reported for joining incubators, with most taking less than four months to join. Seven reported that they had been turned down in their application to join an accelerator and 21 indicated a future intent to apply. Time spent in incubators varied widely.

Most frequently, the accelerator was identified through word of mouth or Internet search and at meetings/events organised by the accelerator. Most (nine) found the accelerator to provide reasonable overall value, with two seeing little or no value. In terms of possible improvements to the accelerators, seven looked for more company-specific training, with one each suggesting a larger program, a longer program duration, access to funding and more

*The Early Investment Ecosystem for Start-ups in Canada, a Preliminary Study*

## Table 20: How Start-ups First Heard About their Angel Investor or VC

| Angel Investor | # | % |
|---|---|---|
| Word of mouth | 10 | 71% |
| Meetings organized by angel groups | 7 | 50% |
| Pitch competition | 6 | 43% |
| Other | 4 | 29% |
| Government | 3 | 21% |
| Internet search | 2 | 14% |
| Online portals | 1 | 7% |
| Universities | 0 | 0% |

| VC | # | % |
|---|---|---|
| Word of mouth | 2 | 40% |
| Other | 2 | 40% |
| Internet search | 1 | 20% |
| Government | 1 | 20% |
| Meetings organized by VCs | 1 | 20% |
| Pitch competition | 0 | 0% |
| University | 0 | 0% |
| Online portals | 0 | 0% |

## Table 21: The Value of the Investor Relationship to the Start-up

| Rank | Criterion |
|---|---|
| HIGH | |
| 1 | Advice/Consultation |
| 2 | Board of directors |
| 3 | Regular mentorship |
| 4 | Feedback to non-selected firms |
| MEDIUM | |
| 5 | New deals/relations |
| 6 | Secure additional funding |
| 7 | Intros to investors |
| 8 | Staff member in company |
| LOWER | |
| 9 | Other |

## Table 22: Start-ups Sources of Funding

| | # | % |
|---|---|---|
| Family friends/self | 34 | 65% |
| Angel group | 12 | 23% |
| Government grant | 9 | 17% |
| Personal relationships | 8 | 15% |
| Crowdfunding | 6 | 12% |
| Venture capital firms | 4 | 8% |
| Banker | 2 | 4% |

## Table 23: Start-ups Criteria for choosing Financial Channels

| Rank | Criterion |
|---|---|
| VERY IMPORTANT | |
| 1 | Long-term cost of capital |
| 1 | Time required to obtain funding |
| 3 | Strategic assistance |
| 3 | Services offered in addition to financial support |
| 5 | Amount of financing available |
| 6 | Influence on daily operations |
| SOMEWHAT LESS IMPORTANT | |
| 7 | Entry barrier/accessibility |
| 8 | Existing channel of the capital |
| 9 | Control rights over the firm |

sion of basic facilities, networks, access to external services, and industry-specific programs being seen as most important.

Working with Angel Groups and VCs

Thirteen start-ups provided feedback on their relationships with Angel groups, with five start-ups provided feedback on their relationships with venture capital firms. The most frequently mentioned method of finding the Angel group that invested in them was by word of mouth, followed by meetings organized by the Angel groups. Word of mouth was also the most frequently mentioned methods of finding the investing VC group (see Table 20). Pitch competitions were important for Angel involvement but not for VCs. One mentioned they met at an incubator Christmas party! The majority met with Angels either monthly or quarterly. Most were happy with the frequency of meetings, with three

follow-up post-program.

In choosing an incubator or accelerator, the most significant criteria were relevance to the business's industry, a trusted referral and location. Table 18 shows the complete ranking. Table 19 shows the relevant importance of the different services provided by the incubator or accelerator, with provi-

Kenneth A. Grant, Divya Padmanaban and Amr El-Kebbi

| MOST IMPORTANT | ENTREPRENEURS | INCUBATORS | ACCELERATORS |
|---|---|---|---|
| Basic facilities support and technology assistance | 1 | 3 | 17 |
| Network/Community of entrepreneurs | 2 | 2 | 3 |
| Common external service providers such as lawyers, accountants and consultants | 3 | 10 | 10 |
| Industry specific programs | 4 | 15 | 8 |
| **QUITE IMPORTANT** | | | |
| Firm specific programs | 5 | 5 | 13 |
| Strategic alliance | 6 | 9 | 6 |
| Alumni network post graduation | 7 | 16 | 9 |
| Business mentoring/training | 8 | 1 | 1 |
| Assistance in formulating business plans | 9 | 7 | 3 |
| Access to bank loans, loan funds and guarantee programs | 10 | 14 | 16 |
| Help in improving company's sales growth | 11 | 6 | 4 |
| Provide feedback to companies if they are not selected into the program | 12 | 17 | 15 |
| Aid in internationalizing company's operations | 13 | 12 | 7 |
| Investor introductions | 14 | 4 | 2 |
| **LESS IMPORTANT** | | | |
| Demo day(s) | 15 | 18 | 12 |
| Pitch competition(s) | 16 | 11 | 18 |
| Patent support | 17 | 8 | 14 |
| Financial support | 18 | 12 | 11 |
| Other | 19 | 19 | 19 |

☐ Accelerator/Incubator ranked 6 or more places lower

■ Accelerator/Incubator ranked 6 or more places higher

**Figure 8: Comparative Ranking of Services Provided by Incubators/Accelerators for Start-ups**

who met quarterly wishing to have had more meetings. Interestingly, the three who met semi-annually or annually were satisfied with that frequency.

Table 21 shows the value attributed to various aspects of the Angel group/VC relationship, with advice and mentorship, board membership and receiving feedback when not selected being seen as the most important.

Access to Funding

As Table 22 shows, the most frequent source of funding was from self and family, followed by Angels and government grants. VCs and banks were the least reported sources.

When asked about the relevant importance of the selection criteria they consider while choosing between financing channels, participants gave all the criteria suggested a significant level of importance. Table 23 shows the split between the most important and the fairly important criteria.

*Ecosystem Interconnection Analysis*

Services Provided by Incubator/Accelerator

Incubators and accelerators were asked to rate the importance of the services each provided and entrepreneurs were asked to rank the importance of the services offered by the incubators and accelerators. (Note: they provided only one ranking for incubator/ accelerator and did not differentiate between the two in their responses). Figure 8 shows the responses from each, using the entrepreneur ranking as the base.

Significant differences can be observed. Differences of six or more places in ranking were chosen to identify the key areas of difference and these are identified in the Figure. Notably, in the entrepreneurs' top four, access to a network/community of entrepreneurs was the only common response in comparison to the views of incubators and accelerators.. Accelerators ranked providing physical space much lower (and only 60% provided such services), with incubators giving much less importance to

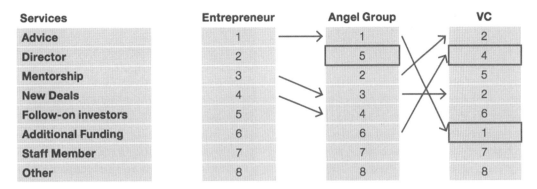

Figure 9: Comparative Ranking of Services Provided by Angel Groups & VCs for Start-ups

providing industry-specific programs (and only about half of either incubators or accelerators provided them). Neither incubators nor accelerators gave access to professional service as having as much importance as entrepreneurs.

Also of interest is that both incubators and accelerators ranked business mentoring/training as their most important service, whereas entrepreneurs ranked it only eighth. Similarly, entrepreneurs ranked investor introductions much lower than incubators and accelerators.

Services Provided by Angel Groups and Venture Capitalists

Angel groups and VCs were asked to rate the importance of the services each provided and entrepreneurs were asked to rank the importance of those services offered. Figure 9 shows the responses from each, using the entrepreneur ranking as the base. With a couple of exceptions, all three were in fairly close agreement as to the most important services, with providing advice, mentorship and access to new deals ranking high. The major differences were that entrepreneurs ranked the provision of a board director higher than the Angels and VCs and that, while VCs saw their top service as providing additional funding, the entrepreneurs did not agree.

SUMMARY OF FINDINGS

Responses were received from 10 incubators and 17 accelerators. Most respondents had multiple formal relationships with other players in the ecosystem, with relationships with universities and Angel groups being most common with incubators, and with corporate partners and universities being the most popular with accelerators. Universities were identified as the most significant sourcing partner for incubators and accelerators, as well as being a major source of education support. Both received financial support from federal and provincial governments; however, universities were more likely to fund incubators than accelerators.

For both incubators and accelerators, the highest level of interest in the stages of evolution of a startup were in the first-generation product and early-growth stages, with incubators more likely to have an interest in companies in the R&D and prototype-development stages. Mature businesses generally were not of interest. In selecting participants, both considered the innovation of the product/service and the quality of the management team to be the most important selection criteria.

Incubators accepted about 22% of applicants (299) in 2014 and accelerators about 18% (410). The period of residence varied significantly in both, anywhere from six to 24 months, with only about one-third having a standard period. Incubators reported "graduating" 156 participants in 2014 and accelerators 167. After graduation, most incubators/accelerators tracked the development of the companies, providing mentorship and alumni events. Overall, incubators and accelerators expected about 45% of the participants to receive equity funding. Typically, the first-round funding ask from an incubator participant was below $300,000, with most asks from accelerators being over $300,000, and several over $500,000.

Responses were received from 24 Angel groups

that had been in operation for an average of five years. By far, the most significant influences in their decision to be investors were financial motivation and strong passion. All had formal relationships with a number of different members of the ecosystem, with incubators and accelerators being the most common and being seen as the primary sourcing partners, followed by universities.

They reported having funded 466 investments in their groups' lives, 169 of these in 2014. They provided deal details for 125 of the deals made during 2014. In choosing investee start-ups, past entrepreneurial experience and being a serial entrepreneur were seen as the most important, followed by participation in incubator and accelerator. The quality of management was seen as a key screening element. Collectively they received 2,112 applications in 2014, of which some 25% of applicants had the opportunity to make pitches, with a nal acceptance rate of about 8%. Most groups reported making between six and 10 deals during 2014, with total investments being in the $500,000 to $5 million range. Individual investments ranged from $15,000 to $2 million, with the median investment being $122,500. About one-third of the deals had co-investors, normally either other Angel groups or individual investors. Very few deals had a pre-planned exit strategy. The total value of the investments was just over $80 million.

Responses were received from eight venture capital (VC) firms; three had been in business for more than 15 years, and four had existed for less than five years. They tended to focus on a relatively small number of industries (two to five), with the most frequent being Life Sciences and Information and Communication Technologies (ICT). Most had formal relationships with other organisations, most commonly with accelerators.

They were most interested in companies in the early-growth and accelerated-growth stages. Of 2,160 applications in 2014, 11 were accepted for investment, less than 1%. Overall, they reported total investments in the range of $2.5–26 million, with an average investment of $1.7 million per deal. All discussed exit expectations with their investee rms, and four had reported successful exits in 2014. In selecting investments, the most important criteria were the startups industry outlook, management team qualifications, product traction and exit expectations

Fifty-four entrepreneurs responded to the survey. A very high proportion (50%) were from the Information and Communication Technologies (ICT) industry, followed by Life Sciences and Services. Most had been in operation for less than four years, and reported three or fewer employees and members of the management team.

Over 60% had joined an incubator, taking anywhere from one month to a year for acceptance. Residence period ranged from a few months to over 24 months. 84% of the startups reported getting significant value from their interactions with the incubator. The most important areas of value were reported to be provision of basic facilities, the network and community, access to external professionals, and industry-specific programs. 20% had relationships with accelerators, typically taking less than four months from application to joining.

The most frequent source of funding was self, family and friends (65%), followed by Angel groups and government grants. Thirteen had relationships with Angel groups and five had relationships with VCs.

## CONCLUSIONS

One of the key objectives for this study was to gain an initial perspective on the early investment ecosystem that provides a baseline for future work. A good level of response was received from each of the ecosystem players, although it would have been useful to have a broader sample of VCs and entrepreneurs. In particular, the sample of entrepreneurs was opportunistic, using a variety of contact methods to solicit input. While the respondents may not be typical of entrepreneurs as a whole, they do seem to represent the higher-growth target start-ups that were the prime interest of the study. A significant proportion participated in incubators and accelerators and were looking for external funding from either Angel investors or VCs. It is also interesting to note that the relative proportions of industries represented (with Information and Communication Technologies being the largest, followed by Life-Sciences) are consistent with other research on the industries most funded by Angel investors and

VCs .

While incubators and accelerators are often seen as quite distinct entities, the responses to this study were more similar than might be expected. For example, both are interested across a similar set of growth stages and offer programs of quite similar elapsed time, with accelerators showing just a slight interest bias toward later stages. This is surprising, as accelerators are often thought to provide fast assistance over a relatively short period of time. Accelerators were, however, significantly faster in accepting new entrants than incubators. Some of these responses may be due to the use of an identical survey for both incubators and accelerators, and the next study will consider using a separate instrument for each

Overall, entrepreneurs, angel groups and VCs held quite similar views as to the importance of the services provided by angel groups and VCs with relatively few differences. the responses confirmed that Angel groups and VCs were highly selective in choosing investments, but the likelihood of success of a given application being very low. The screening process and evaluation criteria used by all groups were very similar.

The study findings demonstrate that the key players within the Canadian early investment ecosystem do work well together in a productive manner and have interactions both between themselves and with the other contributing organizations within the ecosystem, including government, banks and universities. However, it did not provide any significant insight into the reasons for the differences in investment levels and exit barriers between Canada and the United States and this should be a topic of further research, of great importance to Canada.

## LIMITATIONS AND FUTURE WORK

The survey samples, while broad-based, are still quite small, particularly with respect to the VCs and the entrepreneurs. Thus, caution should be taken in generalization of the results. In addition, all respondents did not provide responses to all questions, further reducing the sample size. Where possible, the sample size for particular questions is shown in the study findings. In addition, as is common in the first iterations of surveys, there were a few areas where responses indicated a lack of clarity in some questions. This will be corrected in future surveys.

Future work could focus on the interaction between the various participants through the stages of startup launch and growth, with a particular emphasis on the challenges and barriers that may exist that reduce the opportunities for successful high-value exits.

## ACKNOWLEDGMENTS

This study was supported by the Canadian National Angel Capital Organisation (NACO) and the Canadian Mitacs Accelerate Research Program, with the findings being shared with the NACO Angel Group Members.

## NOTES

1) Mitacs is a Canadian, not-for-profit organization that designs and delivers research and training programs, working with universities, companies, and the Canadian federal and provincial governments.

## REFERENCES

AERNOUDT, R. (2004). Incubators: tool for entrepreneurship? *Small Business Economics*, 23, 127–135.

AMITA, R., BRANDERA, J. & ZOTTA, C. (1998). Why do venture capital firms exist? theory and canadian evidence. *Journal of Business Venturing*, 13, 441-466.

BDC CAPITAL (2017). Canada's Venture Capital Landscape: Challenges and Oportunities. Business Development Bank of Canada.

BERGER, A. & UDELL, G. (1998). The economics of small business finance: The role of private equity and debt markets in the financial growth cycle. *Journal of Banking and Finance*, 22, 613-673.

EISENMANN, T. R. (2013). Entrepreneurship: A Working Definition. *Harvard Business Review*.

FILION, L. J. (2011). Defining the Entrepreneur. In: L.P., D. (ed.) *World Encyclopedia of Entrepreneurship*. Cheltenham, UK: Edward Elgar.

GLOBAL ENTREPRENEURSHIP MONITOR (2018). Global Report 2017/18.

GREATHOUSE, J. (2012). Pssst...Here's How To Become A Venture Capitalist. *Forbes*.

HARRIS, R. S., JENKINSON, T. & KAPLAN, S. N. 2014. Private equity performance: What do we know? *The Journal of Finance*, 69, 1851–1882.

HECHAVARRIA, D. M. & INGRAM, A. (2014). A review of the entrepreneurial ecosystem and the entrepreneurial society in the United States: an exploration with the global entrepreneurship Monitor dataset. *Journal of Business and Entrepreneurship*, 26, 1-35.

ISENBERG, D. J. (2010). How to Start an Entrepreneurial Revolution. *Harvard Business Review*, 1-12.

ISENBERG, D. J. (2011). The Entrepreneurship Ecosystem Strategy as a New Paradigm for Economic Policy: Principles for Cultivating Entrepreneurship—A presentation for the Institute of International and European Affairs, Dublin, May 12, 2011. Dublin: Babson Entrepreneurship Ecosystem Project.

KETIKIDIS, P. H., CHIKHLADZE, K. & BARESEL- BOFINGER, A. (2017). Working Paper No. 03, Early Stage Investment in Southeast Europe: Issues and Challenges. World Business Angels Investment Forum 2016. Istanbul: South-East European Research Centre.

LANDSTROM, HANS (2005). *Pioneers in Entrepreneurship and Small Business Research*, New York, Springer Science.

LERNER, J. (2010). The future of public efforts to boost entrepreneurship and venture capital. *Small Business Economics*, 35, 255-264.

MACK, E. & MAYAR, H. (2016). The evolutionary dynamics of entrepreneurial ecosystems. *Urban Studies*, 53, 2118-2133.

MASON, C. & BROWN, R. (2014). Entrepreneurial ecosystems and growth oriented entrepreneurship. background paper for the International Workshop on Entrepreneurial Ecosystems and Growth Oriented Entrepreneurship.

PATTON, D. & MARLOW, S. (2011). University technology business incubators: helping new entrepreneurial firms to learn to grow. *Environment and Planning C: Government and Policy*, 29, 911–926.

PETERS, L., RICE, M. & SUNDARARAJAN, M. (2004). The role of incubators in the entrepreneurial process. *The Journal of Technology Transfer*, 29, 83–91.

PITELIS, C. (2012). Clusters, entrepreneurial ecosystem co-creation, and appropriability: a conceptual framework. *Industrial and Corporate Change*.

PWC (2018). US Moneytree Report. PwC MoneyTree.

PWC CANADA (2016). MoneyTree Canada Report: Q4 and Full-year 2016.

RIDING, A., L. (2008). Business angels and love money investors: segments of the informal market for risk capital. *Venture Capital*, 10, 355-369.

SCHUMPETER, J. (1934). *The Theory of Economic Development*, Cambridge, Harvard University Press.

SILCOFF, S.(2016). Angel investments on the rise in Canada *Globe & Mail*.

SPIGEL, B. (2017). The Relational Organization of Entrepreneurial Ecosystems. *Entrepreneurship Theory and Practice*, 41, 49-72.

STAM, E. (2015). Entrepreneurial Ecosystems and Regional Policy: A Sympathetic Critique. *European Planning Studies*, 23, 1769-1769.

STANGLER, D. & BELL-MASTERSON, J. (2015). Measuring an Entrepreneurial Ecosystem. Ewing Marion Kauffman Foundation.

STOREY, D. J. (1998). *Six steps to heaven: evaluating the impact of public policies to support small businesses in developed economies*, Centre for Small & Medium Sized Enterprises, Warwick Business School.

TAMASY, C. (2007). Rethinking Technology-Oriented Business Incubators: Developing a Robust Policy Instrument for Entrepreneurship, Innovation, and Regional Development? *Growth and Change*, 38, 460–473.

TANG, J. (2008). Environmental munificence for entrepreneurs: entrepreneurial alertness and commitment. *International Journal of Entrepreneurial Behavior & Research*, 14, 128–151.

THE CENTRE FOR DIGITAL ENTREPRENEURSHIP AND ECONOMIC PERFORMANCE. (2018). *Mapping Canada's Accelerator and Incubator Ecosystem* [Online]. Available: http://

*The Early Investment Ecosystem for Start-ups in Canada, a Preliminary Study*

deepcentre.com/billiondollarfirms/do-accelerators-and-incubators-make-a-difference/mapping-canadas-accelerator-and-incubator-ecosystem-2 [Accessed Janury 3rd 2018].

UNH CENTER FOR VENTURE RESEARCH (2016). Angel Investor Market in 2015 a Buyers Market. In: CENTER FOR VENTURE RESEARCH, U. O. N. H. (ed.).

WONG, A., BHATIA, M. & FREEMAN, Z. (2009). Angel Finance: The Other Venture Capital. *Strategic Change*, 18, 221–230.

WORLD ECONOMIC FORUM (2013). Entrepreneurial Ecosystems around the Globe and Company Growth Dynamics. Davos.

---

Dr. Kenneth A. Crant is a Professor of Entrepreneurship & Strategy in the Ted Rogers School of Management, Ryerson University, Canada. Email:kagrant@ryerson.ca

Divya Padmanaban is a Researcher with the National Angel Capital Organization, Canada.

Amr EI-Kebbi is a Researcher with the Ted Rogers School of Management, Ryerson University, Canada.

*Kindai Management Review* Vol. 6, 2018 (ISSN: 2186-6961)

# Inter-linkages between Educational Institutions and White Collar Labor Mobility: A Comparative Study in Japan, Germany, and the U.S.A.

**Patricia (Tish) Robinson**

*Hitotsubashi University, Graduate School of International Corporate Strategy, Japan*

**Kiyohiko Ito**

*Shidler College of Business, the University of Hawai'i at Manoa, USA*

## Abstract

In this study, we examine how institutions and business practices are interlinked within institutional systems, towards helping explain differences among business systems in Japan, Germany, and the USA. More specifically, we explore how educational institutions and institutionalized corporate practices are inter-related within each of these systems, drawing on data from 2993 managers from large firms in Japan, Germany, and the USA to explore the relationship between educational institutions and institutionalized career path trajectories in firms in these countries. Results showed that business practices and career paths vary in these three countries, and that they are linked with educational institutions, in that managers with various professional certifications are more likely to have worked for multiple firms over their careers, while those with university degrees are not.

**Keywords:** *comparative business systems, systems dynamics, labor mobility, education systems, institutional theory*

## INTRODUCTION

Business practices continue to vary across countries (Lim et al., 2010; Morgan et al., 2001). Might one reason for this variety of business practices be due to the way institutions are interlinked with business practices? This study examines how business practices and institutions might be inter-linked within business systems, as a way of explaining why business practices have not converged despite the prevalence of multinational companies (Whitley, 2003).

This linkage between national institutions and business practices has important implications for why national economies cannot respond more quickly to global economic and technological change. The comparative business systems literature would argue that the interdependent nature of the institutions in a country make it difficult for one institution or set of institutionalized practices to change without having the other interlinked institutions change at the same time, which would cause other practices to change as well. While economists have examined economic change and the interlinkage of institutions in Japan as they

*Inter-linkages between Educational Institutions and White Collar Labor Mobility:*
*A Comparative Study in Japan, Germany, and the U.S.A*

relate to banking and other practices (Aoki, 2001), very little research explores the linkage between educational institutions and the labor practices.

To our knowledge, this is the first comparative study on inter-linkages of educational institutions and white collar labor mobility in these three countries. This study contributes to the comparative business literature by exploring the relationship between institutionalized business practices to another institution in the business system—here, education. We explore the different ways similar institutions and practices are linked across business systems. We argue that not only do countries take a variety of approaches when addressing similar types of issues, but institutions within business systems interact differently with each other, from country to country. This is because systems are complex. We explore how this complexity makes each system address issues differently by exploring inter-linkages between education and white collar labor mobility of major firms in Japan, Germany, and the USA. These three countries make for a good starting point for the comparative explanation because they are three prominent exemplars among advanced market economies. The education and training systems in these three countries are also argued to vary considerably in ways that affect the kinds of skills developed, social identities, and organizational commitments (Whitley, 2003). By exploring linkages between educational institutions and white collar labor mobility in Japan, Germany, and the USA, we contribute to the comparative business systems literature by analyzing the inter-linkages between education and white collar labor mobility in three countries, using a large primary data sample derived from managers of large firms in these three countries.

## LITERATURE REVIEW

### Comparative business systems

The comparative business systems literature argues that business practices and organizational behavior vary across countries in part because they are shaped by differing institutional arrangements across countries (e.g., Aguilera & Jackson, 2003; Dobbin, 1994; Guillen, 1994; Hollingsworth,

Schmitter & Streeck 1994; Morgan, Campbell, Crouch, Pedersen, & Whitley, 2010; Orru, Biggart, & Hamilton 1997; Smelser & Swedberg, 2005; Streeck, 2001; Whitley, 1992). This literature views organizations as well as organizational practices as part of a larger national system that is shaped by a number of institutions, including governmental agencies, banking arrangements, union configurations, venture capital markets, labor markets, social contracts, and societal norms around activities such as cross-shareholding. This raises the question of how institutions are inter-linked with organizational practices, toward explaining how different countries undertake common business practices using different approaches.

Institutions shape organizations and organizational practices in various ways that can be positive or negative, and restrictive or expansive. For example, governmental laws and regulations constrain organizations and organizational practices. Further, educational institutions shape the norms, knowledge base, and practices of organizations, and shared norms and unconscious notions of legitimate behavior shape organizational interactions (e.g., Biggart & Guillen, 1999; Fligstein, 2001; Granovetter, 1985). Distinct national customs and practices are also reinforced when institutions pursue patterns that reinforce their power (Bebchuk & Roe, 1999), existing notions of legitimate behavior are strongly held (Biggart & Guillen, 1999), or the complementarities between institutions make the system self-reinforcing (Aoki, 2001). Guillen (2001) documents how newly industrialized countries such as Argentina and South Korea, and the companies in these countries, excel at different activities in the global economy based on their social organization. This perspective has its roots in several classic comparative analyses of work: *Work and Authority in Industry* (Bendix, 1956), *Peddlers and Princes* (Geertz, 1963), and *British Factory—Japanese Factory* (Dore, 1973).

Awareness has been growing around the variety of institutional arrangements found in different market economies and their varying influence on firms' structure and behavior (Granovetter, 1990; Whitley, 1992). This awareness is reflected in the varieties of capitalism research in political science, which underscores the multiplicities of political

The Institute for Creative Management and Innovation, Kindai University 101 approaches to solving similar problems (Hollings-worth, Schmitter, & Streeck 1994; Polanyi, 1957; Streeck, 1991, 1995). The variety of effective forms of business organizations and their interdependences with key government, financial, educational and social institutions across countries imply that a single rationality or logic of business efficiency is inadequate to explain the development of successful managerial structures and processes in market economies. There is an increasingly widely shared view of economic activities as socially embedded (e.g., Granovetter, 1985; Smelser & Swedberg, 1994; Mizruchi & Fein, 1999; Whitley 1992, 2003). Economic efficiency and success, in this latter view, are socially constructed, and so vary significantly across social contexts. Consequently, a key task in organizational analysis is to understand how different kinds of business organizations and economic rationalities develop and become effective in different institutional contexts.

### Interlinkages, "Reinforcing Loops" and "Unintended Fit" Between Institutions

The idea of interlinkages between institutions, or between institutions and practices, bears some similarity to reinforcing loops in systems thinking, which looks at the whole system of institutions, practices, and other elements, and the relationships between all of these things, specifically how changing one element of a system affects other elements. Reinforcing loops occur when two or more aspects of a system reinforce each other in a vicious/virtuous cycle (e.g., Kim & Anderson 1998; Sterman, 2000; Sterman, Repenning, & Kofman 1997). Interlinkages also complement the idea that institutional arrangements are path dependent, that is decisions in Time 1 limit decisions in Time 2, so that once institutional arrangements are set on a path, it is hard to go back and change course to a completely new direction. Underlying path dependence is observation that the variety of choices for change depend in large part on supporting institutions in the environment. Reinforcing loops reinforce these choices. For example, secondary labor markets may require post-graduate education for workers if there is no incentive for firms to provide training internally. Where there is no post-graduate education, it may be difficult for employees to change

jobs mid-career because they may need to learn new skills, which somebody needs to teach them. Whitley (1992: 240-247) notes: "Cohesive and mutually reinforcing nature of many characteristics of East Asian business systems…suggest that, once established in particular institutional contexts, effective business systems may develop considerable cohesion and become resistant to major changes." Thus, "once a particular business system has become established and certain rules of the game are institutionalized, major changes in firm type and patterns of behavior are unlikely to occur in the absence of substantial institutional changes" (Whitley 1992: 240-247).

Alternatively, interlinkages may also be a result of unintended fit. Aoki (1996) argues that, because Japanese institutions tend to complement each other, and their functioning is often contingent on fitting with other institutions, their effects on firms often interact to influence firms with more concerted force than they would individually. Aoki also argues that the institutional framework inherited from the war period in Japan started to work in the high growth period of the 1950s and 1960s, only when it was found to fit with an evolutionary tendency that had been taking place in the private sector. During the postwar period, "a unique organizational coordination mechanism evolved within and across enterprises, one that would eventually have a significant impact on productivity" (Aoki 1996: 235). Aoki's work here stresses the "unintended complementarity between the evolving organizational mode and the institutional framework" (Aoki 1996: 236). Consequently, "the possible reform of institutions in Japan seems to lie only in an extension of its own evolutionary path and that should be the way for Japan to contribute to the gains from system diversity on a global scale" (Aoki 1996; 235).

In the case of Japan, as documented by Gordon (1985) and Aoki (1996), seniority-based compensation and promotion systems, as well as "lifetime" employment were not just the result of a unilateral rationalistic design by management to prevent the frequent mobility of skilled workers. It was the result of "trilateral interactions involving the government aiming to pacify labor disputes and eliciting workers' cooperation toward war production, management, and workers who aspired to be members of the enterprise" (Aoki 1996: 240). Ad hoc adaptation to severe labor shortages led to job sharing and ambiguous job demarcations. After the war, workers often took over the factory, and management did not have the authority to break up workers and reassign them to different tasks. The "methods of quality control techniques and time-and-motion studies were introduced to the shop floor with the participation of the works as a group rather than by relying exclusively upon the research of industrial engineers and imposing their findings on individual workers" (Aoki 1996: 242; Mantzavinos, 2004; North, 1991). Eventually, there emerged an unintended fit between evolving organizational practices and the institutional framework the government had initially developed for a different purpose, i.e. the centralized control of resource allocation.

### Institutionalized Career Path Trajectories across Countries and the Role of Education in Shaping Them

The nature of work differs considerably across countries in terms of career trajectories, labor mobility, and the importance of certification for advancement (e.g., Aguilera & Jackson, 2003; Guillen, 2001; Hall & Soskice, 2001; Hamilton & Biggart, 1988; Hollingsworth, Schmitter, & Streeck 1994; Kalleberg & Stark, 1993; Streeck, 2000; Whitley, 1992, 2003). As Kalleberg and Stark (1993: 182) note, the nature of work and work values are "rooted in, and largely shaped by the work structures and social institutions in which workers participate and are embedded in." In this study, we argue that the divergent work practices are shaped in part by varying educational systems, which is also related to the norms as well as the skills and expectations of employees.

Two key institutions shaping business systems and the nature of work across countries are formal educational institutions and the structure of labor markets. Education systems shape the expectations of graduates around work. Labor markets, in turn, shape their career paths. For example, in business systems with internal labor markets, employees are more likely to work for fewer firms. In some business systems, this results in working across multiple functions. Also, where there is long-term employ-

ment, there are more incentives for the company to provide internal formal, or on-the-job training (OJT) (Dore, 1973; Whitley, 2003; Witt, 2014). For example, Witt (2014) proposes that Japanese-style OJT is expensive, and that firms only afford to engage in it if they can be reasonably certain that employees will stay within the firm long enough for there to be a positive return on the training investment. The presence of secondary labor markets also shapes the nature of competition in the work place, as employees can find other companies to advance their careers, where employees in systems with largely internal labor markets have very limited options for advancing their careers.

Because of the significance of the characteristics of individual firms and the immense range of alternative career paths in the full labor force, much of the conceptual development and empirical research on work careers has been focused on more limited structures, such as "internal labor markets" (Althhauser, 1989; Doeringer & Piore, 1985). However, even internal labor markets are defined in different ways, such as job ladders in a single firm, within an occupational category, and/or in an industry. It is very unlikely that the more refined categories of internal labor markets can be useful in studies of the full labor force, and clusters of occupations may need to be used to avoid overwhelming complexity (Haller et al., 1985). However, Kerkhoff (1995) notes that the internal labor market suggests some form of orderliness in careers.

Where external labor markets are present, indicated by mid-career "job hopping," educational institutions are also more likely to be present. Educational institutions provide Masters of Business Administration (MBA) degrees or professional certificates of some kind, such as the Chartered Professional Accountant (CPA) certification and financial analyst certifications, allowing employees to retrain themselves or advance their skills for other jobs (Whitley, 2003). These "certified skills" tend to be "owned" and developed by individuals who invest in particular external training programs without much involvement by employers.

However, in countries that lack external labor markets or where external labor markets are not well developed, there are often deeply held social contracts reflected in labor law, the lack of a fully developed social welfare system, or the lack of small business financing to provide alternative employment options. In some countries that lack well-developed labor markets, education is undertaken internally within the firm. For example, in the case of post-World War II Japan, there has been an emphasis on rotations across functions with the goal of creating broad exposure to the company, with the effect of producing generalists who lack skill specialization and whose company-specific knowledge is not very marketable in external labor markets (Ono, 2010; Witt, 2014). Intentionally or not, this reflects post-war employer concerns around maintaining employees and developing employee loyalty. Developed during a period of extended economic growth, "life-time" employment was premised on a pyramidal structure that required constant growth to continually expand its base through the annual hiring of new graduates as life-time employees. Yet, even as the economic conditions have changed, the practices have been slow to change with them.

### Labor mobility in Japan, Germany, and the USA

By international comparison, labor mobility in Japan has remained strikingly low due to various institutional factors and related business practices, such as internal labor markets, firm-specific training, portability of pensions, labor laws, etc. As such, there is a weaker link between white-collar job content and undergraduate education in Japan than in the U.S. Instead, in Japan, undergraduate education is not necessarily professional preparation for a career, and training in the firm is often firm and job-specific. In 2016, the labor separation rate in Japan was 2.04% (Japanese Ministry of Health, Labor and Welfare, 2016). The average tenure of regular male employees continued to hover around 12.8 years for college and university graduates, and the average number of jobs held by men aged 45 to 54 was around 2.1 (Ono, 2010). For regular male employees in Japan, such low mobility is a rational response to the economic incentives of the labor market. Seniority-based wages, internal labor markets, firm-specific training and pension plans make changing jobs economically disadvantageous to employees (Holbrow, 2015; Ono, 2010). Further, good midcareer jobs are hard to find, as

almost half of firms hire no regular employees at the midcareer level (Recruit Works Institute, 2010), and often employ explicit/implicit age cut-offs in hiring (Rebick, 2005). While some full-time job mobility does exist in Japan, it is highest among white-collar employees when they are in their 20s and decreases markedly after age 35. In addition to age playing a factor, labor laws also reduce labor mobility among full-time white-collar employees. Specifically, labor laws make it difficult to fire employees, and pension plans are only now becoming portable (Ono, 2010). Second, salaries are often negotiated *en masse*, and many Japanese firms still utilize some form of seniority pay (Witt, 2014). Third, large Japanese firms average around 5-8 levels of management, ranging from 4 to 11 levels (McCann, Hassard, & Morris, 2010). Fourth, job descriptions are very general, and rotations across functions still exist, although firms are increasingly pursuing specialist career tracks for technical employees up to middle upper manager level with the same compensation and potential for advancement as their management track counterparts. Finally, employee training is still largely done within the firm, and while there are MBA programs in Japan, the number of applicants has not increased noticeably.

In contrast to Japan, in Germany, job vacancies peaked in 2016 at 1.6% (OECD, 2016). Labor mobility has continued to be highest among white collar employees when they are in their 20s (Zimmermann, 1998). Employees in this age bracket often move around a lot to get experience and tend to do so until they find a family-oriented employer that provides for working parents and offers job security, at which point, they settle down. On the average, employees changed firms 7.8 times in their careers in the early 1990s (Zimmermann, 1998). In Germany, labor laws make it difficult for firms to fire employees, except in situations of demonstrable profit loss. Also, there are strong legal restrains on unilateral employer actions and strategies: the expansion of codetermination has encouraged continuous retraining and redeployment of the quite stable labor force as employees become more committed to the success of the firm and internal labor markets dominate external ones (Whitley, 2003). German firms have relatively few ranks and salary grades, and employers use individual contracts for white-collar employees with specific, detailed job descriptions, although salaries for blue collar employees are negotiated through the labor union. Unlike Japan, there is a strong link between education and functional assignment. For example, those who study engineering tend to become engineers or take related jobs in sales involving engineering knowledge, etc. Those who study business often become managers or join the Personnel Department. Those who pursue a PhD signal their efficiency in completing the PhD in the prescribed 3 years (after completing the BA in 2 years, and the MA in 2 years), which can lead to an assistantship to a director or eventually to a directorship around age 45.

In the USA, labor mobility among white-collar employees is higher at every age than in Japan and Germany. In 2016, the labor separation rate in the USA was 3.5% (OECD, 2016; Kambourov & Manovskii, 2008), and over time, men in the 45 to 54 age group had held 5.6 jobs on average (Ono, 2010). These figures are substantially higher than in Japan and Germany. In contrast to Japan and Germany, labor laws make it relatively easy to lay off employees and 401(k) pension plans are portable, which contributes to higher labor mobility. White-collar employees are often functional specialists who advance their careers by changing jobs and companies. Because these employees tend to owe their primary loyalty to their profession, they are reluctant to invest in developing firm-specific skills and acquiring firm-specific knowledge (e.g., Whitley, 2003). This functional specialization and identity decreases organizational commitment and increases labor mobility. In comparison to Japan, US firms have up to 13 layers of general management grades (McCann et al., 2010). Although US firms provide internal training, external training is well developed and exists in the form of professional schools such as business schools, law schools, and certifications such as public accountancy and financial analysis. In part, this may be because there is a weak link between white-collar job content and undergraduate education, and graduates are not necessarily hired on the basis of their undergraduate major.

## Historical Perspective of Higher Education in Japan, Germany, and the USA

In Japan, the present education system was put in place after World War II on the basis of the US model. Japanese education thus reflects both German and American influences: Students go through six years of primary school, three years of junior high school, and three years of high school before moving on to two-year or four-year college, followed by graduate degree programs. There are two types of public four-year colleges: the 96 national universities and the 39 local public universities, founded by prefectures and municipalities. The 372 remaining four-year colleges are private. As of 2005, more than 2.8 million students were enrolled in 726 universities (Japanese Ministry of Education, 2006). In 2008, the average costs (tuition, fees, and living expenses) for a year of higher education in a public university were 6 million yen (US$6000) (Japanese Ministry of Education, 2009). Because large, prestigious Japanese firms often hire only from the top-tier universities, competition for those universities is stiff (Witt, 2014). As a result, entrance examinations are an important part of the education system.

In Germany, while number of university students has more than tripled since World War II, university attendance in Germany lags behind many other European nations. Universities in Germany are part of the free-state education system, which means that there are very few private universities and colleges. German universities focus more on education and less on research, but bear a strong resemblance to American universities. Student selection practices, however, are novel: German university students largely choose their own program of study and students can change universities according to their interests and the strengths of each university. Sometimes students attend two or more universities in the course of their studies. This mobility means that at German universities there is a freedom unknown in Japan or the USA. Setting the stage for career path tracking, there are 50 ways to get into college in Germany. One such way is the *Abitur*, or final examination following secondary school, which can be attained at a Gymnasium, Abendgymnasium or Gesamtschule, and which opens the way to any university. Another way to gain access to a university is via a Berufsoberschule. University placement is usually decided by the *Abiturdurchschnittsnote* (similar to GPA in the USA). Additionally, an institution may quote an entry requirement for a particular course or require entrance exams. In some cases students need to write essays or motivational letters (Haerder, 2009).

In the USA, religious denominations established most early universities in order to train ministers, and most of the universities which opened between 1640 and 1750 form the contemporary Ivy League, including Harvard, Yale, Columbia, and Princeton, and other universities (NCSU, 2009). At the beginning of the 20th century, fewer than 1,000 colleges with 160,000 students existed in the USA. Explosive growth in the number of colleges occurred at the end of the 19th and early 20th century. Today, education in the USA is mainly provided by the public sector, with control and funding coming from three levels: federal, state, and local. Public education is universal at the primary and secondary levels (known inside the USA as the elementary and high school levels). Post-secondary education, (better known as "college" in the USA), is generally governed separately from the elementary and high school system, and there are 4,352 colleges, universities, and junior colleges in the country (Neuharth, 2009). Among the country's adult population, over 85% have completed high school and 27% have received a bachelor's degree or higher (US Census, 2000). Each state in the USA maintains its own public university system, which is always non-profit. Unlike many other nations, there are no public universities at the national level outside of the military service academies.

## HYPOTHESES

The above discussion suggests that two key institutions shaping business systems and the nature of work across countries are formal educational institutions and the structure of labor markets. Education systems shape the expectations of graduates around work. Labor markets, in turn, shape their career paths. We thus expect inter-linkages between educational institutions and white-collar labor mobility in Japan, Germany, and the USA. For

example, more coordinated institutional frameworks tend to restrict labor movement more in Japan and Germany than in the USA. Therefore, the task undertaken in this study is to understand how different organizational rationalities and organizational practices are affected by institutional arrangements in those three countries. Briefly, this study's argument follows two steps. First, although issues facing business systems across the world are similar, institutions are structured differently to deal with them in those countries. Second, institutions and institutionalized business practices have intended or unintended fit. Following the above arguments, we derive six hypotheses to be tested.

Hypothesis 1: White-collar labor mobility demonstrates distinctively different trends across countries, such that the number of companies employees work for in their career differs across Japan, Germany, and the USA, controlling for employee age.

Hypothesis 2: Institutionalized education is linked to white-collar labor mobility, such that employees with public qualifications and certifications, other than educational degrees, tend to have worked for a larger number of companies in their career.

Hypothesis 3: Employees who have work experience in a greater number of functional areas tend to have worked for a smaller number of companies in their career.

Hypothesis 4: Institutionalized education is linked to white-collar labor mobility, such that employees with a college degree tend to have worked for more companies in their career.

Hypothesis 5: Institutionalized education is linked to white-collar labor mobility, such that employees with an MBA degree tend to have worked for more companies in their career.

Hypothesis 6: Trends in labor mobility and innovation have stayed fairly consistent over the past several decades.

# METHOD

## Sample

The data was collected by the Japan Institute of Labor in Japan, Germany, and the USA. A similar sampling procedure was used in these countries. In Japan, the largest 1000 companies (by employee size) were targeted in this study as listed in the *Diamond Company Directory*. In the US, the largest 1000 companies (by employee size) were targeted as listed in the *Ward's Business Directory* (The Reference Press) and Compustat II (Standard and Poor's). In Germany, the largest 1000 companies (by employee size) were targeted as listed in the *Index of Deutsche Gesellshaft fuer Grosunternehmen*.

In Japan, Germany, and U.S., chiefs in the Human Resources/Personnel, Management, and Accounting departments or divisions in the company were surveyed. The sample consisted of 2993 managers in total, with 1567 managers from Japan, 674 managers from Germany, and 752 managers from the US, with respective response rates of 38%, 19%, and 21%. Each chief of division/section was asked about his/her career and the evaluation of his/her career. Questions regarding systems to develop talented persons and labor management systems and their operation were included in the survey of the managerial class (aimed toward division chief for U.S. and Japan, and section chief for Germany) responsible for personnel affairs.

## Dependent Variable

The dependent variable, *Number # of Companies* worked at, was based on a survey question that asked the total number of companies the employee worked for (from one to five or more). The data is thus censored, where values over five are all reported as five. To address the issue of censoring, we report results using both ordinary least square (OLS) and the Tobit estimation procedures.

## Independent Variables

We used two dichotomous independent variables to test H1. *U.S.* takes the value of 1 if the employee is in U.S., and 0 otherwise. *Germany* takes the value of 1 if the employee is in Germany, and 0 otherwise.

To test H2, we use *Certificate*, which is a dichotomous variable that takes the value of 1 if the employee has any public qualifications and/or certifications, other than educational degrees, and 0 otherwise. To test H3, we use *Function*, which is the total number of all the functional areas the employee has experienced in his/her career. To test H4, we use *College*, which is an indicator variable, taking the value of 1 if the employee has a college degree, and 0 otherwise. Similarly, to test H5, we use *MBA*, which is an indicator variable, taking the value of 1 if the employee has an MBA degree, and 0 otherwise.

## Control Variables

We included two control variables to rule out alternative explanations for our results. *Gender* is the employee's gender, which takes the value of 1 if the employee is male, and 0 for female. *Age* is the age of the employee.

## RESULTS

Table 1 summarizes the correlations and descriptive statistics among study variables. Table 2 shows the estimated OLS and Tobit regression coefficients with all data from Japan, Germany, and U.S. The two models produce consistent decisions, which suggest that there is an appealing robustness to the results. The highest variance inflation factor (VIF) for the main variables in the first two columns is 2.02, which is well below the recommended ceiling of 10 (Hair, Anserson, Tatham, & Black, 1998), suggesting that multicollinearity does not have a serious impact on the estimation process.

Hypothesis 1 states that white-collar labor mobility demonstrates distinctively different trends across countries, such that the number of companies employees work for in their career differs across Japan, Germany, and the U.S.A., controlling for employee age. As shown in Table 2, the *U.S.* variable is positively and significantly related to the total number of companies the employee worked for in both models ($p < 0.01$). This result suggests that the U.S. managers on the average work for 1.58 and 1.64 more companies in their career, based on OLS and Tobit estimates, respectively, than Japanese employees. Further, the *Germany* variable is posi-

Patricia (Tish) Robinson and Kiyohiko Ito

## Table 1: Means (M), Standard Deviations (SD), and Correlations

|   |   | M | SD | 1 | 2 | 3 | 4 | 5 | 6 | 7 | 8 |
|---|---|---|----|---|---|---|---|---|---|---|---|
| 1. | U.S. | 0.28 | 0.45 | | | | | | | | |
| 2. | Germany | 0.12 | 0.32 | -.23 | | | | | | | |
| 3. | Certificate | 0.33 | 0.47 | .16 | -.05 | | | | | | |
| 4. | Function | 3.15 | 2.01 | .16 | .09 | -.06 | | | | | |
| 5. | College | 0.89 | 0.31 | .11 | -.00 | -.01 | -.04 | | | | |
| 6. | MBA | 0.17 | 0.37 | .34 | .32 | .00 | .08 | .15 | | | |
| 7. | Gender | 0.91 | 0.29 | -.36 | -.06 | -.07 | -.00 | .00 | -.11 | | |
| 8. | Age | 46.63 | 7.52 | -.22 | -.14 | -.06 | .09 | -.11 | -.17 | .31 | |
| 9. | # of Companies | 1.85 | 1.21 | .51 | .21 | .11 | .20 | .02 | .30 | -.24 | -.09 |

## Table 2: Regression Results (Dependent Variable: Total Number of Companies Each Employee Has Worked for in His/Her Career)

|  | OLS | | | Tobit (5) | | | OLS | | | Tobit (5) | | |
|---|---|---|---|---|---|---|---|---|---|---|---|---|
|  | B | SE | p | B | SE | p | B | SE | p | B | SE | p |
| Constant | 0.64 | .15 | ** | 0.59 | .16 | ** | 0.68 | .16 | ** | 0.64 | .17 | ** |
| Certificate | 0.10 | .04 | * | 0.10 | .04 | * | 0.14 | .05 | * | 0.14 | .06 | * |
| US x Certificate | | | | | | | -0.17 | .09 | † | -0.19 | .10 | † |
| Germany x Certificate | | | | | | | 0.24 | .14 | † | 0.27 | .15 | † |
| Function | 0.04 | .01 | ** | 0.05 | .01 | ** | 0.02 | .02 | | 0.02 | .02 | |
| US x Function | | | | | | | 0.03 | .02 | | 0.03 | .02 | |
| Germany x Function | | | | | | | 0.04 | .03 | | 0.04 | .03 | |
| College | -0.12 | .06 | † | -0.12 | .07 | † | -0.12 | .07 | † | -0.12 | .07 | |
| US x College | | | | | | | 0.07 | .18 | | 0.04 | .19 | |
| Germany x College | | | | | | | 0.10 | .20 | | 0.09 | .21 | |
| MBA | -0.01 | .06 | | -0.01 | .06 | | -0.06 | .27 | | -0.06 | .29 | |
| US x MBA | | | | | | | 0.10 | .28 | | 0.10 | .30 | |
| Germany x MBA | | | | | | | -0.07 | .30 | | -0.08 | .32 | |
| Gender | -0.13 | .07 | † | -0.13 | .08 | † | -0.12 | .07 | | -0.13 | .08 | |
| Age | 0.01 | .00 | ** | 0.02 | .00 | ** | 0.01 | .00 | ** | 0.02 | .00 | ** |
| US | 1.58 | .05 | ** | 1.64 | .06 | ** | 1.49 | .20 | ** | 1.56 | .21 | ** |
| Germany | 1.33 | .07 | ** | 1.37 | .07 | ** | 1.13 | .22 | ** | 1.13 | .24 | ** |
| n | 2508 | | | 2508 | | | 2508 | | | 2508 | | |
| (pseudo) $R^2$ | .390 | | | .358 | | | .393 | | | .467 | | |

Note: ** $p < .01$, * $p < .05$, † $p < .10$

tive and significant for both models ($p < 0.01$), suggesting that the German employees on the average work for 1.33 and 1.37 more companies in their career, based on OLS and Tobit estimates, respectively, than the Japanese employees. To test a joint hypothesis that the *U.S.* and *German* variables are equal, we conducted the test of linear restriction using the F statistics and Wald test for OLS and Tobit results, respectively. The test results show that

they are statistically different ($p < 0.01$) for both models, lending support for Hypothesis 1; the managers in three countries work for different number of companies in their career.

Hypothesis 2 states that institutionalized education is linked to white collar labor mobility, such that employees with public qualifications and certifications, other than educational degrees, tend to have worked for a larger number of companies in their career. The *Certificate* variable is positively and significantly ($p < 0.05$) related to the dependent variable for both OLS and Tobit models, providing support for Hypothesis 2.

Hypothesis 3 states that employees who have work experience in a greater number of functional areas tend to have worked for a smaller number of companies in their career. The *Function* variable is positive and significant ($p < 0.01$) for both OLS and Tobit models. However, this result is contradictory to Hypothesis 3, suggesting that the number of functions the employee experienced is positively related to the number of companies he/she worked.

Hypothesis 4 states that institutionalized education is linked to white-collar labor mobility, such that employees with a college degree tend to have worked for more companies in their career. The education-related variables do not lend support to Hypothesis 4. The *College* variable is negatively and marginally significantly ($p < 0.10$) related to the number of companies the employee worked for both OSL and Tobit models.

Hypothesis 5 states that institutionalized education is linked to white-collar labor mobility, such that employees with an MBA degree tend to have worked for more companies in their career. The *MBA* variable is not significantly related to the total number of companies the employee worked for ($p > 0.10$) for both OSL and Tobit models, and therefore does not lend support for H5. This result suggests that the MBA degree is not related to the number of companies the employee worked, after controlling for the other variables in the model.

Hypothesis 6 states that trends in labor mobility and innovation have stayed fairly consistent over time. As the data in Table 3 show, employee turnover and patent rate tended to be consistent within countries over time, that is, they did not change dramatically.

*Additional Analyses*

Among the control variables, *Gender* is negative and marginally significant ($p < 0.10$), suggesting that male employees tend to work for fewer total companies. The *Age* variable is positive and significant ($p < 0.01$), suggesting that older employees tend to work for a greater number of companies, as

we expected.

In Table 2, the third and fourth columns show the estimated OLS and Tobit regression coefficients with all data from three countries with interaction effects. Pooling the data across all three countries, there were significant interaction effects found for US*Certificate and Germany*Certificate variables ($p < 0.10$), i.e., they are statistically different from Japan*Certificate, and the first two variables are also statistically different from each other ($p < 0.10$).

## DISCUSSION

Hypothesis 1 and 2 are supported, suggesting that white-collar labor mobility demonstrates distinctively different trends across countries, and that institutionalized education is linked to white collar labor mobility.

While we hypothesized that employees with a college degree (H4) and an MBA degree (H5) tend to have worked for more companies in their career, our empirical results do not lend support for this. However, our results indicate that a college degree may afford managers more stability. A recent survey by the US Bureau of Labor Statistics (2016) indicates that employees with college and MBA degrees have longer tenure in the US, suggesting that higher degree holders work for fewer companies in their career. This is contrary to the common perception that they tend to change jobs more often. This perception may stem from the fact that traditional job turnover research has not focused on less educated, minimum wage-type workers who tend to change jobs more often than managers with college degrees.

Interlinkages may offer one explanation for this. Specifically, educational institutions provide benefits that are realized in the form of more stable employment for college graduates. For minimally educated workers, employment may be unstable, due to the part-time, contract, or irregular nature of their work. In contrast, having a college education may afford managers more stability than their less educated counterparts. In addition, our study indicates some areas of research that are important to explore in the future. For example, it may be useful to gather more finely stratified labor market

## Table 3: Trends in Innovation & Labor Mobility in Japan, USA, and Germany 1990-2016

| Year | GDP GROWTH (%) | | | CHANGE IN PATENTS (%) | | | Labor Separations (US & Japan) & Job Vacancies (Germany) | | | Change in Labor Separations & Job Vacancies from previous year (5) | | |
|---|---|---|---|---|---|---|---|---|---|---|---|---|
| | JAPAN | US | GER-MANY | JAPAN | US | GER-MANY | JAPAN Rate of labor separations | US Rate of labor separations | GER-MANY Job Vacancies | JAPAN | US | GER-MANY |
| 1990 | 5.57 | 1.92 | 5.26 | | | | | | 0.80 | | | |
| 1991 | 3.32 | -0.07 | 5.11 | -4.56 | 0.84 | 2.56 | | | 0.91 | | | 14.05 |
| 1992 | 0.82 | 3.56 | 1.92 | 25.83 | 3.61 | 3.10 | | | 0.90 | | | -1.34 |
| 1993 | 0.17 | 2.75 | -0.96 | 14.33 | 4.03 | 3.52 | | | 0.71 | | | -20.79 |
| 1994 | 0.86 | 4.04 | 2.46 | -16.71 | 13.87 | 3.30 | 1.92 | | 0.74 | | | 3.99 |
| 1995 | 2.74 | 2.72 | 1.74 | 3.64 | 17.38 | 1.69 | 1.93 | | 0.83 | 0.52 | | 11.95 |
| 1996 | 3.10 | 3.80 | 0.82 | 1.84 | 0.05 | 7.70 | 1.92 | | 0.85 | -0.52 | | 2.56 |
| 1997 | 1.08 | 4.49 | 1.85 | 2.61 | 17.06 | 4.69 | 2 | | 0.88 | 4.17 | | 3.60 |
| 1998 | -1.13 | 4.45 | 1.98 | 2.13 | -0.30 | 2.37 | 1.96 | | 1.08 | -2.00 | | 23.15 |
| 1999 | -0.25 | 4.69 | 1.99 | -0.14 | 7.23 | 1.74 | 2.04 | | 1.17 | 4.08 | | 8.38 |
| 2000 | 2.78 | 4.09 | 2.96 | 6.11 | 9.99 | 1.20 | 2.09 | | 1.25 | 2.45 | | 6.42 |
| 2001 | 0.41 | 0.98 | 1.70 | 2.01 | 32.29 | -5.02 | 2.15 | 4.0 | 1.19 | 2.87 | | -4.96 |
| 2002 | 0.12 | 1.79 | 0.00 | -2.17 | 5.02 | -9.85 | 2.23 | 3.9 | 1.03 | 3.72 | -2.50 | -12.90 |
| 2003 | 1.53 | 2.81 | -0.71 | -1.49 | 7.25 | -4.86 | 2.17 | 3.6 | 0.74 | -2.69 | -7.69 | -27.89 |
| 2004 | 2.20 | 3.79 | 1.17 | 1.40 | 6.22 | -6.57 | 2.14 | 3.7 | 0.57 | -1.38 | 2.78 | -22.89 |
| 2005 | 1.66 | 3.35 | 0.71 | 0.64 | 5.67 | -5.87 | 2.18 | 3.7 | 0.70 | 1.87 | 0.00 | 22.48 |
| 2006 | 1.42 | 2.67 | 3.70 | -5.47 | 1.76 | -6.98 | 2.14 | 3.8 | 0.95 | -1.83 | 2.70 | 35.51 |
| 2007 | 1.65 | 1.78 | 3.26 | -5.66 | 0.33 | -3.54 | 2.1 | 3.7 | 1.11 | -1.87 | -2.63 | 16.95 |
| 2008 | -1.09 | -0.29 | 1.08 | -2.73 | -3.46 | 1.46 | 2.07 | 3.4 | 1.01 | -1.43 | -8.11 | -9.44 |
| 2009 | -5.42 | -2.78 | -5.62 | -9.75 | -6.72 | -5.06 | 2.13 | 3.3 | 0.78 | 2.90 | -2.94 | -22.58 |
| 2010 | 4.19 | 2.53 | 4.08 | -3.13 | 4.27 | 1.64 | 1.97 | 3.3 | 0.95 | -7.51 | 0.00 | 21.03 |
| 2011 | -0.12 | 1.60 | 3.66 | -1.58 | 7.38 | -0.15 | 1.97 | 3.1 | 1.20 | 0.00 | -6.06 | 27.10 |
| 2012 | 1.50 | 2.22 | 0.49 | -0.24 | 6.94 | -6.30 | 2.04 | 3.1 | 1.22 | 3.55 | 0.00 | 1.52 |
| 2013 | 2.00 | 1.68 | 0.49 | -6.29 | 4.73 | -18.62 | 2.05 | 3.2 | 1.16 | 0.49 | 3.23 | -5.28 |
| 2014 | 0.34 | 2.37 | 1.60 | -7.00 | 0.81 | 10.19 | 1.98 | 3.4 | 1.23 | -3.41 | 6.25 | 6.38 |
| 2015 | 1.22 | 2.60 | 1.72 | -16.12 | -8.40 | 15.04 | 2.03 | 3.4 | 1.41 | 2.53 | 0.00 | 15.02 |
| 2016 | 1.00 | 1.62 | 1.87 | -68.35 | -31.24 | -45.91 | 2.04 | 3.5 | 1.59 | 0.49 | | 12.30 |

data by education level (more data on less educated workforce) and type of education (in orders to compare MBAs, M.A.s, and M.S.s) with respect to job turnover.

This study has some limitations. First, while our analysis draws on rich primary data, we were not able to provide a longitudinal analysis of white-collar labor mobility in these three countries. Sec-ond, several additional factors can influence white-collar job mobility. For example, job stability (unemployment rates) that influences labor mobil-ity varies in these three countries. In particular, various institutional factors embed employees in their organizations and limit labor mobility in Japan. In addition, we have data only from manag-ers in large firms. Thus, it would be interesting to

**Patents**

| | |
|---|---|
| Overview | Count of patent applications per country per year |
| Source | World Intellectual Property Organization (WIPO), PATENTSCOPE database |
| | Japan patent office |
| Data contained within PATENTSCOPE | Patent applications under the Patent Cooperation Treaty, the global patent system which WIPO operates |
| | Patent documents from participating regional patent offices, including ARIPO, EAPO, and EPO |
| | Patent documents from many national patent collections, including China, Japan, Korea, and the United States |
| Data from Japan Patent Office | Supplemental patent totals for Japan, 1990-1993 (WIPO Japan only available from 1993-) |
| Link | https://patentscope.wipo.int/search/en/search.jsf |
| | https://www19.j-platpat.inpit.go.jp/PA1/cgi-bin/PA1SEARCH |

**Labor Turnover, Separations**

| | |
|---|---|
| Overview | Rate of separations, seasonally adjusted, noted from July of each year; The separations rate is computed by dividing the number of workers separated from their jobs by the number of people employed and multiplying the resulting quotient by 100 |
| Sources | Japan Ministry of Health, labour, and welfare Monthly Labour Survey, table TBL-T-4, Labour Turn Over |
| | USA Bureau of Labor Statistics, Job Openings and Labor Turnover Survey, Total separations, non-farm |
| Links | http://www.mhlw.go.jp/english/database/db-l/monthly-labour.html |
| | https://data.bls.gov/pdq/SurveyOutputServlet |
| Notes | UNAVAILABLE FOR GERMANY |
| | US data only available from 2001- |

**Labor Turnover, Job Vacancies**

| | |
|---|---|
| Overview | Total unfilled job vacancies, reported yearly for Germany and monthly for US; US figures are obtained for July |
| | Job vacancy rates for Germany are calculated by dividing the number of job vacancies by the number of people employed and multiplying by 100 |
| Sources | US Bureau of Labor Statistics, Job Openings and Labor Turnover Survey, Job openings, total nonfarm, level, seasonally adjusted |
| | OECD.stat; job vacancies, total, unfilled vacancies (stock), Germany, 1990-2016 |
| | OECD.stat; employed population, aged 15 and over, all persons, Germany, 1990-2016 |
| Links | https://data.bls.gov/timeseries/JTS00000000JOL |
| | https://stats.oecd.org/Index.aspx?DataSetCode=LAB_REG_VAC# |
| Notes | UNAVAILABLE FOR JAPAN |
| | US data only available from 2007- |

include data from smaller firms, and from lower organizational levels. Finally, it would be interesting to explore the relationship between "what employees studied in college" and their turnover.

## CONCLUSION

A key task in organizational analysis is to under-stand why different kinds of business organizations and organizational rationalities operate in different institutional contexts. This study examined how institutions are interlinked within institutional systems, towards helping explain differences among business systems in Japan, Germany, and U.S. Specifically, in this research, we analyzed the relationship between institutionalized career paths and educational institutions in Japan, Germany, and U.S. We found that career paths vary across countries, and that they are linked with educational institutions, in that employees with MBAs, college degrees, and various professional certifications are more likely to have worked for multiple companies over their careers. The results of our OLS and Tobit regression analysis indicate that the total number of companies that employees work for in their career is related to institutional factors associated with social and educational systems. In Japan, Germany, and U.S., we observe different relationships between specific institutional factors and employment patterns, i.e. it appears that our results are mostly consistent with the notion that institutional systems in different countries have different interactions with business practices and employment patterns. This issue has been theorized in the literature, but it has not been explored in depth across business systems in the empirical literature.

In this way, this research explores the "fit" between institutions and business practices within institutional systems (Aoki 1996). In the U.S., for example, external labor markets appear to be supported by certification programs external to the firm that help employees advance their skills to change jobs. Drawing on the results here, we argue that the interaction between institutions underlies phenomena such as internal labor markets. Were there more external opportunities for training in Japan, for example, this might support a transition to create secondary labor markets for mid-career managers to change jobs.

Systemic differences highlight the interlinked nature of institutional systems. Exemplifying this, over time, many national employment systems have evolved to be internally consistent, with many individual practices and policies fitting together and becoming tightly linked. Thus, in Japan, for example, long-term employment and internal training are closely linked, as is teamwork and rotation across functions and seniority employment, and cross share-holding and long-term investment. Thus, in addressing the need to reduce labor costs, for instance, Japanese firms have not resorted to massive layoffs like their western counterparts have. In contrast to American and German systems, Japanese institutions experience impediments to downsizing, such as those provided by social norms, labor law, and the lack of external labor markets. Instead, large Japanese firms have resorted to reduced hiring of new college graduates and increased hiring of part-time and temporary contract employees to achieve flexibility. As a result, the evolution of organizational change in Japan continues on a different path than that of western firms, due to the differing environmental pressures and institutional arrangements in these two business environments.

## ACKNOWLEDGEMENTS

The authors are grateful to R.J. Moore for research assistance and to Vesa Peltokorpi and an anonymous reviewer for valuable suggestions.

## REFERENCES

Abegglen, J. C. (1968). "Organizational change." In *The Japanese Employee*, edited by R. J. Ballon. Rutland, Vermont, Charles E. Tuttle.

Aguilera, R. V. and G. Jackson (2003.) "The cross-national diversity of corporate governance: Dimensions and determinents." *Academy of Management Review* 29:447-465.

Althauser, R.P. (1989). "Internal Labor Markets." *Annual Reviews of Sociology* 15:143-161.

Altschuler, G. and Blumin, S. (2009). *The GI Bill: The New Deal for Veterans*. Oxford University Press.

Aoki, M. (1996). Unintended Fit: Organizational Evolution and Government Design of Institutions in Japan." In *The Role of Government in East Asian Economic Develop: Comparative Institutional Analysis* edited by Aoki, Masahiko and Hyung-Ki Kim, and Masahiro Okuno-Fujiwara, Oxford University Press.

Aoki, M. (2001). *Toward a Comparative Institutional Analysis*. Cambridge, MA, The MIT Press.

BLS. (2008). History of Boston Latin School, the oldest public school in America. http://www.bls.org/cfml/l3tmpl_history.cfm. Retrieved 2008-11-01.

Bebchuk, L. A. and M. J. Roe (1999). "A theory of path dependence in corporate governance and ownership." *Stanford Law Review* 52: 127-170.

Bendix, R. (1956). *Work and Authority in Industry: Ideologies of Management in the course of Industrialization.* New York: Wiley.

Berger, S. and R. Dore (1996). *National Diversity and Global Capitalism.* Ithaca, NY: Cornell University Press.

Berle, A. A. and G. C. Means (1932). *The Modern Corporation and Private Property.* New York, Harcourt, Brace, and World.

Biggart, N. W. and M. F. Guillen (1999). "The automobile industry in four countries." *American Sociological Review* 645: 722-747.

Bureau of Labor Statistics (2016). News Release: For release 10:00 a.m. (EDT) Thursday, September 22, 2016. USDL=16-1867. U.S. Department of Labor.

Cole, R. E. (1979). *Work, Mobility, and Participation: A Comparative Study of American and Japanese Industry.* Berkeley, CA: University of California Press.

Davis, G. F. and M. Useem (1999). "Top management, company directors, and corporate control." In *Handbook of Strategy and Management,* edited by A. Pettigrew, H. Thomas and R. Whittington. eds..

De Bary, William Theodore, Carol Gluck, Arthur E. Tiedemann (2005). *Sources of Japanese Tradition,* Vol. 2. New York: Columbia University Press.

DiMaggio, P. and W. W. Powell (1983). "The iron cage revisited: Institutional isomorphism and collective rationality in organizational fields." *American Sociological Review* 48: 147-160.

Dobbin, F. (1994). *Forging Industrial Policy: The United States, Britain, and France in the Railway Age.* Cambridge, Cambridge University Press.

Doeringer, P.B. and M.J. Piore (1985). *Internal Labor Markets and Manpower Analysis.* ME Sharpe Publishers.

Dore, R. (1973). *British Factory Japanese Factory: The Origins of National Diversity in Industrial Relations.* Berkeley, CA: University of California Press.

Dore, R. (1987). *Taking Japan Seriously: A Confucian Perspective on Leading Economic Issues.* Stanford, CA: Stanford University Press.

Fligstein, N. (2001). *The Architecture of Markets: An Economic Sociology of Twenty-First-Century Capitalist Societies.* Princeton, Princeton University Press.

Fligstein, N. and R. Freeland (1995). "Theoretical and comparative perspectives on corporate organization." *Annual Review of Sociology* 21: 21-43.

Friedland, R. and R. R. Alford (1991). "Bringing society back in: Symbols, practices, and institutional contradictions." *The New Institutionalism in Organizational Analysis.* W. W. Powell and P. J. DiMaggio. Chicago, The University of Chicago Press.

Geertz, C. (1963). *Peddlers and Princes, Social Change and Economic Modernization in Two Indonesian Towns.* Chicago and London: The University of Chicago Press.

Gerlach, M. L. (1992). *Alliance Capitalism: The Social Organization of Japanese Business.* Berkeley, University of California Press.

Gordon, A. (1985). *The Evolution of Labor Relations in Japan.* Cambridge, MA: Harvard University Press.

Granovetter, M. (1985). "Economic Action and Social Structure: The Problem of Embeddedness." *American Journal of Sociology* 91: 481-510.

Guillen, M. (1994). *Models of Management: Work, Authority, and Organization in a Comparative Perspective.* Chicago, University of Chicago Press.

Guillen, M. (2001). *The Limits of Convergence: Globalization and Organizational Change in Argentina, South Korea, and Spain.* Princeton, NJ, Princeton University Press.

Hair, J. F., Anderson, R. E., Tatham, R. L., & Black, W. C. (1998). *Multivariate data analysis.* London: Prentice Hall International.

Hall, P. A. and D. Soskice (2001). "An introduction to varieties of capitalism." *Varieties of Capitalism: The Institutional Foundations of Comparative Advantage.* edited by P. A. Hall and D. Soskice. New York, Oxford University Press: 1-70.

Hamilton, G. G. and N. W. Biggart (1988). "Market, culture, and authority: A comparative analysis of management and organization in the Far East." *American Journal of Sociology* 94 Supplement: S52-S94.

Haveman, H. A. and H. Rao (1997). "Structuring a

theory of moral sentiments: Institutional and organizational coevolution in the early thrift industry." *American Journal of Sociology* 1026: 1606-51.

Holbrow, H. J. (2015). How conformity to labor market norms increases access to job search assistance: A case study from Japan. *Work and Occupations* 42(2): 135-173.

Hollingsworth, J. R., P. C. Schmitter, et al., Eds. (1994). *Governing Capitalist Economies*. New York, Oxford University Press.

Kalleberg, A, and Berg, I. (1987). *Work and Industry: Structures, Markets, and Processes*. Kluwer Academic/Plenum Publishers.

Kalleberg, A. and Stark, D. (1993). "Career Strategies in Capitalism and Socialism: Work Values and Job Rewards in the U.S. and Hungary." *Social Forces*, 72(9):181-198.

Kerkhoff, A. C. (2001). "Education and Social Stratification Processes in a Comparative Perspective." *Sociology of Education* Extra Issue: 3-18

Kim, D. and V. Anderson (1998). *Systems Archetype Basics: From Story to Structure*. Boston, MA: Pegasus Communications.

Kraus, Josef (2008). "Tag des Gymnasiums: "Das Gymnasium - Zugpferd des Bildungswesens" Präsident des Deutschen Lehrerverbandes DL.

Lim, D. S.K., Morse, E. A., Mitchell, R. K. and Seawright, K. K. (2010), Institutional Environment and Entrepreneurial Cognitions: A Comparative Business Systems Perspective. *Entrepreneurship Theory and Practice* 34: 491–516.

Mantzavinos, C., North, D., & Shariq, S. (2004). Learning, Institutions, and Economic Performance. *Perspectives on Politics* 2(1): 75-84.

Mizruchi, M. S. and L. C. Fein (1999). "The social construction of organizational knowledge: A study of the uses of coercive, mimetic, and normative isomorphism." *Administrative Science Quarterly* 44: 653-683.

Morgan, G. Kristensen, PH, Whitley, R. (2001). *The multinational firm: organizing across institutional and national divides*. Oxford: Oxford University Press.

North, D.C. (1991). Institutions. *Journal of Economic Perspectives* 5(1): 97-112.

NCSU. (2009). *Agriculture and Education in Colo-*

*nial America*. North Carolina State University.

Neuharth, A. (2009). "College Decision Day". *Florida Today*. Melbourne, Florida: May 1, pp.11A.

Orru, M., N.W. Biggart and G. Hamilton, eds. (1997). *The Economic Organization of East Asian Capitalism*. Thousand Oaks: Sage Publications.

Pfeffer, J. and G. R. Salancik (1978.) *The External Control of Organizations: A Resource Dependence Perspective*. New York, Harper and Row.

Polanyi, K. (1957). *The Great Transformation*. Boston: Beacon Press.

Repenning, N. and J. Sterman (2000). "Getting Quality the Old Fashioned Way: Self-Confirming Attributions in the Dynamics of Process Improvement," in R.B. Cole and R. Scott, eds. *Improving Theory and Research on Quality Enhancement in Organizations*. Thousand Oaks, CA: Sage.

Schülerzahlen Statistisches Bundesamt Deutschland. http://www.destatis.de/jetspeed/portal/cms/Sites/destatis/Internet/DE/Presse/pm/2009/01/PD09__032__12421,templateId=renderPrint.psml. Retrieved 2007- 07-20

Scott, R. W. (1995). *Institutions and Organizations*. Thousand Oaks, CA: Sage.

Selznick, P. (1949). *TVA and the Grass Roots*. Berkeley, CA: University of California Press.

Smelzer, N. R. Swedberg (2005). *The Handbook of Economic Sociology*, 2nd Ed. Princeton, N.J.: Princeton University Press.

Spenner, K.I. (1995). "Technological Change, Skill Requirements, and Education: The Case for Uncertainty," *The New Modern Times: Factors Reshaping the World of Work*, edited by. David Bills. State University of New York Press.

Spilerman, S. (1977). "Careers, Labor Market Structure, and Socioeconomic Achievement." *American Journal of Sociology* 83:551-593.

Sterman, J. (2000). *Business Dynamics: Systems Thinking and Modeling for a Complex World*. New York, NY: Irwin/McGraw-Hill.

Sterman, J., N. Repenning, and F. Kofman (1997). "Unanticipated Side Effects of Successful Quality Programs: Exploring a Paradox of Organizational Improvement." *Management Science* 43: 503-521.

Streeck, W. (2001). "Introduction: Explorations into the origins of nonliberal capitalism in Germany and Japan." *The Origins of Nonliberal Capitalism*, edited by W. Streeck and K. Yamamura. Ithaca, NY, Cornell University Press: 1-38.

Thompson, J. (1967). *Organizations in Action*. New York, McGraw-Hill.

Tiberghien, Y. (2002). State Mediation of Global Economic Forces: The Politics of Corporate Restructuring in Japan, France, and South Korea. Doctoral dissertation in political science. Stanford, Stanford University.

United States Census 2000.

Useem, M. (1998). "Corporate leadership in a globalizing equity market." *Academy of Management Executive* 12: 43-59.

Veysey, Laurence (1970). *The Emergence of the American University*. University Of Chicago Press.

Westney, D. E. (1987). *Imitation and Innovation: The Transfer of Western Organizational Patterns to Meiji Japan*. Cambridge, MA: Harvard University Press.

Whitley, R. (2003). The institutional structuring of organizational capabilities: The role of authority sharing and organizational careers. *Organization Studies* 24: 667-695.

Whitley, R. (1992). *Business Systems in East Asia*. London, Sage.

Whitley, R. (2001). The Institutional Structuring of Innovation Strategies: Business Systems, Firm Types and Patterns of Technical Change in Different Market Economies. *Organization Studies* 21: 855-886

Witt, M. A. (2014). Japan: Coordinated capitalism between institutional change and structural inertia. In M. A. Witt & G. Redding (Eds.), *The Oxford Handbook of Asian Business Systems* (pp. 100-122). Oxford, UK: Oxford University Press.

Zimmermann, K. F. (1998). German job mobility and wages. In I. Ohashi & T. Tachibanaki (Eds.), *Internal Labour Markets, Incentives and Employment* (pp. 300-332). Springer.

Dr. Patricia (Tish) Robinson is Associate Professor at the Graduate School of International Corporate Strategy, Hitotsubashi University, Japan. Email: probinson@ics.hit-u.ac.jp

Dr. Kiyohiko Ito is Shidler College Distinguished Professor at Shidler College of Business, The University of Hawai'i at Manoa, U.S.A. Email: k.ito@hawaii.edu

*Kindai Management Review* Vol. 6, 2018 (ISSN: 2186-6961)

# Growth Aspirations and Financing Choices of Immigrant-Owned New Ventures in Canada

## Miwako Nitani

*Telfer School of Management, University of Ottawa, Canada*

## François Neville

*DeGroote School of Business, McMaster University, Canada*

### Abstract

The job-creating growth of new firms depends critically on access to financial capital; however, access to capital can also be limited—and growth constrained—if business owners choose not to apply for funds. External financial capital funds both working capital and fixed asset expansion, both of which are required for growth. New firms founded by recent immigrants contribute disproportionately to growth of small- and medium-sized enterprises (SMEs). Immigration policy lies at the heart of current international debates it is essential to ensure that the policy discussions are well informed. Among key issues in these debates is the extent to which immigrants add to prosperity. Neville et al. (2014) are among those who have shown that growth of young immigrant-owned exporter firms adds disproportionately to job creation and economic welfare, at least in Canada. Because growth requires financing this paper examines, conceptually and empirically, financing choices of young firms with particular emphasis on firms owned by recent immigrants. It finds that immigrant owners of growth-oriented young firms were less likely to apply for financing than growth-oriented firms owned by non-immigrants. This is important because immigration policies often encourage "business immigrants," those immigrants who intend to start a business. Such applicants are often presented with strenuous requirements in order to be granted a visa (including minimum levels of wealth and experience, and a viable business plan with the intention to hire employees). It is therefore essential to determine the extent to which the financial system allows for the provision of the resources that are necessary to fuel growth among young immigrant-owned enterprises. Immigration policy might be compromised if immigrants are discouraged from accessing the forms of financing consistent with realizing growth aspirations. Growth-oriented immigrant owners—precisely those who ought to be seeking capital—are less likely to apply for growth-enabling financing.

**Keywords:** *Entrepreneurs, risk, leadership, intellectual capital, effectuation, triple loop learning*

## INTRODUCTION

The growth of new firms is widely regarded as a key element in the formation of new jobs and economic prosperity (Haltiwanger et al., 2010). It has also been noted that many of the most successful growth-oriented firms have been founded and managed by recent immigrants (Dalziel, 2008, Neville, Orser, Riding, Jung, 2014) and that immigrants appear to be a catalyst for international trade from their host countries (Co, Euzent, & Martin, 2004; Dunlevy & Hutchinson, 1999; Head & Ries, 1998; Mundra, 2005; Neville et al., 2014; Partridge & Furtan, 2008). The widely held belief that immigrants are particularly entrepreneurial has prompted more than 30 countries to adopt policies that encourage and facilitate immigration of entrepreneurs (Ley, 2006) and is further exemplified in the popular media.[1]

In order to nourish growth, however, external capital is usually required to finance the need for additional working capital and for additions to the asset base (Vos et al., 2007, among many). Accordingly, the growth of immigrant-owned firms—and, indeed, the growth of firms not owned by immigrants—depends critically on access to financial capital. However, recent immigrants tend to lack credit histories, have relatively more limited business networks and are focussed on different market segments compared with those of resident entrepreneurs. Accordingly, immigrants may make different financing choices, some by necessity and some by preference, than non-immigrants. Choices may even self-limit certain financing sources. Therefore, this work compares the financing choices of recent immigrant business owners with those of counterpart non-immigrant business owners.

This is an important issue because access to capital fosters wealth-creation. However, it is has been found "that the most innovative firms are less successful in loan markets than their less innovative peers" (Freel, 2007, p. 23; see also Binks and Ennew, 1996; among others). To the extent that immigrant-owned enterprises are over-represented among high growth SMEs, the financing of immigrant-owned businesses is a research question that also contributes to the discussion regarding owner-level influences on SME financing structures and decisions. The recognition of the need for capital among growing SMEs has prompted virtually all developed countries to intervene in the credit markets through establishing development banks or by means of loan guarantee schemes. Therefore, this paper's focus on the financing choices of young growth-oriented firms, with special reference to immigrant-founded new ventures, lies at the heart of immigration, commercial, banking and trade policies.

Moreover, immigration policy lies at the heart of current debates around the world. One extreme is exemplified, perhaps, by countries such as the United States, those nations that are arguably becoming less friendly to immigration than many. At the other extreme, Germany may be illustrative of countries that are currently more welcoming. A key issue in these debates is the extent to which immigrants either add to prosperity or are economic burdens. To this point, Neville et al. (2014) has shown that, in the Canadian context, the growth of young exporter firms owned by recent immigrants adds disproportionately to job creation and economic welfare. This research, which also lies in the Canadian context, represents a nation in which the vast majority of residents are in fact immigrants. This work therefore examines the extent to which immigrant owners of new firms are able to access the financial capital necessary for job-creating enterprise growth.

To examine these questions, the paper opens with a short review of the salient research literature that leads to a conceptual rationale and to the development of testable research hypotheses. A detailed description of data and empirical methods follow along with the empirical findings. This work reports on secondary analysis of data drawn from a large-scale stratified survey of business owners. The analysis focuses on 2,915 enterprises that had been founded within the five-year period previous to the administration of the survey. Of these, 132 business owners had immigrated during the same five-year period. The survey data include comprehensive information about the business owners, including owners' growth aspirations, demographic information about the firm, and whether the firm had sought external financing (as well as the specific type of financing sought). The paper closes with a summary of results and a discussion of the implications, limitations and future directions of this research.

## REVIEW OF THE RESEARCH LITERATURERE

### Financing growth-oriented new ventures

Financing growth-oriented new businesses is an important element with respect to attaining national and regional goals of economic development. It is generally recognized that the development of new firms contributes disproportionately to economic welfare and job creation (Haltiwanger et al., 2010); however, it has also been found that the inability to access financing acts as a constraint to enterprise growth (Demirguc-Kunt, 2006; OECD, 2006). Traditionally, academic literature's consideration of SMEs' access to capital is vested in the presumption of market failures (Stiglitz and Weiss, 1981) or credit rationing (Storey, 1994). The conceptual model that governs most of this research literature presumes that businesses advance loan applications to commercial lenders and then explores the impacts of the asymmetrical information that is understood to permeate the lender-borrower relationship. However, access to capital can be limited for a variety of other reasons. Often, business owners make choices that result in self-limitation of access to financing. Kon and Storey (2003) address a situation whereby some potential borrowers, who they describe as "discouraged borrowers," choose not apply for bank loans because they feel they will be rejected. To this point, Kon and Storey cite Levenson and Willard (2000) to the effect that more than twice as many small firms are "discouraged" as are rejected for loans from financial institutions in the United States. Similarly, Wynant and Hatch (1991) describe a situation they term "informal turndowns" in which loan applications are discouraged on the basis, for example, of a social conversation between a business owner and bank employee: again a formal loan application does not necessarily ensue. While their data is dated, Wynant and Hatch suggest that informal turndowns occur approximately as frequently as formal rejections of loan applications. Furthermore, some business owners—especially owners of innovative firms—may eschew

debt financing in favour of equity capital (Freel, 2006). Brierley (2001) describes the converse, where firms that ought to apply for equity financing inappropriately apply for commercial loans. Brierley maintains that commercial lenders may perceive firms seeking growth as relatively informationally opaque (risky) and are best advised to seek equity financing (see also Binks & Ennew, 1996). This paper therefore focuses on the choices business owners make with respect to seeking financing.

Historically, the theory of financing choices and of capital structure, the outcome of such choices, comprises one of the most extensive literatures in finance. In the context of large public firms the classical works of Modigliani and Miller (1958, 1963), amended later by Miller (1977), suggest that there is an optimal capital structure for a given firm, one that reflects trades-offs among the costs and benefits of debt financing, personal and corporate taxation of dividend and interest income, costs of financial distress and agency costs. Myers (1984) and Myers and Majluf (1984) developed an alternative paradigm known as the "pecking order" theory, which argues that internal financing is preferred over external; debt is the preferred source of external finance; and external equity is issued only as a last resort. Both sets of theories provide important insights; however Brealey and Myers (2000) and Graham and Harvey (2001) maintain that neither theory fully explains observed capital structures.

These classical theories were developed in the context of capital markets in which firms have recourse to public markets for debt and equity, where information is widely available and in which markets provide liquidity. However, Romano et al. (2001) indicate that new and small firms do not usually operate in the public equity and debt markets that are typically the paradigm of financial theorists. Uzzi and Gillespie (1999) add that social capital and the inseparability of entrepreneurs from their businesses make obtaining financing a much different proposition than the act of securing capital for major corporations. Accordingly, several researchers have tried to adapt the classical theories to the small business context. For example, Howorth (1999), Berggren, Olofsson and Silver (2000), Berggren (2009), Robb and Robinson (2009) and Beck and his colleagues (2008) all report evidence that the pecking order theory may hold for small firms—but for quite different reasons than those which form the basis of the theories as they apply to large firms.

In examining the capital structure of SMEs across various countries, Psillaki and Daskalakis (2009) concluded that capital structure choice was a result of firm characteristics and not financial or institutional attributes of the country in which the firm operated. While commercial loans appear to be the mainstay of SME external financing Robb and Robinson (2009), Psillaki and Daskalakis (2009) as well as Beck et al. (2008) report that firm size is associated with financial leverage: smaller firms were relatively less likely to be highly levered. This implies that smaller firms may be relatively less likely to seek traditional forms of debt financing from banks and financial institutions. Other research has found that firms operating in certain industries, specifically knowledge-based firms, are relatively more likely to employ equity financing (Baldwin & Johnson, 1995; Ben-Ari & Vonortas, 2007).

An important *caveat* to the empirical literature on SMEs financing structures, however, is that virtually all findings are based on the types of financing actually obtained by firms. The conclusions based on observations of types financing obtained make the tacit assumption that the types of financing obtained are the same as the types of financing that had been sought. This assumption is conceptually inconsistent with capital rationing (borrowers are refused the form of capital they seek) and is at variance with the understanding that financing applications from small firms (and especially new firms) are frequently rejected. For example, new firms typically face high turndown rates of debt financing requests: rejected firms must resort to less preferred alternatives. Hence, the types of financing sought and the types of financing obtained are likely to differ.

Conceptually, it seems reasonable to expect that growth aspirations are central to SME owners' desire for external financing. Growth can only be accomplished by adding to the asset base, the labour base (or both) and growth invariably involves additions to net working capital. Financial resources are required in order to add to the stock of assets or of labour, often prompting the need for external capital. Additions to the left side of the balance sheet either draws down cash or requires additions to the right side of the balance sheet: new financing. Arguably, this is especially true for young firms, the focus of this study, where cash flows are typically insufficient to finance growth. These arguments are to a large extent common sense but have also been confirmed empirically (see, among others, Demirguc-Kunt, 2006; OECD, 2006; Cosh, Cumming and Hughes, 2009; and Neville et al., 2014). Because growth intention is an antecedent of the need for finance, it is important to ensure that growth intention is a precursor for financing in the data to be used in this analysis.

*Proposition 1. Growth aspirations are a primary driver of applications for external capital.*

### Financing immigrant-owned business ventures

Business ownership by immigrants is reportedly higher in developed countries such as the United States, Canada, Australia and the United Kingdom (SBA, 2008). In the United States, the Small Business Administration Office of Advocacy reports that immigrants account for 12.5% of the total population of US business owners and immigrants are also 30% more likely to start a business than non-immigrants (SBA, 2008). Among immigrant-owned firms, 51.6% are service-based (compares with 45.6% of all US businesses). According to Canadian data, 15.3% of immigrant-owned firms are in professional services, 11% in educational and health services, 10% in arts, entertainment and recreation, and 15.3% in other services (Industry Canada, 2009). Immigrants' businesses also appear to be relatively highly oriented towards international trade (Portes et al., 2002) and immigrant-owned firms were found to be significantly more likely to export than counterpart businesses not owned by-immigrants (Orser *et al.*, 2008).[2]

According to previous research, immigrant-owned firms tend to be smaller than non-immigrant owned firms (SBA, 2008; Kushnirovich & Heilbrunn, 2008). This can be linked to the reality that immigrants may be pushed into entrepreneurial endeavours as a form of economic adaptation. Consequently, firm growth may not be as pressing as salary substitution or generating enough income to support family members (Portes et al., 2002). Moreover, initial investments made by immigrants in their start-up ventures were found, on average, to be smaller than those of non-immigrants (Kushnirovich and Heilbrunn, 2008). Bates (1997) also observed that Korean and Chinese immigrants in the US raise less debt than nonminority borrowers. Moreover, immigrants may face particular difficulties accessing external financial capital because, not having resided in their host countries for very long, immigrants are likely to have relatively short banking relationships, relatively inchoate networks and poor credit histories. To this point, Avery, Brevoort, & Canner (2009) report that immigrants receive relatively low credit scores, putting them at a disadvantage in obtaining financial capital. Accordingly, immigrant entrepreneurs may feel constrained with respect to their financing choices and this might compromise the viability and growth of their enterprises.

In summary, it is argued that immigrant business owners may hold preferences for the types of external financing they seek. However, factors such as firm size, firm age, and sector have been cited as factors that may also relate to choice of financing. With respect to these factors, previous research suggests that immigrant-owned firms are smaller, tend to be concentrated in services and knowledge-based industries and are more likely to be export oriented than non-immigrant owned firms. Immigrant firm owners probably demonstrate relatively limited financial track records, given their less established period of residence in their host country. For these reasons, it is expected that immigrant-owned firms would be less likely to seek formal sources of financing than non-immigrant owned firms. Consequently, the following research propositions are advanced.

*Proposition 2. Controlling for growth, and other potentially salient factors such as firm size, business age, and sector, immigrant-owned firms are less likely to apply for formal types of financing than non-immigrant-owned firms.*

In spite of this discussion, there is virtually no previous research regarding the financing of immigrant-owned enterprises. Previous research regarding immigrant entrepreneurs has predominantly investigated firm and owner characteristics, start-up opportunities, behaviours and management strategies (Waldinger et al., 1990; Portes and Jensen, 1989; Portes et al., 2002; Ram & Smallbone, 2003).

*SME financing choices—supply-related factors*

For new firms, notions of information asymmetry and credit rationing provide a key conceptual framework underlying the financing process. A related aspect of the financing process is the relationship between borrowers and lenders. Relationships potentially mitigate information asymmetries. Petersen and Rajan (1994) found that stronger banking relationships typically led to increased credit availability for borrowers, less onerous collateral requirements and lower interest rates (see also: Borheim and Herbeck, 1998; Cole, 1998; Voordeckers and Steijvers, 2006). This is consistent with Binks & Ennew (1996) who argued that information asymmetries may be higher in the case of small and growing businesses but that perceptions of trust between these businesses and lenders reduce the extent to which owners of these businesses feel credit constrained. Accordingly, firms with weaker and shorter banking relationships – such as those of immigrant-owned enterprises – seem to be at a distinct disadvantage in terms of acquiring financing. Likewise, firms undergoing high growth may present relatively greater levels of information asymmetry.

For relatively small loans, maintaining a relationship with a commercial lender is onerous from the lenders' perspective. Consequently, credit scoring is now in widespread use throughout financial industries because it creates efficiencies for lenders by shortening (or even eliminating) due diligence for certain types of loans.[3] Credit scoring lowers the likelihood of loan defaults (DeYoung, Glennon, & Nigro, 2008) and Frame et al. (2001) argued that credit scoring increases credit availability for small businesses and pushes banks to focus of small business loans. Berger and Frame (2007) found that most banks in the US made use of credit scoring for small business loans: that 100% of banks scored loans under $100,000 and that 74.2% of banks scored loans between $100,000 and $250,000. In addition, 87.1% of banks used scoring models from an external vendor. Consequently, almost all small business loans are being assessed using a statistical algorithm with a common root that is vested in the accumulation of historical data; however, immigrants' present short histories. Credit scores are based on measures that include: payment history (ability to maintain healthy credit), amount of credit owed, utilization of credit (proximity of balances to credit limits), length of time credit is established, searches for acquisition of new credit, and types of credit established. Consequently, a good credit score is largely contingent on having established a considerable and arguably flawless financial track record. For recent immigrants, generating a sufficient credit history could be a challenge, an expectation confirmed empirically by Avery et al. (2009). Therefore, the following hypotheses are advanced:

> Proposition 3. Immigrant-owned firms are less likely to apply for debt financing than non-immigrant owned firms.
> Proposition 4: Immigrant-owned firms are less likely to apply for equity financing than non-immigrant owned firms.

As a result of the influence of the lending relationship and the usage of credit scoring, owner-managers of young firms may also be more likely to believe that financing requests will be turned down. According to Kon and Storey (2003), information availability impacts screening errors by lenders and the potential for discouraged borrowers is at a maximum when the availability of information is at an intermediate level for both the borrower and lender. Therefore, new firms led by an owner who is relatively young and less experienced, less educated, potentially hindered by language and cultural barriers, and with a relatively limited financial track record (maximizing intermediate levels of information) would arguably be at higher risk of assuming that their financing request would be turned down. Consequently, it would seem that these firms would be relatively likely to be discouraged from seeking financing.

Han, Fraser and Storey (2009) found that in concentrated markets higher risk borrowers—such as those undergoing rapid growth or those whose owners have short credit histories—are particularly likely to be discouraged. Other potential factors in discouragement include certain industries and firm types: larger firms are at a distinct advantage over smaller firms (Zambaldi et al., 2009; Voordeckers and Steijvers, 2006). In summary, it seems reasonable to expect that immigrant-owned firms are at a relative disadvantage in terms of financing accessibility and terms and that the owners are aware of this disadvantage. It follows that they are more likely to be discouraged, and may therefore be more likely to use trade credit as a substitute for formal sources of capital. Therefore, the final two research propositions are advanced.

> Proposition 5. Immigrant-owned firms are more likely to believe that their requests for external financing will be denied.
> Proposition 6. Immigrant-owned firms are more likely to apply for trade credit than non-immigrant-owned firms.

The following section describes the data and methodology to be employed in testing the hypotheses advanced above.

## DATA AND METHODOLOGY

### Data

Data for this work were drawn from the "Survey on Financing of Small and Medium Enterprises" conducted by Statistics Canada between September 2004 and March 2005 on behalf of Industry Canada (Industry Canada, 2006). The population of interest comprised 1.3 million Canadian enterprises listed on the Business Register maintained by Statistics Canada (mandatory for all Canadian firms reporting a minimum of $30,000 in revenues during any 12-month period) from which a sampling frame of 34,509 firms were randomly drawn. Eligible firms had fewer than 500 full-time-equivalent employees and annual gross revenues of less than $50 million. Data collection was undertaken in two phases. First, computer-assisted telephone interviews collected extensive firm demographic data along with

**Table 1: Population Estimates of Salient Attributes of Sample Firms**

|  | Immigrant-Owned (N=104) | Benchmark new firms (N=2,057) | Chi-Square p-value |
|---|---|---|---|
| Size distribution of firm |  |  | 0.642 |
| < 5 employees | 0.825 | 0.858 |  |
| 5 to 9.9 employees | 0.087 | 0.083 |  |
| 10 to 19.9 employees | 0.039 | 0.031 |  |
| 20 or more employees | 0.049 | 0.029 |  |
| Sectoral distribution |  |  | 0.775 |
| Goods | 0.214 | 0.223 |  |
| Services | 0.709 | 0.681 |  |
| Knowledge-based | 0.078 | 0.096 |  |
| Export Propensity | 24.3% | 8.0% | 0.000 |
| Growth-oriented | 68.9% | 56.2% | 0.000 |
| Start-ups (< 2 years old) | 58.3% | 40.0% | 0.000 |
| Majority male-ownership | 44.2% | 63.4% | 0.002 |
| Urban location | 88.3% | 76.9% | 0.007 |
| Conducts R&D | 57.3% | 32.6% | 0.000 |

attributes of the primary owners of the firms (the key respondents). Subsequently, financial statement data were collected using a fax-back questionnaire. Telephone follow-up was used to increase response rates and reduce non-response bias. Valid responses were received from 12,047 SMEs, a response rate of 47 percent of in-scope potential respondents.

As noted, the focus of this work is on young firms. Accordingly, of the 12,047 respondents, this unit of analysis for this work concentrates exclusively on the 2,915 firms that had been started between 2000 and 2004 (the five-year period preceding administration of the survey). Fewer than 10 per cent of Canadian business owners have more than one primary business; moreover, fewer than 18 per cent of Canadian SMEs report more than two owners. This period was chosen because the survey had asked all respondents whether they had immigrated to Canada during this five-year period. Therefore immigrant status is known for the young firms as defined here.[4] Of these, 132 primary owner respondents reported having immigrated to Canada within the five-year interim. Responses were weighted according to region (the ten Canadian provinces are each defined as a region with the Northern Territories—the Yukon Territory, the Northwest Territories and Nunavut—collectively defined as an eleventh region), size, and sector to best represent the underlying population while ensuring minimum data counts for particular cells. Employing sample weights, Table 1 provides a comparison of population estimates of salient attributes based on 104 young firms owned by immigrants and 2,057 young firms that serve as a basis of comparison (because of skip patterns intentionally built into the data to ease respondent burden, some results may be based on fewer than 132 observations).

First, it is seen that, firms owned by immigrants were significantly more likely to be growth-oriented, to conduct R&D and to be exporters. Compared to other new firms, immigrant-owned new businesses were also more likely to be situated in urban locations and to be owned by women. It is also notable that, contrary to the literature, firm size did not differ significantly between immigrant-owned firms and counterparts even though a relatively higher proportion of immigrant-owned firms were start-ups (defined here as firms trading for less than two years as of date of survey administration). In addition, the sectoral mix did not differ significantly between immigrant-owned and counterpart firms. This again is at variance with the literature that contends that immigrant-owned firms tend to be concentrated in the services sector. However, previous research has generally not been based on as

*Growth Aspirations and Financing Choices of Immigrant-Owned New Ventures in Canada*

large a sample as is employed here.

Business owner respondents were asked: *"During the past 12 months ... did the business or its owners approach any type of credit supplier to request new or additional credit for business purposes?"* Firms not seeking external capital were asked why they chose not to apply and firms that did seek external financing were asked detailed questions about the source of financing they had sought. Employing sample weights, it was found that:

- 66.0 percent of firms did not apply for external financing because they did not require it;
- 5.8 percent of firms did not apply for external financing because they thought that they would be turned down (that is, were discouraged);
- 26.5 percent of owners sought some form of financing. The vast majority of these sought debt financing (commercial loans or leasing); 1.6 percent of owners sought external equity capital.

Firms that reported applying for capital but which sought government grants were excluded from analysis. Multinomial and binary logistic regressions were employed to explore the systematic differences among these groups.

## EMPIRICAL FINDINGS

As noted, three categories of firms are of interest for this analysis: those firms that did not need financing (these serve as the base case for analysis); those firms that applied for financing; and those firms that did not apply because they perceived that their applications would have been turned down (discouraged borrowers, six percent of respondents). These three categories comprised the dependent variable in a multinomial regression model. Control variables included:

- size of firm (natural log of the number of employees, including the owner);
- sector (a binary variable according to whether the firm was in the goods (=1) or services (=0) sector;

- age of firm (binary variable =1 if the firm had been founded in the previous two years, 0 otherwise); and,
- A binary variable according to whether (=1) or not (=0) the firm had invested in R&D.

As a first stage, the multinomial model was estimated with these control variables only. In the second stage, the model was augmented by adding the two variables of interest: owners' growth intention and immigrant status of the owners. Growth intention was measured as a binary variable connoting whether (=1) or not (=0) the owner had expressed growth aspirations according to his or her answer to the question: *"Do you intend to expand the size or scope of your business within the next two years?"* Immigrant status was based on the owners' response to the question: *"Did the primary owner of the firm immigrate to Canada within the last five years?"* These binary variables were added to the base case multinomial model by means of a categorical variable comprising:

- Immigrant owners with growth intentions (N=93);
- Immigrant owners without growth intentions (N=38);
- Non-immigrant owners with growth intentions (N=1630);
- Non-immigrant owners without growth intentions (N=1121).

The results of the hierarchical estimation are reported in Table 2, which shows systematic ways in which firms that did not need financing differ from financing applicants and from discouraged borrowers. Discouraged borrowers did not differ as to size from firms that did not need financing *(p-value=0.786)* but were significantly smaller than firms that did seek financing *(p-value=0.000)*. Compared with firms that did not need financing, discouraged borrowers were relatively more likely to be start-ups *(p-value=0.004)*. In addition, owners with growth aspirations were also more likely to be discouraged borrowers than owners who did not seek growth. This was particularly true of immigrant owners with growth intentions who were relatively likely to be among discouraged borrowers

**Table 2: Multinomial Logistic Model of Financing Choices**

| | | Base Model | | | | Expanded Model | | | |
|---|---|---|---|---|---|---|---|---|---|
| | | Coefficient estimate | Std. Error | p-value | Exp(B) | Coefficient estimate | Std. Error | p-value | Exp(B) |
| Financing Applicants | Intercept | -2.117 | 0.098 | 0.000 | | -2.535 | 0.122 | 0.000 | |
| | LN(employees) | 0.277 | 0.053 | 0.000 | 1.32 | 0.280 | 0.055 | 0.000 | 1.32 |
| | Goods sector | 0.410 | 0.129 | 0.001 | 1.51 | 0.329 | 0.131 | 0.012 | 1.39 |
| | Startups (< 2 years old) | 0.295 | 0.116 | 0.011 | 1.34 | 0.323 | 0.119 | 0.007 | 1.38 |
| | Invests in R&D | 0.281 | 0.113 | 0.013 | 1.32 | 0.063 | 0.119 | 0.596 | 1.07 |
| | Immigrants owners with Growth aspiration | | | | | 0.388 | 0.346 | 0.261 | 1.48 |
| | Non-immigrant owner with growth aspirations | | | | | 0.841 | 0.120 | 0.000 | 2.32 |
| Discouraged borrowers | Intercept | -4.102 | 0.266 | 0.000 | | -4.301 | 0.309 | 0.000 | |
| | LN(employees) | 0.007 | 0.170 | 0.969 | 1.01 | -0.048 | 0.176 | 0.786 | 0.95 |
| | Goods sector | -0.289 | 0.418 | 0.489 | 0.75 | -0.366 | 0.419 | 0.382 | 0.69 |
| | Startups (< 2 years old) | 0.940 | 0.293 | 0.001 | 2.56 | 0.865 | 0.298 | 0.004 | 2.38 |
| | Invests in R&D | -0.064 | 0.319 | 0.842 | 0.94 | -0.253 | 0.329 | 0.442 | 0.78 |
| | Immigrants owners with Growth aspiration | | | | | 1.563 | 0.556 | 0.005 | 4.77 |
| | Non-immigrant owner with growth aspirations | | | | | 0.509 | 0.320 | 0.112 | 1.66 |
| Pseudo R-Square | | | | | | | | | |
| | Cox & Snell | 0.020 | | | | 0.042 | | | |
| | Nagelkerke | 0.030 | | | | 0.064 | | | |
| p-values | | | | | | | | | |
| | Step | 0.000 | | | | 0.000 | | | |
| | Model | 0.000 | | | | 0.000 | | | |

Notes: Reference category comprises firms not needing external capital. Base case is non-immigrants that do not have growth aspirations. The category corresponding to immigrant owners who were also discouraged borrowers comprised no respondents and is therefore suppressed in the above.

(p-value=0.005).

Table 2 also shows that financing applicants differed from firms that did not need financing in several systematic ways. Firms in the goods-producing sectors, larger firms, and firms founded within the last two years were relatively more likely to seek formal sources of capital (p-values < 0.05 in each case). The most important factor, however, appears to be the owners' growth aspirations: firms whose non-immigrant owners had expressed an intention to expand the firm were more than twice as likely to apply for capital than counterpart firms that did not espouse growth intentions (p-value=0.001).

Because of the relatively small number of discouraged borrowers who were also immigrants, the above analysis does not provide information about the relative propensity of immigrants to seek formal

## Table 3: Binary Logistic Model of Financing Choices

| Variable | N | Base Model | | | | Expanded Model | | | |
|---|---|---|---|---|---|---|---|---|---|
| | | Coefficient estimate | Std. Error | p-value | Exp(B) | Coefficient estimate | Std. Error | p-value | Exp(B) |
| NAIC Category | | | | 0.000 | | | | 0.000 | |
| Primary | 133 | 0.743 | 0.222 | 0.001 | 2.10 | 0.689 | 0.225 | 0.002 | 1.99 |
| Construction | 256 | -0.170 | 0.175 | 0.330 | 0.84 | -0.341 | 0.179 | 0.056 | 0.71 |
| Manufacturing | 163 | 0.039 | 0.239 | 0.870 | 1.04 | -0.114 | 0.243 | 0.639 | 0.89 |
| Wholesale & Retail | 364 | -0.247 | 0.170 | 0.147 | 0.78 | -0.352 | 0.173 | 0.043 | 0.70 |
| Finance, Insurance, etc. | 83 | -1.764 | 0.364 | 0.000 | 0.17 | -1.732 | 0.368 | 0.000 | 0.18 |
| Professional Services | 540 | -0.955 | 0.174 | 0.000 | 0.39 | -1.064 | 0.178 | 0.000 | 0.35 |
| Accommodation & Food Services | 264 | -0.667 | 0.205 | 0.001 | 0.51 | -0.672 | 0.207 | 0.001 | 0.51 |
| Other Services | 335 | -0.303 | 0.159 | 0.056 | 0.74 | -0.461 | 0.163 | 0.005 | 0.63 |
| LN (Number of employees) | | 0.312 | 0.047 | 0.000 | 1.37 | 0.303 | 0.048 | 0.000 | 1.36 |
| Invests in R&D | | 0.399 | 0.092 | 0.000 | 1.49 | 0.242 | 0.096 | 0.011 | 1.27 |
| Startup (< 2 years old) | | 0.312 | 0.095 | 0.001 | 1.37 | 0.300 | 0.097 | 0.002 | 1.35 |
| Immigrant/growth status | | | | | | | | 0.000 | |
| Immigrants, growth intentions | 79 | | | | | 0.288 | 0.267 | 0.281 | 1.33 |
| Immigrants, no growth intentions | 33 | | | | | 1.093 | 0.331 | 0.001 | 2.98 |
| Non-Immigrants, growth intentions | 1166 | | | | | 0.682 | 0.095 | 0.000 | 1.98 |
| Constant | | -1.132 | 0.136 | 0.000 | 0.32 | -1.375 | 0.144 | 0.000 | 0.25 |
| Goodness of fit measures | | | | | | | | | |
| Cox & Snell R-squared | | 0.057 | | | | 0.074 | | | |
| Nagelkerke R-squares | | 0.083 | | | | 0.108 | | | |
| p-values | | | | | | | | | |
| Step | | 0.000 | | | | 0.000 | | | |
| Model | | 0.000 | | | | 0.000 | | | |

## Table 4: Frequencies of Financing Applications

|  | Sought supplier financing* | Sought debt financing | Sought equity financing |
|---|---|---|---|
| Immigrant Owner | 14.2% | 21.5% | 0.1% |
| Non-Immigrant Owner | 13.1% | 20.0% | 1.6% |
| *p-value of difference* | *0.360* | *0.348* | *0.000* |
| Growth aspirations | 15.9% | 12.1% | 0.2% |
| No growth aspirations | 9.8% | 26.8% | 2.7% |
| *p-value of difference* | *0.000* | *0.000* | *0.000* |
| All firms | 13.1% | 20.1% | 1.6% |

*Some firms may have sought both trade credit as well as institutional finance.

financing. Specifically, the dependent variable was a binary variable corresponding to the primary owner's response to the question: *"During the past 12 months ... did the business or its owners approach any type of credit supplier to request new or additional credit for business purposes?"* (=1 if the firm had applied, =0 if the firm had not needed financing; discouraged borrowers were omitted from this portion of the analysis). This approach, because it is not limited by the relatively small number of discouraged borrowers, also allows more detailed specifications of the control variables which included: size of firm (log of the number of full-time-equivalent employees, including the owner); sector (a categorical variable corresponding to one-digit NAICS classifications); a categorical variable corresponding to whether (=1) or not (=0) the firm had been founded within the last two years; and a binary variable equal to 1 if the firm had invested in R&D (=0 if not). In the second stage of the model estimation the sequence of dummy variables, described above, that which corresponds to growth intentions of immigrant and non-immigrant owners, was added to the model. The results are presented in Table 3.

Table 3 confirms that larger firms, firms that invest in R&D, firms in goods-producing sectors and new firms are relatively more likely to apply for formal financing *(p-values all < 0.05)*. It also shows that non-immigrant owners who seek growth of their firms are also significantly *(p-values all < 0.000)* more likely to seek financing than counterpart owners who do not seek growth. It also shows that non-immigrant owners who hold growth aspirations are approximately 48% more likely to apply for finance than immigrant owners with growth

intentions (=1.98/1.33), although this result is only weakly significant *(p-value < 0.10, calculated from Table 3)*. The table also shows that immigrant owners without growth intentions are significantly more likely to seek financing than counterpart non-immigrant owners.

The results listed in Tables 2 and 3 strongly support Hypothesis 1, that growth aspiration is a key determinant of firms' needs for external finance. They partially support and partially refute Hypothesis 2, that immigrant owners are less likely to seek formal financing in that immigrant owners who seek growth are less likely to seek capital but those who do not seek growth are more likely to apply for formal sources of financing. The results are also consistent with Hypothesis 5, that immigrant owners are relatively likely to be among discouraged borrowers. To test the remaining hypotheses, Table 4 presents a breakdown of the specific forms of financing according to immigrant status and growth orientation.

Table 4 again confirms that growth aspirations are strongly linked to applications for all forms of financing (Hypothesis 1). While it is also seen that immigrant owners are relatively less likely to apply for equity financing (consistent with Hypothesis 4) they are neither more nor less likely to seek debt (Hypothesis 3) or trade credit (Hypothesis 6).

### SUMMARY, DISCUSSION AND IMPLICATIONS

Immigration, commercial, banking and trade policies of many developed and less developed nations now recognize that the growth of young firms contributes disproportionately to economic welfare

*Growth Aspirations and Financing Choices of Immigrant-Owned New Ventures in Canada*

## Table 5. Summary of Research Findings

| | Hypothesis | Findings |
|---|---|---|
| 1 | Growth aspirations are a primary driver of applications for external capital. | Supported for non-immigrant owners. Growth intentions and applications for financial capital were strongly correlated. |
| 2 | Controlling for growth, and other potentially salient factors such as firm size, business age, and sector, immigrant-owned firms are less likely to apply for formal types of financing than non-immigrant-owned firms. | Supported for immigrant owners with growth intentions and refuted for immigrant owners without growth intentions, the latter being more likely to seek financing. |
| 3 | Immigrant-owned firms are less likely to apply for debt financing than non-immigrant owned firms. | Not supported. Overall, immigrant owners were neither more nor less likely to seek debt financing than non-immigrant-owned firms. |
| 4 | Immigrant-owned firms are less likely to apply for equity financing than non-immigrant owned firms. | Supported. Immigrant-owned firms were significantly less likely to seek equity financing than firms owned by non-immigrants. |
| 5 | Immigrant-owned firms are more likely to believe that their requests for external financing will be denied. | Supported for the case of immigrant owners with growth aspirations. |
| 6 | Immigrant-owned firms are more likely to apply for trade credit than non-immigrant-owned firms. | Not supported. Overall, immigrant owners were neither more nor less likely to seek supplier financing than non-immigrant-owned firms. |

and job creation. However, the growth of new firms, those owned by immigrants and non-immigrants alike, depends critically on access to financial capital. Much of the literature views financial constraints in terms of market failures or credit rationing; however, access to capital can also be limited if business owners choose not to apply, either because they are discouraged or had been informally dissuaded from applying or because they sought other forms of capital. Therefore, this paper examined, conceptually and empirically, financing choices of young firms with particular emphasis on firms owned by recent immigrants. On the basis of a review of literature and a conceptual argument, six research hypotheses were advanced. These, along with the related empirical findings, are summarized in Table 5.

An important finding of this work is that growth aspirations are strongly correlated with the need for financing. Additional financial capital funds both working capital and fixed asset expansion, both of which are required for growth and confirming previous research findings (for example, Demirguc-Kunt, 2006; OECD, 2006; and Cosh, Cumming and Hughes, 2009). This work found that, overall, applications for trade credit, debt and equity capital were significantly higher for growth-oriented businesses (Table 4). While evidence of market failure and credit rationing remains a topic of considerable

debate (Parker, 2002; Cressy, 2002) immigrant-owners and owners of growth-oriented young businesses may be discouraged from seeking capital, whether or not capital rationing might apply. This is an important finding because immigration policies often encourage "business immigrants," those immigrants who intend to start a business. Such applicants are often presented with strenuous requirements in order to be granted a visa (including minimum levels of wealth and experience, and a viable business plan with the intention to hire employees). However, this type of policy may be compromised if immigrants are discouraged from seeking the forms of financing consistent with achieving their growth aspirations. Perhaps this explains why Ley (2006) found that immigrant business owners admitted to Canada under the terms of the immigrant entrepreneur policy were less than satisfied with the development of their businesses.

Therefore, this work informs commercial and trade and lending policies of governments as well as lending policies of financial institutions. It appears that current lending practices discourage applications for growth financing from young firms. Perhaps borrowing criteria for young immigrant-owned firms might need to be modified in order to stimulate more business creation in what is often described as an industrious segment of the entrepreneurial population. For financial institutions, it would seem that they might benefit, over the longer term, from initiatives that encourage more growth-oriented immigrant business owners to seek financing. This is especially true if, as is often thought (Dalziel, 2008) that immigrant-owned firms go on to achieve superior performance.

The work also shows that personal factors such as immigrant status and growth orientation figure prominently in SME owners' financing choices. This is consistent with Uzzi and Gillespie (1999) who point out that the inseparability of entrepreneurs from their businesses affects financing decisions among SMEs. This is a step towards achieving a yet better understanding of the factors that lie behind financing decisions. It was interesting to find that overall, immigrant owners were neither more nor less likely to apply for formal sources of capital. This would appear to be an "averaging out" of the two groups of immigrant owners: immigrant owners with growth intentions who were less likely to seek financing and immigrant owners without growth intentions, the latter being more likely to seek financing. What is important is that it is the growth-oriented immigrant owners—precisely those who ought to be seeking capital—are not those who, like non-immigrant growth firms, are applying for capital most often.

Finally, the work documents financing patterns among early-stage entrepreneurial ventures. Consistent with previous findings, the work shows that only a minority of businesses seek financing in a given year and that external debt capital is by far the most frequently sought form of capital. Only a small minority of enterprises seeks external financing, although growth-oriented firms are relatively more likely to seek equity.

*Limitations and future directions*

The work is limited in that, in spite of a large-scale carefully weighted stratified sample, the small number of immigrant business owners precludes certain breakdowns that could be yet more informative (for example, across finer gradations of sector and in terms of immigrant owners' ability to access the financing they sought relative to non-immigrant owners). As with interpretation of many

survey results, the work can only speak to associations among variables and causation can only be imputed. On the other hand, the work is based on a large carefully representative sample of businesses. Response rates were high so as to mitigate non-response biases and, unlike many previous studies, the analysis examines the types of finance for which firms actually applied (as opposed to the types of financing they eventually obtained).

For future research, it should be noted that the unit of analysis is the firm, not the ownership. Immigrant status used here reflects responses to the question: *"Was the majority ownership of the business held by someone who had resided in Canada for less than five years?"* There is no information about the likelihood of other firms being owned by the same owner. This is a potentially important distinction because business owner(s) may have more than one business and other companies he or she owns could underestimate the available financial, social, etc. resources. In addition, this work focusses on new firms and on immigrants defined as those who have resided in Canada for less than five years. The research literature on immigrants uses a wide variety of definitions, including analyses of second and even third generation immigrants. This work employs a five-year criterion for three reasons. First, long term residents would be less likely to lack the track records and credit history that facilitates access to capital while recent immigrants would arguably be more likely to lack the track records that facilitate access to capital. Second, this work focusses on new firms: those that began trading within the most recent five years. Third, Neville et al (2014) show that recent immigrants whose firms trade internationally add disproportionately to job creation and economic welfare and it is these firms that are most likely to need financing.

Finally, because immigration policy lies at the heart of current international debates it is essential to ensure that the policy discussions are well informed. Among key issues in these debates is the extent to which immigrants add to prosperity. Neville et al. (2014) are among those who have shown that growth of young immigrant-owned exporter firms adds disproportionately to job creation and economic welfare. It is therefore essential to determine the extent to which the financial system allows for the provision of the resources that are necessary to fuel such growth. This work examines this question.

## NOTES

1) See, for example, Geoffrey Cameron and Ian Goldin (2011), More immigrants are in Canada's national interest, *The Globe and Mail*, August 4, 2011, http://www.theglobeandmail.com/news/opinions/opinion/more-immigrants-are-in-canadas-national-interest/article2118755. This is true in many countries, but it is especially true in Canada. Immigration policy in Canada is closely connected to economic welfare policies. Immigration policy in Canada is selective; those who seek entry into Canada typically have to meet criteria related to economic welfare.

2) In Canada, Industry Canada identifies recent immigrant-owned SMEs as representing roughly 2.6% of the entrepreneurial population in Canada (Industry Canada, 2009). In the UK, the Household Survey of Entrepreneurship (2007) reports some causality between entrepreneurial intentions and London's concentrated immigrant and ethnically diverse population.

3) In North America, two of the predominant credit scoring specialists, TransUnion and Equifax, characterize credit scores as a three-digit number, derived from a statistical formula, which helps lenders make decisions (Equifax Consumer Services Canada; TransUnion Canada.). Interestingly, both also use the same model pioneered by Fair, Isaac & Co. This credit scoring model (FICO Score), is deployed in 21 countries (including the US, Canada, the UK, and South Africa), but is also used by approximately 90% of the largest lenders worldwide (Fair, Isaac & Co.).

4) Of course, people who had immigrated at some point in their lives start some firms. Dalziel (2008) chronicles several case studies of successful immigrant entrepreneurs; however, in many cases startup and subsequent success (or failure) occurs many years after immigration.

## REFERENCES

Avery, R. B., Brevoort, K. P., & Canner, G. B. (2009). Credit scoring and its effects on the availability and affordability of credit. *Journal of Consumer Affairs*, 43(3), 516-530.

Baldwin, J. R., & Johnson, J. (1995). Business strategies in innovative and non-innovative firms in Canada. *Analytical Studies Branch Research Paper*, (73)

Bates, T. (1997). Financing small business creation: The case of Chinese and Korean immigrant entrepreneurs. *Journal of Business Venturing*, 12(2), 109-124.

Beck, T. and A. Demirguc-Kunt, 2006. Small and medium-size enterprises: Access to finance as a growth constraint. *Journal of Banking and Finance*, 30(2), 2931-2943.

Beck, T., Demirgüç-Kunt, A., & Maksimovic, V. (2008). Financing patterns around the world: Are small firms different? *Journal of Financial Economics*, 89(3), 467-487.

Ben-Ari, G., & Vonortas, N. S. (2007). Risk financing for knowledge-based enterprises: Mechanisms and policy options. *Science and Public Policy*, 34(7), 475-488.

Berger, A. N., & Frame, W. S. (2007). Small business credit scoring and credit availability. *Journal of Small Business Management*, 45(1), 5-22.

Berger, A. N., Frame, W. S., & Miller, N. H. (2005). Credit scoring and the availability, price, and risk of small business credit. *Journal of Money, Credit and Banking*, 37(2), 191-222.

Binks, M. R., & Ennew, C. T. (1996). Growing firms and the credit constraint. *Small Business Economics*, 8(1), 17-25.

Bornheim, S. P., & Herbeck, T. H. (1998). A research note on the theory of SME - bank relationships. *Small Business Economics*, 10(4), 327-331.

Brierley, Peter (2001), The financing of technology-based small firms: A review of the literature, Bank of England. *Quarterly Bulletin*, Spring, 41-76.

Brenner, G. A., Filion, L. J., Menzies, T. V., & Dionne, L. (2006). Problems encountered by ethnic entrepreneurs: A comparative analysis across five ethnic groups. *New England Journal of Entrepreneurship*, 9(2), 25.

Churchill, N. C., & Lewis, V. L. (1986). Bank lending to new and growing enterprises. *Journal of Business Venturing*, 1(2), 193-206.

Citizenship and immigration Canada. (2010), Government of Canada, Ottawa.

Co, C. Y., Euzent, P., & Martin, T. (2004). The export effect of immigration into the USA. *Applied Economics*, 36(6), 573-583.

Cole, R. A. (1998). The importance of relationships to the availability of credit. *Journal of Banking and Finance*, 22(6-8), 959-977.

Cosh, A., Cumming, D. and Hughes, A. (2009). Outside Entrepreneurial Capital. *The Economic Journal*, 119: 1494-1533.

Cressy, R., (2002). Funding Gaps: A Symposium. *The Economic Journal*, 112(477), F1-F16.

Dalziel, M. (2008). Immigrants as extraordinarily successful entrepreneurs: A pilot study of the Canadian experience. *Journal of Small Business and Entrepreneurship*, 21(10), 23-36.

DeYoung, R., Glennon, D., & Nigro, P. (2008). Borrower-lender distance, credit scoring, and loan performance: Evidence from informational-opaque small business borrowers. *Journal of Financial Intermediation*, 17(1), 113-143.

Dunlevy, J. A., & Hutchinson, W. K. (1999). The impact of immigration on American import trade in the late nineteenth and early twentieth centuries. *Journal of Economic History*, 59(4), 1043-1062.

Equifax consumer services Canada. Retrieved 04/03, 2010, http://www.equifax.com/home/en_ca, accessed January 31, 2011.

Fair, Isaac & Co. Retrieved 04/03, 2010, http://www.fico.com/en/Products/Scoring/Pages/FICO-score.aspx, accessed January 31, 2011.

Frame, W. S., Srinivasan, A., & Woosley, L. (2001). The effect of credit scoring on small-business lending. *Journal of Money, Credit and Banking*, 33(3), 813-825.

Freel, M. (2006). Are Small Innovators Credit Rationed? *Small Business Economics* (2007) 28:23–35

Han, Liang, Stuart Fraser, David J. Storey (2009). Are good or bad borrowers discouraged from applying for loans? Evidence from US small business credit markets. *Journal of Banking & Finance*, 33 (2009), 415–424.

Haltiwanger, J. C., Jarmin, R. S., & Miranda, J. (2010). Who creates jobs? small vs. large vs. young. SSRN eLibrary, 1-47.

Head, K., & Ries, J. (1998). Immigration and trade creation: Econometric evidence from Canada. *Canadian Journal of Economics*, 31(1), 47-62.

Household survey of entrepreneurship 2005. (2007). *DTI Research Report*, Government of the UK, London.

Industry Canada. (2009). Key small business financing statistics - December 2009. Retrieved from http://www.sme-fdi.gc.ca/eic/site/sme_fdi-prf_pme.nsf/eng/h_02169.html

Jones, T., Ram, M., Edwards, P. (2006). Ethnic minority business and the employment of illegal immigrants. *Entrepreneurship & Regional Development*, 18(2): 133-150.

Kon, Y., & Storey, D. J. (2003). A theory of discouraged borrowers. *Small Business Economics*, 21(1), 37-49.

Kushnirovich, N., & Heilbrunn, S. (2008). Financial funding of immigrant businesses. *Journal of Developmental Entrepreneurship*, 13(2), 167-184.

Ley, D. (2006). Explaining variations in business performance among immigrant entrepreneurs in Canada. *Journal of Ethnic and Migration Studies*, 32(5): 743-764.

Levenson, A. R., & K. L. Willard, (2000). Do Firms Get the Financing They Want? Measuring Credit Rationing Experienced by Small Businesses in the US. *Small Business Economics*, 14(2), 83–94.

Manove, M., Padilla, A. J., & Pagano, M. (2001). Collateral versus project screening: A model of lazy banks. *RAND Journal of Economics*, 32(4), 726-744.

Mundra, K. (2005). Immigration and international trade: A semiparametric empirical investigation. *Journal of International Trade and Economic Development*, 14(1), 65-91.

Neville, F., Orser, B., Riding, A., & Jung, O. (2014). Do young firms owned by recent immigrants outperform other young firms? *Journal of Business Venturing*, 29(1), 55-71.

OECD (2006). The SME Financing Gap: Theory and Evidence, Brasilia.

Parker, Simon (2002). Do Banks Ration Credit to New Enterprises? Should Governments Intervene? *Scottish Journal of Political Economy*, 49(2): 162-195.

Partridge, J., & Furtan, H. (2008). Immigration wave effects on Canada's trade flows. *Canadian Public Policy*, 34(2), 193-210.

Petersen, M. A., & Rajan, R. G. (1994). The benefits of lending relationships: Evidence from small business data. *The Journal of Finance*, 49(1), 3.

Portes, A., Guarnizo, L. E., & Haller, W. J. (2002). Transnational entrepreneurs: An alternative form of immigrant economic adaptation. *American Sociological Review*, 67(2), 278-298.

Portes, A., & Jensen, L. (1989). The enclave and the entrants: Patterns of ethnic enterprise in Miami before and after Mariel. *American Sociological Review*, 54(6), 929-949.

Portes, A., & Zhou, M. (1996). Self-employment and the earnings of immigrants. *American Sociological Review*, 61(2), 219-230.

Psillaki, M., & Daskalakis, N. (2009). Are the determinants of capital structure country or firm specific? *Small Business Economics*, 33(3), 319-333.

Ram, M. & Smallbone, D. (2003). Ethnic minority enterprise: policy in practice, Introduction to Special Issue. *Entrepreneurship & Regional Development*, 15: 99-102

Riding, A., Orser, B. J., Spence, M., & Belanger, B. (2010). Financing new venture exporters. *Small Business Economics*, 1-17.

Robb, Alicia (2009) The capital structure decisions of new firms. Kaufmann Foundation Working Paper.

Roszbach, K. (2004). Bank lending policy, credit scoring, and the survival of loans. *Review of Economics and Statistics*, 86(4), 946-958.

SBA: Office of advocacy research report - estimating the contribution of immigrant business owners to the U.S. economy. (2008).

*Survey on financing of small and medium enterprises, 2004.* (2006). Small Business and Special Surveys Division, Statistics Canada.

TransUnion Canada. Retrieved 04/03, 2010, from http://www.transunion.ca/ca/home_en.page

Uzzi, B., & Gillespie, J. (2002). Knowledge Spillover in Corporate Financing Networks: Embeddedness and the Firm's Debt Performance. *Strategic Management Journal*, Vol. 23 Issue 7, 595-619

Voordeckers, W., & Steijvers, T. (2006). Business collateral and personal commitments in SME lending. *Journal of Banking and Finance*, 30(11), 3067-3086.

Vos et al., 2007 Vos, E., Yeh, A., Carter, S., Tagg, S., 2007. The happy story of small business financing. *Journal of Banking and Finance* 31, 2648–2672.

Waldinger, R., Aldrich, H., & Ward, R. (1990). Ethnic Entrepreneurs. Beverly Hills, CA: Sage.

Wynant, Larry & James Hatch (1991). *Banks and Small Business Borrowers.* Richard Ivey School of Business, The University of Western Ontario, London, Ontario, 1991

Zambaldi, F., Aranha, F., Lopes, H., & Politi, R. (2009). Credit granting to small firms: A Brazilian case. *Journal of Business Research*, forthcoming.

---

Dr. Miwako Nitani is an assistant professor at Telfer School of Management, University of Ottawa, Canada. E-mail: Nitani@telfer.uottawa.ca

Dr. François Neville is an assistant professor of Strategic Management at DeGroote School of Business, McMaster University. E-mail: nevillef@mcmaster.ca

# BOOK REVIEW

## My Adventures in Marketing: The Autobiography of Philip Kotler

By Philip Kotler
Printed in the United States of America. Idea Bite Press, 2017. ISBN 978-0-9905767-6-1. 307 pages

*Fangqi Xu*
*The Faculty of Business Administration, Kindai University, Japan*

This book was published by Philip Kotler, the Father of Modern Marketing. It is his 66th book. He wrote it after receiving an offer of publication from the Nikkei, a Japanese daily newspaper at the beginning of 2013. The Nikkei wanted Dr. Kotler to write a series of articles about his life for its column *My Resume*, with a proviso that he would write an article (600~800 words) and add a photo to it on a daily basis for a month. Although Dr. Kotler had published so many books previously, he had never looked back on his life in order to write a book. As he would turn 82 in 2013, however, he thought that it was time for him to write an autobiography. So, he got intrigued by the offer, accepted it and started to write one. In fact, he wrote 54 articles, 30 of which were published in the newspaper in December, 2013. In the following year, the Nikkei published a book, *My Life of Marketing*, in Japanese, which included the 30 articles and some unposted ones. Last year, Dr. Kotler added some more articles to the Japanese version of the book and decided to publish it in English. So, this book is the first English version of Dr. Kotler's autobiography.

In this book, Dr. Kotler introduced many interesting stories. For example, one day, when he received a call from Peter Drucker, he was very pleased as well as surprised. He wrote, "Because I had closely read his book that are rich in insight and I had great respect for him although I never met him. A call from Peter Drucker meant more to me than if our U.S. President called." (p.81) He respects Drucker. When someone praised him as the "Father of Modern Marketing," he always said, "I would call Peter Drucker the 'Grandfather of Modern Marketing'."(p.255)

Needless to say, we can learn a lot of things in terms of Dr. Kotler's marketing theory by reading this book. He has constantly taught us new perceptions on marketing. He emphasizes, "Marketing is a philosophy centered on serving customers and includes a set of skills and activities to solve economic and social problems." (p.11) I think this is a very important point of view. According to my hypothesis, if a scholar of management is deeply researching, or a top manager is successfully practicing in a certain field, his/her perspectives will sublimate into the level of philosophy. For example, Dr. Ikujiro Nonaka, the Father of Knowledge Creation Theory and a professor emeritus at Hitotsubashi University, and Kazuo Inamori, the founder and honorary chairman of Kyocera, both emphasize management as philosophy. Fortunately, my hypothesis was verified once again by Dr. Kotler's opinion.

Also, the book includes many photos of Dr. Kotler's family, colleagues and friends in the world. I believe that each piece of photo contains a story related to his life.

I would like to recommend this book not only to scholars, Ph.D. candidates, but also to top managers and consultants. Finally, I am very grateful to Dr. Kotler for providing me with a copy of this book.

# BOOK REVIEW

## Wise Family Business:
## Family Identity Steering Brand Success

By Joachim Schwass and Anne-Catrin Glemser
Hampshire, UK: Palgrave Macmillan, 2016, 284 pages.

*Joachim Schwass*
*Professor emeritus of Family Business, IMD*

The purpose of this book is to help families in business identify better ways of assuring longevity, sustainability and lasting performance by linking the owning family's identity to the business brand. Family businesses have a unique opportunity to position themselves as a family business brand by building on their family history, identity, values and long-term vision. But to what extent should they be visible? Are they better off staying beneath the radar or should they promote their heritage and position themselves as family businesses?

The starting point is that family firms face predictable and highly impacting challenges – potentially endangering their survival – as they transition through the generational changes from the founder or controlling owner stage to the siblings and then to the cousin generation. The typical configuration shows that the identity link between family and business is strongest during the early stages when the family is still small. As the family continues to grow, the risk of an identity loss clearly increases. This is caused by the centrifugal forces arising from the increasingly diverse interests of a growing family, a larger number of owners and a growing business. While this is a predictable evolution, the vast majority of family businesses fail to appropriately understand and address this challenge.

The authors have studied and worked with family-owned and family-controlled businesses from all over the world for more than 25 years and witnessed them navigate through both difficult and happy times. In this book they share a wealth of knowledge about the inside perspectives and dynamics that families in business are exposed to. They take a look at the external forces and analyze how these put pressure on family systems and their next generations. The book includes a truly global set of company cases from Ayala Corporation of the Philippines to Zegna from Italy and presents a varied portrait of leading branded family businesses such as Henkel, Patek Philippe and Bata Group. It demonstrates concrete examples of how family businesses can undertake the often difficult path of leveraging the family's identity, their values and vision for the benefit of their business and the solutions these industrial families have found.

The book reveals how successful, multi-generational family businesses have in fact identified and applied a centripetal strategy – countering the negative centrifugal evolution – by leveraging the family identity for the benefit of a family business brand. A structured process and a practical toolbox highlight how to start by analyzing the family identity and expressing it in meaningful, value-added ways for the business.

A special chapter provided by the Brunswick Group is dedicated to the relevance and impact of strategic reputation management for families of wealth, family businesses and at the intersection of family, ownership and business. As Warren Buffet pointed out, "*It takes 20 years to build a reputation and five minutes to ruin it.*"

A values-based vision can be extremely beneficial for a family business in a rapidly changing competitive environment. An important insight gained from this study is the additional strong benefit for the family itself when confronted with the task of crafting a family business vision based on the family identity.

The key conclusion is that family identity matters in multiple ways and for a large number of stakeholders, potentially over generations. This book helps owning families to gain a better understanding of their current and future long-term family business challenges and how to wisely address them in a carefully planned and comprehensive strategic process.

# The International Conference on Creativity and Innovation 2018
## From the Perspective of Interdisciplinary Research and Practice

**Osaka, Japan  September 10-12, 2018**

## Official Organizers

Japan Creativity Society

The Institute for Creative Management and Innovation, Kindai University

## Official Partners

American Creativity Association

European Association of Creativity and Innovation

German Association for Creativity

Deutsche Gesellschaft für Kreativität

Crea-France

Portuguese Association for Creativity And Innovation

Creativity Foundation of South Africa

International Center for Studies in Creativity (ICSC)

## Official Sponsors

Japan Federation of Management Related Academies (JFMRA)

Osaka Government Tourism Bureau

## Official Partners

Creative Education Foundation

## Day and Venue

September 10-12, 2018

International House, Osaka, Japan.
Tel: 81-6-6772-5931

Address: Uehommachi 8-2-6, Tennouji-ku, Osaka 543-0001, Japan
URL: http://www.ih-Osaka.or.jp/

## Important Dates

Submission of Abstract by May 9, 2018.     Notification of Acceptance by May 31, 2018
Submission of full Papers by July 31, 2018
All submissions should be made to info@ICCIosaka2018.net using the abstract and full paper templates available on the conference website. http://www.ICCIosaka2018.net/

## Keynoters

Prof. Ikujiro Nonaka
Hitotsubashi University

Prof. Masaaki Kotabe
Temple University

Prof. Tudor Rickards
Manchester Business School

Prof. Gerard Puccio
State University of New York

## Registration Fees

| Participation Category | Japanese Yen(¥) | Early Bird* |
|---|---|---|
| Delegates from all low income countries | ¥20,000 | ¥18,000 |
| Delegate from all other countries | ¥40,000 | ¥35,000 |
| Full time graduate student** | ¥15,000 | ¥13,000 |
| Gala Dinner | ¥6,000 | — |

* Payment from June 15 to July 9, 2018.     ** Please attach a copy of your student ID card.

## Contact

Email: info@ICCIosaka2018.net   or   icmi@bus.kindai.ac.jp
URL: http://www.ICCIosaka2018.net/

# ORDER SHEET

## *Kindai Management Review* Vol. 6  2018

ISBN 978-4-86345-375-3 List Price 2,500 Japanese Yen

**Please make a photocopy of this page and send to us.**

We would like to place an order of _____ copy (copies)

• *Ship to:*

Name

Address

City                              State                    ZIP

Country

Telephone

e-mail address

• *Postage (by Surface Air Lifted)*

| Area | 1 copy | 2 copies | 3 copies | Additional copy |
|------|--------|----------|----------|-----------------|
| N. America | 890 JPY | 1,490 JPY | 1,990 JPY | +600 JPY/1 copy |
| Europe | 890 JPY | 1,490 JPY | 1,990 JPY | +600 JPY/1 copy |
| E. Asia | 810 JPY | 1,380 JPY | 1,780 JPY | +500 JPY/1 copy |
| Other | 1,190 JPY | 1,900 JPY | 2,495 JPY | +700 JPY/1 copy |

**Please fill the above form and send it with check or money order to following:**

## Maruzen Planet Co., Ltd.

17, Kanda Jimbo-cho 2 chome, Chiyoda-ku, TOKYO 101-0051 Japan

Tel: +81-3-3512-8516  Fax: +81-3-5212-1168  e-mail: marupura@maruzen.co.jp